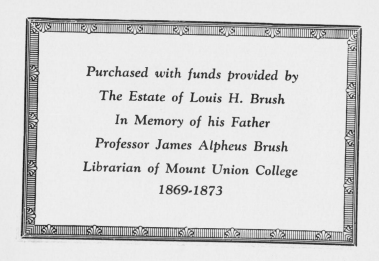

THE CORONA LIBRARY

NYASALAND

LAKE NYASA

NYASALAND

The Land of the Lake

BY

FRANK DEBENHAM

LONDON

HER MAJESTY'S STATIONERY OFFICE

1955

First published 1955
Second impression 1958

Published by
HER MAJESTY'S STATIONERY OFFICE

To be purchased from
York House, Kingsway, London W.C.2
423 Oxford Street, London W.1
13A Castle Street, Edinburgh 2
109 St. Mary Street, Cardiff
39 King Street, Manchester 2
Tower Lane, Bristol 1
2 Edmund Street, Birmingham 3
80 Chichester Street, Belfast
or through any bookseller

Price £1 5s. od. net.

Printed in Great Britain under the authority of Her Majesty's Stationery Office by
William Clowes and Sons, Limited, London and Beccles

THE CORONA LIBRARY

A series of illustrated volumes under the sponsorship of the Colonial Office dealing with the United Kingdom's dependent territories, the way their peoples live, and how they are governed. The series has been designed to fill the place between official Blue Books on the one hand and the writings of occasional visitors on the other, to be authoritative and readable, and to give a vivid yet accurate picture. The books are being written by established authors whose qualifications include, where possible, experience of colonial administration and first-hand knowledge of the territory concerned. Neither Her Majesty's Government in the United Kingdom nor the Governments of the territories necessarily associate themselves with the personal views expressed by the authors. Each volume will contain maps and be fully illustrated.

ACKNOWLEDGMENTS

On my four different visits to Nyasaland I have received so much hospitality and so much help in whatever inquiries I was making that it would be quite impossible to mention even a tithe of those kind people by name, and many, no doubt, would prefer to remain anonymous.

It almost goes without saying that the Administrative Service, from successive Governors down to the African drivers who were allotted to me, were uniformly helpful. Of the seniors I would like to pick out for special mention Mr. K. W. Simmonds (Financial Secretary), Mr. Frank Brown (former Chief Secretary), Mr. V. Fox-Strangways (former Secretary of African Affairs), Mr. R. W. Kettlewell (Director of Agriculture) and Mr. M. J. Morris (former Director of Public Relations).

Those were all attached to the Secretariat in Zomba, but in the provinces I owe a special debt of thanks to Mr. R. H. Keppel-Compton and to Mr. W. H. J. Rangeley, both of them Provincial Commissioners as well as to a number of District Commissioners who put up with my presence and my questions and became friends as well as counsellors.

Of permanent residents, locally called 'settlers', I owe a great deal to Mr. and Mrs. G. D. Hayes, who made me welcome on every visit, as well as to their neighbours—in a Nyasaland sense—Mr. and Mrs. Reginald Sharpe, and Sir Malcolm and Lady Barrow, all of whom have followed the fortunes of the territory for a long time.

The paramount chiefs whom I met are all mentioned in the text and I hope that Chief Mbelwa of the Angoni, Chief Mwase of the Chewa and Chief Msusa of Kota Kota will believe that my account of our meetings is full of the friendly regard which I shall always feel towards them. The late Chief Gomani of Ncheu also received me with that courtesy which seems to be innate in the chiefly caste of modern Nyasaland.

Those readers who consult the general map at the end of this book will notice certain discrepancies in the spelling of place names in map and text: they may take it that the form used in the text is that used in the territory itself.

Finally I would like to mention help from my wife, my daughter and my cousin, Miss Christina Wanklyn, who at different times shared with me the ups and downs of travelling round Nyasaland, with equanimity and zest.

Frank Debenham,
Herne Lodge, St Eligius Street,
Cambridge

March 1955

CONTENTS

ILLUSTRATIONS

PLATES

ILLUSTRATIONS

Acknowledgment is made to the following for the use of photographs :
Dr. Amy Laws, Plate III(b) ; Methuen & Co., Jacket (Angoni man),
Plate XVI ; Royal Geographical Society, Endpaper ('Ma Robert'),
Plate II, Plate III(a) ; Universities Mission to Africa, Plate XX(b).

DRAWINGS

MAPS AND DIAGRAMS

Black and white maps and diagrams drawn by Reitz M.S.I.A.

Folding Maps at end of volume
Nyasaland (General) by Directorate of Colonial Surveys
Nyasaland (Shadow relief) by Geographical Projects Limited

ENDPAPERS
Front:

Dr. Livingstone's 'tin can', the *Ma Robert,* encounters an elephant
on the Shire River (1859). Painted by T. Barnes from a description by Mr. Rae. *Reproduced by permission of the Royal Geographical
Society.*

Back:

The exhibits include the territory's coats of arms, old and new,
Central Africa's earliest newspapers, and a print of the steamer
Ilala off Cape Maclear, the first site of the Livingstonia Mission.

1. INTRODUCTION

To a passing visitor a country is what he makes of it, compounded of his reception, his own background, and a welter of other influences on his mind.

To a reader seeking knowledge of a country it is apt to become what smart phrases in the Press have given him, whether they be quips of sarcasm or puffs of praise.

This book, therefore, can only present Nyasaland as what the author made of it, biased no doubt in some directions, ignorant perhaps in others, but it can at least begin with a word or two on what others have made of it.

In this age of hustle we like our descriptions to be brief and cryptic, and we are apt to accept headlines in the tabloid Press as the background for the picture we hope to fix in our minds. If we lay on enough of such potted phrases, balancing the fulsome ones against the derogatory, we may, I suppose, arrive at a reasonable canvas, but if we pick and choose our paragraphs to suit our fancy we may go very wrong indeed and end with a scene which is far too gaudy or far too sombre, or more likely still, just plain muddle.

When planning this book I did, I believe, promise a V.I.P. at the Colonial Office that I would do my best to avoid calling Nyasaland the 'Switzerland of Africa', yet here it is on the very first page. It is culled, of course, from a guide book, and, like most phrases from such a source, it requires pruning. We can lop off snow-capped peaks at once and glistening glaciers and funiculars and indeed most of the trappings of the Alps as we know them, and we can, if we like, snort with impatience at the glib simile. Yet if we do not push it too far we have one necessary element in our impression of the country, which is one of sharp contrasts in relief and in climate and, therefore, like the Switzerland of our holidays, it has mountains to be climbed, scenery for the artist, and the whole gamut of temperatures and vegetation that one associates with a range of altitude from nearly sea-level to 10,000 feet above it.

If we must cling to the faint analogy, since it is always easier to describe by resemblances than by opposites, then we must be ready to replace the stark white beauty of the Jungfrau with the sheer grey cliffs of Mlanje, the sparkling glaciers of the one with the lush greenery of the cedar forests of the other, both filling their respective valleys, and standing out against the grassy shoulders which overlook them.

There is a quality of breath-taking beauty in the view as one first sees the Jungfrau from Interlaken which is hard to match anywhere, yet with due allowance for the manifest differences due to latitude there is the same surprise to the traveller in the train toiling and twisting up steep valleys from the Lower Shire River to the area known as the Shire Highlands.

As he tops the rim of the 4,000 foot plateau he spies away to the east the suddenest mountain mass he has probably ever seen, rising straight out of the flat but lofty plateau, a Pelion upon Ossa indeed, quite unreal in its sheer domination of the scene, a mountain of character if ever there was one, worthy of the books and the lyrics which will yet be devoted to it, for it is a challenge to the imagination, food for the emotions.

Like any other notable mountain it has its moods and can convey them to the artist and the poet in different guises, the guise depending largely on the temperament of the viewer.

To one prose-poet of my acquaintance it appeared as 'terrific, grand, wizard', so much so that 'one must stop when one sees Mlanje for the first time. It is one of the great views of Africa.' To such a sensitive man it developed at the very first glance a personality which in his rich phraseology he describes as 'a great, grey, compelling Jurassic sort of personality, a character of ill-suppressed rages, a petrified brontosaurus-like grinding and gnashing of teeth, that made everything near it shrink and cower; it presented itself to my senses as a giant striding through time with the plain, like a mongrel, at its heels.'

Such imagery is beyond the compass of normal men, no doubt; in the words of the faint but willing disciple, I would say, 'I know what you mean, though I can't see it that way myself.'

To the local inhabitant it does not mean all that much perhaps; to the African dwelling in his village at its foot it is a cold misty place to be shunned, while to the European it is a challenge to be climbed. To the managers of the tea estates beneath its southern end it is a godsend, for it brings them the frequent rain which gives their plants the flushes they need every few weeks with which to earn their dividends.

Like many mountains, perhaps all, its real glory is most apparent when the clouds it fosters add height or mystery to its shape. It is a sober fact that for anyone living within sight of Mlanje up to 40 miles radius the first automatic glance on coming out on to their verandah each day is towards the mountain and its complement of clouds; always is there some new phase or trick of lighting to make it different from yesterday's view.

We shall meet other mountains of character in this book but we have said enough perhaps to show that while the easy phrase of the guide book is extreme yet Nyasaland has a combination of mountains and lakes unmatched in scenic value anywhere else in Africa. The Drakensberg in Natal has higher mountains and so has Morocco but they have no lakes; the three giants of Equatorial Africa, Kilimanjaro, Kenya and Ruwenzori, are splendid in their isolation and their permanent snow, but the combination of lake and mountain in Nyasaland is almost unique in that vast continent. We know then that it is no Switzerland but it has some of that lucky country's attributes, not the least being that nowhere can one call it monotonous.

From its scenic qualities we may pass easily to another descriptive phrase for the territory which I heard lately from one who had much to do with the coming of federation in Central Africa. Comparing the assets which each of the three countries can put in the common pool of resources, he said, 'Poor little Nyasaland, she has nothing to sell but scenery and labour.'

Like the aphorism about Switzerland this, too, requires modification, yet it is true in the main. It needs expansion rather than pruning because, whether true or not at present, it will not always be true, as this book hopes to show.

But the statement does emphasize the fact that unlike the other two territories in the Federation, Northern and Southern Rhodesia, the country has received no boost from mineral wealth. The history of pioneering and, to some extent, of colonization, is full of instances of lands which would never have been settled or exploited but for the lure of gold or diamonds or their lesser equivalent in the mineral needs of the world. Arctic wastes in Canada, semi-desert areas in Australia, forbidding and hostile coasts in South Africa all owe their exploration to those apostles of Mammon, the prospector and the fossicker, followed, of course, by the engineer and the financier. But that combination has passed Nyasaland by, and, to date at all events, she has exposed no mineral riches to consolidate into a foundation for development as the two Rhodesias have done.

Instead she has had to provide the labour for the natural resources of her neighbours to the south and west. One cannot travel for long in Nyasaland without meeting parties of men on the way to or from the farms of Southern Rhodesia or the mines of the Union, or without noticing that there is a deficiency of young men in the villages. We shall see later that this export of labour has great disadvantages to the country, yet it is also responsible for the high reputation of the Nyasa 'boys' throughout Southern Africa.

It is an export which has, until recently, had but little reward in any form that can be shown in financial returns.

One can, of course, quote instances where a man returning from a sojourn in the Transvaal has brought back with him savings or even handicrafts which have started him in a trade in his homeland. It is easier, however, to quote other instances of the opposite character, like this one. A Customs officer was examining the contents of a tin trunk of one such African, just returned from two years' work in Johannesburg, and came across no less than a dozen bottles of a very costly preparation for inducing sun-tan on European glamour-girls. These, explained the proud owner, were presents for his wife and in the choice of them he had asked the Jo'burg shopkeeper what was the most desired beautifier demanded by the white women, something by which he could improve the appearance of his wife and, no doubt, be a means of acquiring other wives. The Customs officer was furious at the deception of the wily trader but since he had told a half-truth in proffering an undoubted requirement of European lovelies there was nothing to be done about it. It was, in fact, only to be laughed at as another version of carrying coals to Newcastle.

The fact remains that in a broad economic sense my friend was correct in describing scenery and manpower as the chief

4

natural assets of Nyasaland at present, but we shall find room for hope of other ones as we go on.

Someone once said that the history of Nyasaland was an epitome of slavery, disease and war, and if that were written in the early years of this century it would have been a fair picture of its recent past. Wise administration and self-sacrifice by missionaries have changed all that, and, until the last year or so, it might perhaps have been rightly pronounced the most contented territory in all Africa. Yet it is as well to remember that such a dictum was true less than 50 years ago, if only as a reminder that we must not expect too much or too quickly. There are still plenty of old men in the villages who remember those far-off unhappy days, men who are somewhat puzzled and confused at the rate at which we British want them to scurry through centuries of slow development in a few years, but who will admit handsomely that the *bwanas** have changed the tenor of their lives beyond all belief. We need not take seriously, therefore, the summing-up of Nyasaland's past of 50 years ago, nor should we accord any but the briefest notice to another statement that Nyasaland is merely a picturesque gash on the face of Africa consisting mainly of cliffs and water. That may be what it would look like from the moon but we shall find it both very habitable and densely inhabited.

By this time the intelligent reader will be accusing us of dodging the sacred duty of describing where Nyasaland is, of avoiding the sound but dull maxim of geographers of beginning with a recital of a country's limits—'bounded on the North by etc., etc.'

It is a very necessary preliminary to a study of this country, yet a very difficult one, since Nyasaland has practically no natural boundaries. For African territories this is a common complaint, as so many of the frontiers were settled by diplomats in Europe arguing over inadequate maps and bargaining one slice of country for another, generally with the most suspect of motives. So it is not surprising that they often followed the principle of 'When in doubt rule a straight line as a frontier', or else the fashion of describing a boundary as the dividing line between two watersheds or river basins.

Nyasaland suffers from both these short cuts to boundary

* The universal name of the Africans in Nyasaland for whitemen.

5

settlement, including a line up the centre of the Lake itself in its northern section, and along its western side a boundary trying to follow a divide between two river basins. The practical result of the latter is that the road to the North wanders across the boundary in several places, so that you may easily be in Portuguese East Africa or in Northern Rhodesia when you think you are in Nyasaland. It is true that Portugal tries to remind you of these crossings into her territory by erecting very handsome boundary pillars stating the fact in the clearest terms, sometimes even in gold lettering, but even so one leaves the district with the firm impression that 'a divide' is a very loose definition, especially when it runs across a plateau.

In fact, long before anyone has got far with describing the boundaries in words he will say, with any geography master, 'Let's cross all that out and draw a map instead.' And that is what we will do here, putting Nyasaland on top of Great Britain, which at least gives a clear idea of its shape and size.

But however we describe it or picture it, Nyasaland remains as a wedge of territory based on a long lake or as a palpable afterthought in the minds of diplomats, something left when the larger territories had grabbed what they wanted.

That was not quite the way of it as we shall see, but the effect is the same, namely, that Nyasaland is indeed the Land of the Lake because in the main it is the basin of the lake and its outlet river, the Shire.

And here we might satisfy the frequent question of the general public concerning why the recent Federation of Rhodesia and Nyasaland was called, temporarily, the Central African Federation, when no part of it is anywhere near the centre of Africa, a vague area anyhow but certainly far to the north of the newly-federated group.

When that gallant and confirmed Empire-builder, Mr. Harry Johnston, came to Nyasaland in 1889 he had grand ideas and, in spite of all obstacles, he at once set about claiming a sphere of influence for the British by his own journeys up Lake Nyasa and across to Lake Tanganyika. On this journey he made treaties of friendship, shadowy 'friendships' perhaps, with all the paramount chiefs he could reach and it was his firm intention to do so up the whole length of Lake Tanganyika itself, by which time he would have indeed reached the 'centre of Africa'.

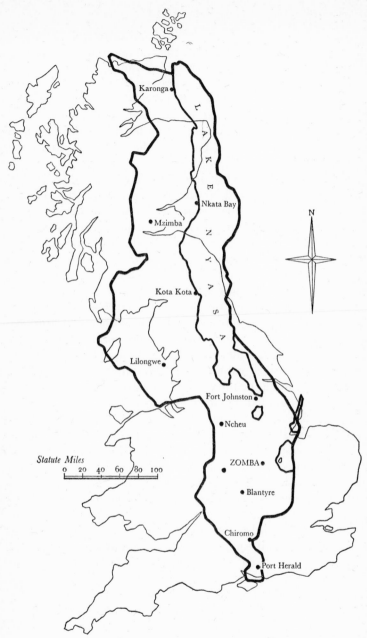

Map showing comparison between Great Britain and
Nyasaland, drawn to the same scale

7

Stirring events back in Lake Nyasa recalled him a few weeks too soon and he had to delegate the extension of these 'treaties' to another great traveller, Mr. A. J. Swann. He, however, was delayed and the evidence for Tanganyika being a claimed sphere of influence for Great Britain, in that Mr. Swann had planted the Union Jack at its northern end, arrived at the Anglo-German Convention in 1890 a few weeks too late to be seriously considered as a pawn in the game of partitioning Africa.

Nevertheless, it was because of these claims to Tanganyika that Johnston proposed to the Foreign Office the name of British Central Africa for this as yet visionary Protectorate, and that name persisted long after the British South Africa Company under the tutelage of Cecil Rhodes had taken over the neighbouring territory now known as Northern Rhodesia.

So we owe this curious title of Central Africa to the dreams of Sir Harry Johnston and Cecil Rhodes.

We may well lament the fact that there was a partition of Africa, a shameful grabbing of territory there by European nations, under the excuse of such vague terms as Spheres of Influence, but it is, unfortunately, the fashion now to decry or disown those British explorers and administrators who saw so clearly what would be the result if they did not take part in it—an Africa dominated by Germany.

The wedge of Nyasaland, shorn of its truly Central African ambitions, was but one of the obstacles to such a wholesale rule of the German, and at one time, as we shall see, in chapter 14, it was utterly saved only by a grant of money from Cecil Rhodes himself. If we had not stepped in, some other nation would have done so, and we cannot be accused of pharisaical talk when we say the effect on the Africans themselves would have been unpleasant and possibly disastrous.

With regard to its shape and size we might follow the Prince of Denmark and liken it to a camel or a weasel or a whale and still be as puzzled as was Polonius.

In length from north to south Nyasaland fits neatly into Great Britain but its area is only a little more than half. If we take the lake away, since it is not habitable, the area of Nyasaland, in fact, is only 36,000 square miles or rather more than that of Scotland, which has double Nyasaland's population.

So, by comparison with its neighbours, Nyasaland is very small indeed, being only one-eighth the size of Northern Rhodesia or of Mozambique and one-tenth that of Tanganyika. As it is long and narrow you can never be more than about 50 miles from the frontier, and in the southern half of the country you have some part of Portuguese territory in view in almost every direction that you may look.

The shadow relief map at the end of this book gives perhaps a rather exaggerated idea of its relief but it does sustain the remark that Nyasaland has a large lake and plenty of steep slopes. Wherever you are in the country you have only to go a score of miles or so to get up from typical tropical low country to the comparative coolness of 4000 feet above sea-level or even a Yorkshire moorland type of country at 6000 feet and over. In fact, if you like to do a certain amount of climbing you can get any climate you like short of an alpine one.

The seasons are simply the wet and the dry parts of the year. The rains may begin any time after October and last until March or April; then comes the long dry season, the most pleasant part of the year. Curiously enough, the most trying time of the year is not in January, when the sun is highest but before the rains, in September and October. The countryside looks very beautiful then with the flush of young leafage coming out in vivid reds but it is hot and oppressive; in fact it used to be called the 'suicide season'.

The same map also calls attention to the fact that Nyasaland is really the southern extension of the series of rift valleys which zigzag or stagger down Africa, starting at the Jordan in Palestine and petering out a little south of the Zambezi. Broadly speaking, the bottom of the rift is black man's country while the higher shoulders are suitable for white people and originally were not popular with the black.

The name of the lake, Nyasa, is the Bantu word for a 'broad water' and we meet it in other parts of Africa, sometimes as Nyanza or Nyanja. The purists rightly assert that we usually pronounce it wrongly as *nigh-assa* whereas it should really be *ne-assa*, in nasal fashion, but even the white inhabitants vary, so we need not be too precious about a small point like that. A large number of words in Chi-nyanja, the chief language of the country, begin with *ny*, such as *nyala*, a rare antelope, and *nyama*, meat, and in all these the pronunciation should be *ne* rather than *nigh* for the prefix. Incidentally, the main river, the Shire, is pronounced *Shee-ray*.

For a land which is so long and narrow and of which one-third of the area is water there is a natural tendency to divide it into the land and the lake. The administrative division is into Northern, Central and Southern Provinces, which explain themselves. For our first tour round the country we shall, however, divide it into the Land below the Lake, that is to say south of the lake, not all of it at a lower level. Then we shall visit the Land beside the Lake and finally the Lake itself.

Let us conclude our introduction by saying something about the Arms and Motto of this picturesque and pleasant little country, which has had such a brief but pregnant history.

The original coat of arms, designed and drawn by that most versatile of Governors, Sir Harry Johnston, can be seen in the back end-paper of this book. It was a little complicated since it had a shield supported by two Africans with pick and shovel, all standing on a perspective map of Africa. On the shield there was an 'inescutcheon' or small shield showing the Royal Arms, while the crest above was a Coffee Tree with Berries.

It was at least one way of telling the world where Nyasaland was, as the point of the shield rested in the lake on the map, but when coffee failed as a main crop owing to disease the crest was at least a little reminiscent of failure, so in 1914 a new and simpler coat of arms was granted by Royal Warrant.

A very appropriate animal was chosen, a 'Leopard statant proper' for the central theme, since in such a hilly country leopards are common and frequently troublesome.

If this leopard is made of metal sheet and with its back sloping at an angle of 15 degrees to the horizontal it forms a very appropriate sundial for the capital, Zomba.

When the leopard is placed facing true south the shadow cast by its back and tail will tell the time as faithfully as any other sundial, the hour lines being ruled in with the aid of a watch on the first sunny day.

In the dining-room at Government House there is a magnificent specimen of a leopard in this pose, as shown opposite.

The original coffee tree has given way to the rising sun, which in the heraldic phraseology is 'on a Chief wavy Sable the

Rising Sun Or' and this is related to the Motto, chosen by Johnston for his design, *Lux in Tenebris*. The association is, of course, with the fact that Dr. Livingstone discovered Nyasaland when it was one of the darkest parts of Darkest Africa and it was the intention of the founders of the Protectorate that it should throw 'light in the darkness' of that unhappy region, one which it has steadily fulfilled.

Leopard statant at Government House

2. THE LAND BELOW THE LAKE

WHEN first good fortune directed me to Nyasaland, in 1945, I was told by a former high officer of the Protectorate that the simplest way to get there, short of flying, was by mail boat to Capetown and by train the rest of the way.

He had to add, 'Of course it means about five days in trains, but they're quite comfortable ones.'

Doing a sum in mental arithmetic, I said, 'But surely that means about 2000 miles by rail to reach a country which is only 200 miles from the Indian Ocean?'

But he was right and it took us only 19 days from England, whereas if we had gone by Suez and down the East Coast it would have taken four or five weeks. By slower boats you can go round via the Cape and miss the long rail journey, but it still takes a longer time.

By rail you go 800 miles through the Union, 400 miles through the Bechuanaland Protectorate, 700 miles through Rhodesia and 160 miles through Portuguese East Africa (Mozambique) and arrive at the port of Beira several days before the round-Africa boat of one or two shipping lines steams into that harbour, and if you had stayed on it you would have eaten your rail fare.

All that is very different if you go by air, and if you're in a hurry you can get to the territory in a couple of days from England, for after all it's only 5000 miles away. If you have heavy luggage you must still go about 7000 miles and for freight Nyasaland will always be round the bulge of Africa from Europe.

Whether you go East-about or West-about or overland by train you have to go through Beira, in Portuguese territory, a port which until quite recently had a very unsavoury reputation.

When you had said that it had a broad harbour (by East African standards) you had said all you could for the place, and you went on to complain of scrubby hotels, inefficient transport, lack of sanitation and so on. But it is different now. Whether it is the result of managing to keep out of the war or whether

Portugal has renounced its former attitude of 'leave it till to-morrow' the fact is that Beira is now almost a first-class port, the hotels are reasonable and you feel you are, if not exactly a welcome passer-by, at least not the nuisance you once were. The passenger train to Nyasaland goes only on Mondays and Fridays so you are almost certain to have to put in a day or so. If you're wise you spend most of the time at the ocean beach, a short bus ride from the port, but even if you spend it on the spacious wired verandah of the hotel you will find something to see. At one season it will be thousands of flamingoes stalking about on the tidal flats to seaward of the town, sieving the insalubrious mud in their curious upside-down bills.

Beyond the mud flats there are cargo boats anchored in the stream with lighters and launches fussily puffing to and fro, while to seaward there are sandy points and African fishermen busy at certain stages of the tide and resting, as only Africans can, in the intervals. If you go to the wharves, increasing in length every year, you find impressive up-to-date machinery and a general air of 'We will now show you that we are efficient'.

One may say, unkindly, that it has taken Beira a long time to realize that it is the sole port for Central Africa, but that it has now almost caught up with that high status. It is even, in the winter, a seaside resort where Rhodesians and Nyasalanders have a rest from their highlands and cold weather. This is all very different from only a few years ago. There was the sad tale of a perambulator sent out in time for the arrival of a grandchild due to be born in Southern Rhodesia. It got to Beira in six weeks but there it stayed, only 150 miles from where it should have been, for 18 months, and arrived just in time for the second grandchild, by which time the correspondence concerning it must have exceeded the weight of the pram and the child together. All this shows that Nyasaland is somewhat difficult of access and we emphasize it in this way because it is a basic economic fact.

Old timers in the Rhodesias will tell you that on at least one occasion in the past we could have bought up Beira for a song. It's a good story, but only the diplomatic files at the Foreign Office could say whether it's a reliable one.

The rail service up to Rhodesia is also vastly improved now and you may travel by an air-conditioned coach if you are careful to take a greatcoat with you to combat the shock of sitting in a temperature of 60° F after coming out of one of 90°. There's still no nonsense with such luxury in the train which takes you the 300 miles to Nyasaland, however, and it can still provide most of the discomforts which are inseparable from pioneer railway travel, including the liability to delays of many hours *en route*. It is, therefore, usually some 12 to 15 hours' journey up to the Zambezi where you rise with the sun so as not to miss the 'longest railway bridge in the world'. There are two other bridges over the Zambezi but the nearest is at Churundu, some 800 miles upstream, which gives an idea of the distances one has to be prepared for in Africa.

The one you are rumbling over is two miles long, but only in a flood season are you passing over water for that distance. In the dry season the Zambezi here is a trifle disappointing for it is then not much wider than the Thames at London and winds rather sluggishly over miles of sandbanks. The bridge was built by a British firm in 1935, and paid for by British money, but being in Portuguese territory it is to be handed over to Portugal at the end of 99 years, from which one learns how well it pays to possess the coastal belts of Africa. In fact, south of the equator Portugal possesses about 40 per cent of the coast line of Africa and Beira is only one of several toll-gates for all traffic from the interior.

Before the days of the railway up from Beira the only route to Nyasaland was via the Zambezi itself which, like the other big African rivers, is barely navigable, and highly temperamental. In those days one of the chief difficulties was to find the mouth of the river, there being a choice of many entrances, most of which had bars, unhealthy swamps of mangrove trees and shifting sandbanks. Dr. Livingstone, on his second long expedition, had infinite trouble in finding his way into the river and since then the best entrance has changed two or three times.

The Zambezi has been declared an international waterway, a fine-sounding phrase, but even when it is controlled higher up by large barrages such as those projected at Kariba Gorge in the Rhodesias and another one on its large tributary the Shire it will be little better than it is now from the point of view of navigation.

Every account of their journey to the country by the early missionaries and administrators is full of the scenes and the hazards of the river transport, and most of them reflect a sense of frustration and delay. Truly the major difficulty for a Nyasaland officer was to get to the scene of his labours; once there life was, by comparison, a simple matter.

With such stories in the traveller's mind he will not be unduly surprised at the mode of starting the train from the picturesque junction of Dona Ana just across the bridge, where a branch line goes off towards Tete, another 130 miles up river, and the coal mines there. There is always a concourse of Africans to greet the train, which has to stop on an incline; in fact the station is literally on the sloping north bank of the river, and no doubt one of the reasons for the gathering is interest in whether the train can surmount the slope.

The procedure is to take off the brakes and let the train run back down the bank and out on to the level bridge. When the driver judges he has gone far enough for the 'run-up' he starts forward again and clatters over a half-mile or so of the bridge to gain impetus. The crowd, of course, remains to see whether the first attempt is successful and, as the laboured panting of the hard-pressed engine drops to the 'I-think-I-can' stage of the climb, little totos run alongside the track watching the wheels and encouraging them with voice and mime. Even when the ascent is made it is a mile or so beyond the station before the engine can puff out its confident little 'I-knew-I-could ... I knew-I-could', and the passengers sit down again to observe a rather deserted prospect of thin bush country with few signs of habitation. They have other occupations as well, because they are approaching the frontier of Nyasaland and can be kept quite busy filling in the forms of exit and entrance, immigration permits and Customs declarations which are the bane of rail travel in Southern Africa. You always seem to be asking permission to leave one country and enter another, and the authorities always seem to be loth to let you either go or come.

By this time you will have become accustomed to the odd profiles of the baobab trees, 'those upturned carrots', as Livingstone called them, which flourish in the low country betwixt swamp and mountain all the way from Natal to the Sudan. The baobab can provide bark for clothing, seed pods for

tartaric acid, and even hollow trunks in which to store water—
a tree of character indeed.

A change comes over the scene as soon as the train crosses the
border to British territory, the miles of cultivation and the
frequent villages proclaiming that you have now entered the
most densely-populated region of all this zone of Africa.

The railway has been gradually edging towards the Shire
River, and as the train steams into the dense cluster of mango
trees, native huts and a sparse scattering of European houses
with an avenue of road that is Port Herald, you find yourself
alongside that river. As you travel farther you will come to
realize that the Shire, together with the vast lake for which it is
the sole outlet, is Nyasaland. You already have rather imposing
hills on either side of you and can easily picture that you are
now entering the southern end of the Great Rift Valley of Africa,
which with a few branches and digressions and interruptions
runs all the way up to the Red Sea and the Dead Sea and the
Jordan valley.

First impressions of a new country have some interest and
even importance, so here are some from a visitor in 1945. Port
Herald has an atmosphere of its own, small though it is, with
only a dozen or so Europeans and perhaps 2000 Africans. Its
tempo is leisurely for it is always hot there. There is a sense of
orderliness without any obvious signs of discipline; the native
police may carry a cane but never a revolver. Lest we become
too proud of our rule, however, it must be recorded that there
was no begging by Africans at Dona Ana—that only began at
Port Herald. There is a certain official formality in passing the
Customs and Immigration officers which has its comic side. On
that occasion I thought I recognized one of them as a former
student of mine, but there was not the least sign of recognition
on his part as he asked me who I was and what was my purpose,
so I concluded there must be a twin brother.

When the official business had finished with this decorum,
the officer came along to the dining-car with his colleagues for
drinks and I was welcomed with hearty handshakes and all his
news since I had last seen him years before. This particular
district officer was typical of most and since the contentment of
the Nyasaland African is linked closely with the type of administrator we have given him we may say more about it here,

and indulge in a little pride. To begin with, they do not rely on a uniform to proclaim their authority, though they have one which looks mighty fine on festivals and parades. Quite often they are more carelessly dressed than the settlers, or the Indian merchants or even the more enlightened chiefs, but they wear their khaki shirts and wide-awake hats, however old, with an air. Even at the risk of misunderstanding I would describe their attitude as 'public school', which is not the same thing as 'old school tie'. The D.O. has that outlook or approach which is so hard to describe, compounded perhaps of being devoted to his job but loth to show it, of hiding his real feelings at all times, of being fond of his people but showing it with humour, of being a ruler in fact but not a fussy one. He is there to govern but he does it with raillery in his tone rather than bluster. He knows his word is law so he uses few words, he knows his orders to his police and messengers will be obeyed so he issues them quietly. Only as magistrate is he stern and implacable, in ordinary affairs his tone is rather that of what took place on that occasion, when he saw his hunter guide in the crowd.

'You lazy old scoundrel, what are you doing here? You ought to be out in the bush finding where the game is for our next Sunday hunt.'

The grins and flood of words in reply showed that there was perfect understanding between him and his Bwana D.C. and that he much preferred to be called 'a lazy scoundrel' with a smile than something more polite without a smile.

To the real villain in his community he may show severity but no animosity. And there certainly are villains at that southern end of Nyasaland, many of them seeking a kind of refuge after crimes committed in Mozambique, for the international boundary runs down the middle line of the Shire here, only a few hundred yards from the centre of the township.

You may notice the large number of birds in this and other native villages in Central Africa, for they are not molested. Thus there is a large baobab near the station which has almost a dozen storks residing in it, and the flash of royal blue wings across the street shows that the 'blue starling' of Africa is nearly as cheeky as his duller cousins in England. Any pronounced chorus of twittering means a colony of the yellow and black weaver birds who will build just outside your window if you oblige them with a weeping kind of tree so that their nests can be out of reach of snakes.

Port Herald has always had a bad name for malaria, and is trying to live it down, but the District Commissioner's house is sited about three miles outside the town on one of the foothills to the west, whence he can look over his narrow dominion of fertile plain and swamp and savour what breezes there may be. He may have far more breeze than he likes at times as this end of the Rift Valley is notorious for its storms in the early part of the rainy season. It was at that D.C.'s house that I witnessed and endured the most vivid storm that has come my way in Africa. We had seen it and its colleagues circling all over the plain as we had dinner, with lightning so continuous that one could see mountains 40 miles away nearly all the time, but it did not come our way till two in the morning. It introduced itself by blowing in my window beyond repair and soaking my bed, whereupon I adjourned to the wide verandah (or *khonde*) to spend the rest of the night on a long chair watching the horizontal rain and the branches of trees and the thatch of the 'boys'' huts sweeping across my line of vision. I thought I was alone but found I had a companion. I had just been wondering what leopards and baboons did for shelter in such a hurricane when something furry brushed against my hands. It seemed safer to sit absolutely still until, at the next flash of lightning, I saw it was a ridge-backed hound whose acquaintance I had not made before and we spent the night in company. Perhaps this alarum had overstimulated my imagination because it was soon followed by another bogus one.

Looking floorwards during some flashes I saw a veritable snake wavily gliding towards the edge of the verandah beside my chair and its size meant that it was a python. Again it seemed best to keep quiet, stealthily drawing my feet up on to the chair. At the next flash it was still moving, larger than ever and at the third, it declared itself as a rapid runnel of water which had overflowed some gutter or other and was pouring down the wall behind me and across the verandah.

Local residents must be accustomed to such displays because the D.C. himself had slept through the turmoil and was not unduly disturbed to find that his 'boys'' huts were bare to the sky in the morning and his road to the township blocked by fallen trees.

By some curious inversion of logic, district officers stationed in a less pleasant part of their territory often take a liking to it and ask to remain there, especially if they are bachelors. To listen to two or more administrators discussing the relative merits of their stations is, at all events, no guide as to what these really are like. As one of them said to me, 'At least you see new white faces at Port Herald when the train passes through and you get the newspapers first.'

Drying fish on the banks of the Shire River

From there to the next place of importance, Chiromo, the train puts on some speed over the flood-plain and its track is flanked by native gardens most of the way, while the meandering line of the river marked by its waving papyrus heads is rarely more than a mile to the eastward.

Chiromo is at the junction of the turbulent Ruo with the Shire, and long before you get to it you see mountains rising higher and higher to the north and east. Conspicuous amongst these, because it is isolated, is Mount Chiperone, in Portuguese territory, and this is not only graceful in shape but has achieved fame by being the alleged cause of local rainy or at least showery weather right in the middle of the dry season, which is a godsend to the peasant cultivators. Certainly the clouds seem to come from the mountain and when you are held up by bad weather on the roads and you complain that it's quite wrong to have rain in July you are told. 'Oh, it's one of our "Chiperones", and it will probably last for four days.' The railway crosses the Shire at Chiromo by an iron bridge which has to be strong to withstand the floods of the river which here contracts to about 100 yards in width and runs at up to three knots. Consequently, the first bridge passed through many critical times, not without damage, until in 1949 it was completely carried away by the pressure of water banking up behind floating islands of vegetation (sudds) which catch on the pillars.

A new and better bridge has now been put in its place (see Plate V (c)). In the interim there would have been a complete barrier to rail traffic, a serious matter, but for the ingenuity of an officer of the Public Works Department and the railway engineers. In a very few days a ferry service was organized. It looked impossible but worked perfectly. Two stern-wheel paddle boats were available and a few large barges which would stand the weight of a railway truck but not that of an engine. There was a great scene of bustle when we arrived at the broken bridge: passengers got out and walked to the boats while an army of porters carried the luggage. The freight cars were gently backed on to lines laid across the barge, athwartships, a ticklish operation but done quickly with practice. One of the attendant stern-wheelers had to be downstream during this transfer, the other being firmly moored on the outside of the barge. Native passengers then swarmed aboard the same barge and the hawsers were cast off. The strong current at once caught the barge and its steamer and, while it appeared to be drifting helplessly at a queer angle, the other steamer glided up and moored itself quickly to the other side of the barge. It took only five minutes for the whole assemblage to be carried down to the mouth of the Ruo and disaster always seemed to be imminent. But the skilled Portuguese skippers of these stern-wheelers knew their job and edged their clumsy tow into the comparatively quiet waters of the Ruo with no mishap. The whole manoeuvre rarely lasted more than 15 minutes before the truck was being hauled up another ramp and the passengers were climbing into another set of carriages.

The new bridge has a wider span and a higher rail level than the old one and, therefore, should have a longer life, but even while it was building I watched one day an unusually large sudd coming down which barely cleared the span, and heard one of the construction engineers murmur that a run of such sudds would be distinctly awkward.

Sitting on the bank of the Shire when floods are running is nothing less than absorbing, remotely similar to watching the

Lily-trotter

traffic along an arterial road in England, for each little island of vegetation is different from the last. It is all one-way traffic, of course, except for the birds which float down on the islands, and then fly back upstream for another trip. Amongst these are the *jacanas* or lily-trotters, with their eight-inch spread of foot enabling them to walk over all but the thinnest of flotsam. They are handsome birds when seen close by, the patterns of reds and browns and yellows being neat though subdued, while at a distance and in flight they look like giant wasps with their yellow feet hanging down instead of being streamlined behind as with cranes and storks.

The sudding of the river may be taken as the sloughing off of the surplus growth of the rest of the year. Every still lagoon or lazy reach of the streams has been busy producing this vegetation during the dry season, till the rising level and increasing current has floated it off into the main stream on its way to a resting place farther down the river or even to death in the salt sea hundreds of miles away.

The most prominent of all the plants to be seen is the small *pistia stratiotes*, which is found on nearly all African rivers and is called locally the 'Shire cabbage'. Its light green crinkly leaves liken it more to the lettuce tribe and it is a true floating plant, growing like wildfire and covering thousands of acres of water surface in the season, so that lagoons may be completely covered with it until the floods come to disperse them, either as single plants turning ceaselessly round in the current or as small carpets of a few score plants matted together.

At the other end of the scale there are the reeds and the papyrus with stems up to 15 feet long, neither of which are really floating plants, preferring some kind of soil in or under the water to give both food and anchorage until the flood surge buoys them up from their hold on the mud and carries them off in islands up to half an acre in extent, together with a wealth of smaller grasses, arums and even small shrubs, all entwined enough to stand bumps against the banks or other obstructions without coming to pieces.

The real menace of these sudds is not only their size but the fact that they are still growing and if they get held up in shallow water they take root again and may thus cause a complete blockage for a season or two, through which it is very difficult to cut a passage. Incidentally, if a paddle-steamer gets really entangled in a large sudd it is likely to be carried down a long way before it can extricate itself.

In African rivers, in fact, it is the sudds rather than the sandbanks which cause the channels to change and their courses to become meandering.

Chiromo is not an impressive place, rather straggly and unkempt in spite of many large trees growing well on the low sandspit which is the basis of the settlement. With the rapid Ruo River on one side and the swamps of the Shire on the other, it is apt to suffer from the floods of each river and when they coincide in time as they did in 1951 they leave their mark in a reddish stain some three feet from the ground on all the houses at the lower end of its one street. Not a salubrious township either, with so much water about, yet it possesses historic interest in the brief history of the country.

Chiromo has always been more truly the gateway to Nyasaland than Port Herald, for it was here that the early visitors had the choice of climbing up the 4000 feet to the Shire Highlands or of making the tedious passage for 80 miles farther up the river, risking the hazards of malaria and rapid currents, not to mention unfriendly reception by tribal autocrats on the banks or hippos in the water.

On one occasion it took Dr. Livingstone six weeks to do that 80 miles in his 'tin can', the *Ma Robert*, while in the very next year Bishop Mackenzie made his last fatal journey down it. His canoe was upset by a hippo, the medicine chest was lost and the bishop arrived at Chiromo after seven days of wet misery only to die of fever there.

Later it was one of the strongholds of chiefs descended from Livingstone's Makololo carriers who played their somewhat undistinguished part in the proclaiming of the Protectorate by being fiercely hostile to the Portuguese.

We will, on this occasion, choose the easier route to the Highlands, sitting in the train winding along the rugged valley of the Ruo, which descends from the 9800 feet of Mlanje to the 150 feet above sea-level of Chiromo in a matter of some 60 miles. It is, therefore, a picturesque river with many rapids of which one catches a glimpse of the Soa Falls about half-way up, impressive in the wet season, and promising to be a tourist centre some day in the future.

It is as much as the powerful engines can do to negotiate the inclines and the curves of small radius, so that it is a noisy journey. Occasionally there are a few native huts to be seen clinging to sandy flats near the river, but for the most part the steep slopes produce nothing but trees and it seems very wild and uninhabitable country.

As the edge of the plateau is approached the view broadens and the scene changes. Not only does the impressive mass of Mlanje appear to the east, as mentioned in the first chapter, but

23

there are wide grass lands, the dense green of plantations and an air of settlement and prosperity.

We are now in the Shire Highlands where had settled the spearhead of British effort in this part of Africa, in the form of missionaries and traders, many years before Southern Rhodesia had been thought of, or British East Africa, later to be known as Kenya.

Dr. Livingstone, as usual, was the first man to discover this promising area in 1859 and, as usual, he recognized its value as a centre for white people, for the trade which he hoped would undercut slavery, and for the teaching which he knew would give the people relief from the rule of witchcraft and superstition that bound them almost as firmly as the bonds of slavery.

He understood also that some form of political protection would be needed but he was cautious about public utterance on that topic for it was a no-man's-land he had discovered, encircled by Portuguese claims, shadowy enough but boldly stated, and his own Government was little likely to share his visions for the future of that inaccessible pocket in Africa.

These highlands have been the heart of British development in the country and probably always will be so, and it is as well that we should remember what it was when Livingstone chose it to be so, though because he moved a little too fast for the African his first missionary plans failed.

In the first place it was a comparatively empty land, with villages few and far between, so no one would be dispossessed if traders, missionaries and settlers occupied it.

It is hard to believe, as one rumbles along towards Blantyre, the economic capital, that the numerous villages were not there 50 years ago, any more than the wide acres of tea and tung and tobacco, or the occasional homestead of a settler to be seen from the railway line. The fact of the matter is that the African nearly always preferred the lower levels of the rift valley, where there was no cold season, where things would grow all the year round, and he would occupy the uplands only when driven there by war. So the villages of the Manganja tribe on the Shire Highlands were hard to find, and in 1861 Bishop Mackenzie had to go to the lower area of Magomero towards Mount Zomba before he could find a large enough gathering of villages amongst which to begin his labours. In those days you could look across from Mount Zomba 40 miles towards Mlanje and see the smoke of less than a dozen villages, representing fewer than 2000 people. Now, there are hundreds of villages and something like 300,000 Africans, and nearly all of them are late-comers, immigrants largely from Portuguese East Africa. What has brought them there has been the white man, with his labour requirements, his guarantee of security, his gifts of education, law and order.

There is nothing new about such a state of affairs, it has happened all over the world, the most striking case being Hong Kong, where the most densely-populated island in the world was uninhabited until, little more than a century ago, the white man came and established a trading centre.

To get a closer view of these highlands we had better descend from the train at Luchenza, some 30 miles short of Blantyre, and visit one of the settler's houses in Cholo, the district where most of the white farms are to be found. We drive there 20 miles by car over the first surprise, a tarmac road, stretching all the way to Limbe, the twin town to Blantyre and centre for the railway administration and workshops.

We drive quickly past groves of Australian eucalypts, now become the staple fuel for Nyasaland tea estates, past thickets of an Asiatic bamboo, and through young townships with lines of Indian stores, with the District Commissioner's headquarters or Boma discreetly off the main road. Then past the neatly-clipped acres of large tea estates with their shade trees of *grevillea* or other exotic trees, past plantations of tung oil trees, and even one of olive trees from the Mediterranean which, however, have not proved suited to the local climate. A mile or so off this busy road one glimpses an occasional European homestead, always one-storeyed with wide verandah and always on a hill to catch the breezes and to secure a view.

The homestead we are heading for is some miles off the main road and, though typical, it is smaller than most, still bearing all the marks of the pioneer days of 30 years ago. The road to it, therefore, is still little more than a track and it passes by a dense thicket or two where leopards may lurk and then turns in suddenly through young tung trees to reach our destination. It is really a bungalow, built of local material in every sense of the word, for the bricks were made of clay dug from the hillside and the thatch came from the coarse thatch grasses that still cover much of the ground. All planned and built by the owner in days when every penny had to be accounted for and when the 600 acres of his estate boasted only a few acres of tung and a few more of mealies for his employees, usually called 'boys' in Central Africa, and one had to be an optimist to see any future for such a small holding.

I believe that I was the first guest to stay in this bungalow but even then it had all the elements of an English home far away from England, and now, eight years later, it has the quintessence of that spirit.

The house faces to the northward and has, like most houses in the Cholo district, a superb view. Seated on the low verandah or on the carefully-trimmed lawn just beyond it one looks down the sloping garden with its rose bushes to remind one of England, oleanders on the right to add a slight hint of the Mediterranean and, on the left, a row of the jacaranda, the ornamental tree of all southern Africa, so covered with its mauve mist of flowers that it almost hurts the eyes. Lower still there is the plantation of banana trees, looking like overgrown arum shoots, and on beyond are rolling hills which were forest until a few years ago and now have villages or small estates all over them. Some miles away there are half a dozen bare rocky hills looking in the distance so conical and so naked that I always called them the 'lunar landscape'. On beyond these are high mountains, with old Chiradzulu standing up to take the morn like some African Olympus, with its wisp of cloud at the summit trailing off towards the leaden mass of Mount Zomba 7000 feet above the sea and over 50 miles away.

Only to the eastward is the view restricted by trees but a walk of two minutes would expose the magnificent fortress of granite that is Mlanje some 30 miles distant, seen over an apparent plain which looks wooded but, in fact, is crowded with villages wherever there is permanent water. This view was always best before breakfast and to complete the picture the reader must imagine he can whiff the fresh air of his 4000-feet altitude, can watch the owner in shirt and shorts and battered hat walk up the hill from inspecting his young tung trees, hear his jubilant tones as he announces that there was a little rain last night so planting can be begun. At that hour, too, there come from all sides sounds of a myriad birds—the chatter of the tiny manakins flying like a swarm of large bees out from their colony in the thatch, the impossibly liquid note of the golden oriole, the querulous challenge of the native partridge (*nkhwale*) and the harsh call of a guinea fowl down by the vegetable garden.

There is Jim, the tall Angoni boy, starting off on his 12-mile walk to get the mail and there is the head house-boy, Ben, clearing away the early morning tea-tray.

Yet in spite of these very African sights and sounds, in spite of all these high mountains with their strange native names, the impression remains, insistently, that this is an England overseas, a transplanted England.

In neighbouring Rhodesia a man, even if he has been resident for only a year, will proudly and rightly proclaim that he is a Rhodesian—British, of course, but a Rhodesian. In Nyasaland the handful of British settlers has not yet reached that stage of cousinly independence, and they are determinedly British overseas, and all their bonds with home are kept religiously.

There are good reasons for this intensely British atmosphere, and we shall discover them as we study the country, but a very obvious one is the desperately small number of Europeans in the country. Thus in 1891, when the British Government declared the Protectorate, there were only 57 whites in the country, though there were already six small steamers on the lake. Ten years later the number had risen to 341 and in the 1914–18 war over half the total European population joined the Army.

It used to be said, in joke, that you could meet half the whites in the whole country at any good-sized party in Blantyre. Even now, with something over 4500 Europeans, the number is merely that of a small country town in the homeland, and for every white there are one-and-a-quarter Asians and 540 Africans. If we confine ourselves to the true settlers, omitting the administration service and the missionaries, the proportions are still more striking. It is little wonder, therefore, that the link with the United Kingdom is far stronger than with Rhodesia or South Africa, in spite of their proximity.

Had we stayed in the train instead of visiting a Cholo homestead we should have passed through more and more occupied country till we reached Limbe which, with its twin Blantyre, five miles farther on, is the commercial centre of the country.

27

As a corollary they are also the centres for the Indian population, for, as elsewhere in Africa, these are the traders, and the lines of Indian shops in both these towns are the busiest parts and the most untidy parts.

There is some rivalry between these two towns which is probably healthy, but before very long they will be almost continuous. There is a fine broad tarmac road between the two, bus services and a constant stream of cars which are always in a hurry. Hence this is the most dangerous part of the country and road accidents are frequent, the jay-walkers and wobbling cyclists being the chief victims.

The railway does not stop at Blantyre but goes on, to plunge once more down into the rift valley, cross the Shire at Mpimbe and run on for another 150 miles to Lake Nyasa.

Vidzumo, Counsellor of Chief Mwase. Reputed to be over ninety years of age, he must have been a small boy when Livingstone was in Nyasaland

3. ZOMBA

IF the twin towns of Limbe and Blantyre represent the heart of the business activity of the territory—its City of London —we have to make a long step to its Whitehall, 40 miles away, with no railway to it.

So we take to the road again, now a first-class tarmac one, and drive past a large mission out into the country, past many a striking hill with views of more distant ones at every turn, the most distant being in Portuguese territory on either side.

It is really rather a historic road and in our modern haste we are apt to forget that fact. Indeed it is hard to imagine that just over 50 years ago this road was a robbers' road where you were liable to have your carriers scattered in an ambush and lose half your goods. You pass below old Chiradzulu, always a handsome hill, and forget that it was the haunt of petty chiefs who were bandits or slavers or both. You see on the right a signpost to Magomero, the scene of Bishop Mackenzie's first mission effort, and the Livingstone tradition is here still warm, as his eldest daughter married the owner of a large estate there in later years.

You pass a few villages in which the centre-piece is usually a rather unkempt Indian store, and it is clear that there are plenty of others a little off the road, as there is ceaseless traffic of Africans, always walking. One comes to the conclusion that when an African has nothing else to do he walks along the road and back again. The women, of course, have baskets or bundles on their heads but the men, no longer having to carry spears, are usually empty-handed.

This is too busy a road for the innate politeness of the Nyasa peoples to show up strongly but even so most of the old men doff their hats if they have them, and if you were not going so fast you would hear a '*M'oni, Bwana*' (Greeting, Master) as you passed. Here, at least, there is an air of security and contentment which is unmistakable.

With so many hills in the way, hills which would be classed as high mountains in England, you do not see much of Zomba

Mountain until you are within a few miles of it, when it looks like a threatening wall blocking your farther passage.

As you come closer and look up to its plateau at 6000 feet above sea-level you see a few bungalows on the edge even before you see much of the town below where, indeed, most of the houses are so surrounded by large trees that you rarely see them as a group. In fact, you don't take in Zomba properly until you look down on it from the plateau which overhangs it. Yet it is the finest residential site in all Central Africa, and from every verandah of every house you have the best of Nyasaland scenery before you. To the east there is the shimmer of Lake Chilwa, in the midst of which there is a hill on an island, to the south-east there is Mlanje, 50 miles away, with its pattern of clouds changing every day. Nearer are the high hills we passed through on our way and, to the west, there is the unmistakable drop to the Shire valley, beyond which is the jagged outline of the Kirk Range which marks the Portuguese border in that direction.

Zomba had been chosen as his residence by Consul Hawes in 1886 and its beauty was not lost on Consul Johnston when he arrived in 1889, by which time the 'Residency' was by far the best house in the country. He soon set about improving it further and with the skilled help of Dr. Whyte, the elderly botanist who did so much exploration in the early days, he laid out the gardens which are now one of the sights of Zomba. Lest this should be thought a straightforward task, we must add that during that period there were wars with slaver-chiefs within a few miles of the Residency, and the Consul himself was absent at least half of his time making treaties or wars with unruly elements far afield in the territory.

More remarkable still, the original part of the house was built by John Buchanan, who came out as a young Scottish gardener for the Blantyre Mission in 1876, introduced coffee as a crop to the country in 1880, became acting-Consul, was captured and flogged by a lakeshore chief, took part in much of the fighting, proclaimed the provisional protectorate when threatened by the Portuguese and died in 1896, having done as much as anyone to lay a foundation for the country.

The architecture is a little unusual, with its terraces, its bow-fronted centre, and a hexagonal tower at each end; but some of these features were necessary as it had to be readily convertible into a fortress. Sir Harry Johnston replaced the original thatch with red corrugated iron (now painted green), which has lasted well but does give a rather untidy appearance.

Zomba is proud of the neat gardens below the Old Residency, as it is called, but one has the impression that it looks a little sideways at the queer and somewhat unkempt-looking building overlooking them.

Yet the building is even more historic than the famous church in Blantyre and it is to be hoped that the Government will not only cherish it carefully, but will take the proper steps to preserve it from decay, whatever the cost. There is a period in the life of all pioneer countries when the inhabitants are a little apt to be ashamed of the early structures and to replace them with modern ones. Nyasaland, one feels, has got beyond that stage, and will become increasingly proud of a building created by its famous gardener son and his brother at a time when few people saw any future for the country.

During Johnston's six years of residence the house and its backyard were rather crowded with the pets which he as an ardent naturalist collected, including leopards, cats and baboons, crested cranes, geese and guinea-fowl. His skill at rendering them docile and affectionate will be best realized from the fact that one of his guinea-fowl was known as 'the Sergeant', attending parades of the guard with its master, and following him for walks, pecking at Africans who came too near.

A crested crane of his accompanied him on his journey from Lake Nyasa to Lake Tanganyika in 1889–90, being carried on the march but rejoining his master in camp. Versatile pets of an even more versatile Governor!

Even now Zomba is delightfully wild as far as animal and bird life is concerned. Not many colonial capitals can claim to have lions parading their streets at night, but this still happens in Zomba, though they are usually satisfied with taking a dog or two. In 1945 I went to dine at a farm a few miles out where a night watchman asleep on a verandah had been seized the night before by the foot but released at the uproar of his companions' yelling. So I had the interesting experience of being driven back to Zomba by the Chief Secretary, very slowly, in hopes of seeing the lion, though we had no weapons with which to deal out punishment.

The private houses are all on the steep slopes of the mountain with winding roads leading to them, and so embowered with trees that you rarely see the next-door house unless it is the roof of the one below your own.

The trees in these gardens are mostly indigenous and illustrate very well how many and various are the species in the territory, running to over a thousand in number. On a climb

Crested cranes

from the Shire to the top of Mount Zomba one passes through every type of vegetation, from the papyrus, the palms and the baobabs of the riverside right up to the moorland grasses and the groves of Mlanje cedar on the summit.

This cedar, which was first discovered by the botanist, Dr. Whyte, and therefore rejoices in the name of *Widdringtonia whytei*, is a very valuable timber and grows best on the mountain of that name in dense patches filling the higher valleys. It has a fine straight trunk, bleached white, with widespread branches and rather scanty tufts of dark green leaves at the ends. The wood is easily worked and looks like that of our lead pencils. The Forestry Department is cherishing the comparatively small areas of cedar, and, besides regulating its cutting, is planting it in other suitable parts of the country. On the well-watered slopes of the Zomba mountain there are examples of the giant evergreen fig-tree which is such a favoured one in the native villages. It provides a dense shade for rest or gossip or liquid refreshment and is, in fact, the equivalent of the bar at the 'local' with us.

The most universal trees of the countryside are those which can withstand the annual bush-fires and of these the commonest are the graceful acacia-leaved group known as the *Brachystegia*, which rarely have straight trunks or tall ones. They are deciduous but the new leaves come very quickly after the old ones have fallen and they burst out in the most brilliant shades of red, capable of setting a whole hillside aglow with rich colour in September, comparable only to that of our Virginia creeper in autumn garb.

Amongst them are found the even more fireproof *Musuku* trees with large and heavily-ribbed leaves, curiously curved and a fruit growing in rich red clusters. When ripe, this fruit, the size of a plum, has a pleasant sub-acid taste very much favoured by all animals from monkeys to elephants. It is of little value as a food, yet it has held off starvation many a time, including periods in Dr. Livingstone's journeys through Nyasaland. Another typical tree is the silvery-leaved *Napini*, whose wood is tough enough for native weapons and which is none other than the silky-tufted *Terminalia sericea*, found all over Central Africa, even in the semi-arid wastes of the Kalahari.

Lastly we must mention the untidy but useful common bamboo, sometimes growing in dense thickets but more often to be found sprouting out of ant-hills, every hill with its bamboo. It has the very curious life-cycle of growing for about 30 years and then suddenly seeding and dying all over a single district, so that at regular intervals there are liable to be bamboo famines. It is small compared with the giant Asiatic species but very strong and has a myriad uses.

Central Africa is to be congratulated on its trees, so varied in

33

form and colour, so different from those of Australia where the universal eucalypt is liable to be monotonous in the extreme. With all this wealth of species one can expect a good deal of interest in forestry in the country and the Forestry Department, though small, is very active. It is one of the few departments that earns revenue in excess of its expenditure.

There is something very farseeing and selfless about foresters, who are for ever sowing where they cannot hope to reap themselves. The Director is one such and his policy for the future of the territory's forests has all the elements of statesmanship in a technical field. It may seem to be a contradiction in terms to talk about a forestry policy for a country which is becoming densely populated, but that is precisely why long-term planning at this stage is so essential. Forestry policy wraps up very neatly with water conservation policy because tree-cover in the uplands and on steep slopes is the very best way of holding up water and preventing rapid run-off and its concomitant, soil erosion.

Briefly stated, its three key timbers in a planting policy are the Mlanje cedar, which, of course, is indigenous, pines and eucalypts, both of which are imported. The cedar is the most valuable but it takes 60 years to mature; it is resistant to the attacks of the white ant and its fame, as well as its seed, is spreading over the world. Moreover, it regenerates itself very happily in Nyasaland. Pines grow at an exceptional rate in the plateau areas and the variety *Patula* can pay for its cost by thinnings at seven years after planting-out and thereafter makes a clear profit. The eucalypts grow even faster, up to 15 feet in height in three years, and plantations of them are to be seen wherever white settlers are found.

Its value is chiefly for firewood and for poles; it is not a good building timber on account of its tendency to split and warp. When cut down it throws up strong shoots from the stump, which are ready for cutting again as poles in three or four years. The best altitude for the cedar seems to be above 6000 feet, for the pine groups from 3000 upwards and the eucalypt at almost any altitude provided there is ample water.

For building-timber, therefore, the pines seem to be the most economic, as they reach maturity in 30 years yet pay for their keep long before that. On the other hand they are much more sensitive to fire and the universal fire hazard is the chief bugbear

34

of the forester. The African has relied on fire for so many centuries for his hunting methods and for his agricultural clearings that he has become what we might call fire-happy, so it will take a long time and possibly a good deal of legislation to subdue his enthusiasm for causing a good old blaze by the very simplest means. Experiments are being made, mainly in Northern Rhodesia, to find out what happens in a natural forest when no burning-off is allowed over a number of years. It appears that undergrowth then gets a chance of taking hold but so far the trees do not seem to grow any straighter or larger than before. It must be remembered, too, that grass fires are one of the best ways of controlling insect pests, especially the ticks which flourish under grassland conditions.

The Zomba gardens are watered by babbling brooks and rills led from the mountain side and consequently they are equivalent to bird sanctuaries.

You may sit on your host's verandah and see, or at least hear, a good percentage of birds of Nyasaland, from the tiny blue waxbill, not much larger than a humming-bird, to the curious hammerkop, the hammer-headed wader which builds its enormous nest in large trees up the ravines of the mountain.

I saw one of the biggest of these nests in Government House Gardens in a large tree just above a pleasant bouldery stream and at the same time I was told of one of its forms of food. While His Excellency and I were trying to get close to the hammerkop's nest, which looked rather like a heap of twigs set for a bonfire in the tree, his eleven-year-old daughter was trying to find me a sample of the landcrabs from under the boulders. The search was assiduous but unsuccessful, so I told the determined young lady that I would do my best to imagine her alleged 'crabs as large as saucers'.

I hadn't bargained for the persistence that no doubt she had inherited from her father and I had a sharp reminder of it some months later when I was staying at another house close by. Just as I was leaving for an evening engagement a large but light parcel arrived for me from Government House, which I took to be socks or a handkerchief which I must have left behind there. So I did not open it till I was going to bed and in a dim light, when my fingers at once discovered the weapons of offence of a saucer-sized crab. Hidden underneath it was a brief note: 'An alleged crab and I hope it gives you an alleged nip.' She had scored heavily and I doubt if she minded the answering note from me—'Hell knows no fury like a woman scorned.'

The present Government House, which succeeded the old Residency in 1902, is of noble proportions and of a style best described as baronial with its battlements and towers, its terraced gardens and wide lawns. It is approached by a neat road in sweeping curves up from the guard-house at the main gate. If you are staying more than an odd day or so in Zomba you call at the guard-house to sign in the visitors' book.

The Central African climate is rather hard on public buildings, which are apt to look seedy just before the periodic cleanings and paintings, but Government House at Zomba has an air which is only equalled by that at Lusaka, and for scenic outlook it excels all others in Africa that I know.

For grandeur of site and beauty of scenery Zomba is, therefore, unique but it would be foolish to blind oneself to some of its disabilities.

It is, for instance, somewhat isolated from the economic centre of the territory, Blantyre, a fact which has been already recognized by placing some of the departmental headquarters, such as Forestry, at Limbe. There was even a movement to move the centre of Government from Zomba to the railway.

Its isolation is, however, accidental in a way since when the railway was continued from Blantyre it was a moot point whether it should go via Zomba to the lake or in the direction it now follows, by-passing the south end of the lake altogether. It may be that a branch line via Zomba to Fort Johnston may yet be built, but even without it the 40 miles by road has already been greatly reduced in time by the laying of a first-class road. Opinions will still vary over the world on whether it is better to have the centre of business and centre of Government in the same city as at London, or to separate the two, as in U.S.A. with New York and Washington. Circumstances, aided by Sir Harry Johnston, favoured the latter course for Nyasaland.

Another quite definite drawback at Zomba is its being under a very high mountain which is at times a focus for catastrophic storms. One such in 1946 caused great havoc and some loss of life and it is no good pretending that similar visitations will not recur from time to time.

The private houses are distributed along the steep lower slopes of the mountain and, therefore, have to be reached by roads which have sharp curves and steep gradients, and pass over innumerable bridges. In the 1946 storm every one of these bridges went and not a few cars were marooned for weeks between two broken bridges on the mountain, while the lawns in the lower levels, including the golf course, were covered with astonishingly large boulders brought down from above by the deluge. The private residences suffered less than one would expect in a storm which registered 28 inches of rain in 44 hours, because they have to be on the little ridges between the ravines.

Nevertheless, there is a certain sense of imminence in that plateau 2000 feet above the houses, a loom of impending masses of rock which, when the mountain is wreathed in swirling mists, can be awe-inspiring if not actually alarming to the newcomer.

The residents make light of it, and in fact hardly any part of the mountain is too steep to scramble up on a Sunday morning, a favourite diversion for many of those who are doomed to sit at a desk the whole of the week.

There was an Attorney-General not so long ago, who was my host for a week, whose custom for the week-end, in spite of his weight and status, was to spend Sunday climbing all over Mount Zomba, possibly as an antidote or corrective for the amazing curry for lunch the day before, which he himself prepared during Saturday morning. He was indeed a tribute in himself to the climate of Zomba which allowed excesses of this kind in the direction of putting on weight one day and taking it off the next, and being the soul of every party that could capture him during the week. For those who are less athletic there is an easier way, the winding road six miles long which climbs half-way up on a westerly bearing and then turns sharply eastward for the rest of its serpentine route.

You have to time your start from the bottom since at the half-way turn you meet a large clock and a signboard which together tell you that those going up must not start before the hour, since a similar clock at the top will have sent off cars starting down at the half-hour. This is because the road is very narrow, built out on ledges and brackets with buttresses of rock on one side and vacant space on the other, and there are practically no passing-places.

Even so there are occasional 'incidents' on this road, such as one when we started off five minutes too early because we heard from an African walking down that there was a leopard on the road half a mile ahead. Our luck was out, the leopard had vanished and we met a descending car. We survived the impasse by our front wheels climbing a few feet up a sloping buttress,

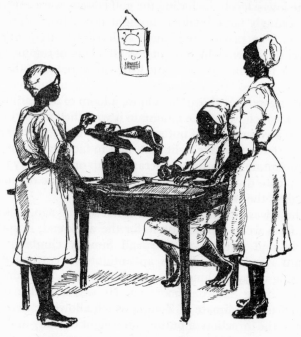

Child welfare at Zomba

which gave the other car a couple of inches to spare on the precipice side. More alarming to the passengers was another occasion when we obeyed the timing rule but after a mile or so met a walker who told us a large car had broken down a little farther on and completely blocked the road. Even Chief Secretaries become hardened to such awkward situations in Africa and he let gravity take us backwards down the road for the mile-and-a-half without turning a hair of his head, though ours was certainly erect at every corner. At one point you pass under a steel cable far overhead, which is the means of sending down the timber from the forests on the plateau.

At the top you have plenty of room, of course, but only a few roads to take you anywhere beyond the dozen or so bungalows which are the summer or week-end resorts of a few Zomba people. The serried lines of the man-made forests of conifers and the grassy downs take you back to Scottish highlands, for here you are far higher than you can get in Scotland though only 15 degrees from the equator. A few hundred feet below you there is the equivalent of a loch in the form of a tree-fringed reservoir, which furnishes the power for the electricity supply of Zomba, the power house being at least 1500 feet below the dam. It is being increased in capacity not without the fears expressed by some of the citizens below that one of the rare earthquakes which do occur along rift valleys might break the dam and empty it on to their heads.

You drive along the road till you get near the edge and then walk to see a view which for once really deserves the epithets 'majestic' and 'sublime'. The whole of Mlanje lies 50 miles away across what appears to be a flat plain, often flecked with cloud or shadows or obscured by the smoke of burning fires. In the direction of Blantyre are minor mountains, but several of these are only 1000 feet lower than your viewpoint.

Immediately below you Zomba itself is spread out but still so shrouded by its own large trees that you have difficulty in picking out individual buildings. Government House, of course, stands out with its lofty Union Jack flying, and farther away the neat patterns of the Police Lines and the cantonment of the King's African Rifles (K.A.R.).

The Secretariat can be seen, getting old but still rather handsome; in the upper storey there is the Legislative Council Room, with its portraits of former Governors.

Above it are the broad roofs of the hospital and below it those of the government departments, but most of Zomba is definitely hidden by trees. The golf course and athletic ground of the Club are only partly hidden, the Club being the social centre of Zomba, whereat nearly every communal meeting has to be, whether it is the weekly cinema film show, the games of cricket and football or ceremonial parades.

The place is growing fast and already has the shadow of a new suburb which is farther round the eastern face of the mountain, and is at present a neat cluster of modern smallish houses reserved for junior officials and their families. All these, too, have views to be seen from their pleasant if small verandahs overlooking their gardens which are rapidly becoming individual under the care of their tenants. Truly the married Secretariat officials of junior grade have their feet in pleasant places even though feet will hardly take them to their daily work two miles away in that warm climate.

Zomba is thus distributed over nearly 1000 feet in altitude, the lowest part being just under 3000 feet above sea-level. Because of this low altitude, for Africa, Zomba was not uniformly healthy in the early days when the amenities of life were less.

There is one definite lack in the town which is a curious one for a place which must have many official visitors, if few of the commercial kind. There is still no residential hotel there, though the small 'Pig and Whistle' is doing its best to turn itself from a restaurant with bar into an embryo hotel. One is forced to the true conclusion that nearly all visitors are so official that they are put up by one or other of the resident officers whom they have come to see, and that a hotel would soon be bankrupt.

This arrangement may have been necessary in the past but it can also be embarrassing to both hosts and visitors, while the casual visitor who merely wants to see the place has nowhere to lay his head nearer than Limbe, 40 miles away. Clearly this is not the best way to encourage a tourist industry, and no doubt steps will soon be taken to rectify it, for, as the above description must have indicated, Zomba is one of the sights of Nyasaland and ought not to be omitted, even if it would disturb the atmosphere of official calm which certainly veils the capital and, according to some, even smothers it.

I have been lucky enough to visit it always in some official capacity and have been received by charming hosts in their delightful houses, so it is hard to criticize from this point of view. Nevertheless, one senses the usual defects of a town which is almost entirely for civil servants, and where business people have no business to reside, and certainly no encouragement.

It is only to be expected, therefore, that Blantyre is sometimes very vocal about the inaccessibility of Zomba in all senses of the word and feels that when it goes there it is liable to be treated with the kind of benevolent arrogance with which, in Victorian times, the local lord of the manor would treat the village grocer.

One must add that this is only discernible if you stay some time in the country and it is very far from the state in which Canberra, the federal capital of Australia, found itself a few years ago. There the whole layout, though planned by an American architect, proclaimed that civil servants were not only to be served first but also in well-defined order of precedence, one suburb for junior clerks, another for the senior ones, while the business centre was discreetly distant from the Houses of Parliament and the Governor-General's dwelling far removed from the city.

But in so far as this character of aloofness is present at all in Zomba it is one which time will cure, the first step to be hoped for being the building of a good residential hotel.

Another difficulty for the visitor is the distance to be covered in the town and the lack of taxis. This is less of a hindrance than would be expected, since you have to have a car in order to reach the place at all, but you cannot always be asking your host to take you about from one department to another. It was characteristic of Dr. Livingstone and Dr. Kirk that, on their very first visit to the present Nyasaland, they walked right across the Shire Highlands and climbed Mount Zomba. It way well have been as a result of the view from its summit that they wrote of it as 'that rich and pleasant country, the Expedition's happiest discovery and the field of its greatest hope'.

Baobab trees

4. THE LAND BESIDE THE LAKE

AFTER reading the last chapter you may suggest that Nyasaland should have been satisfied with its rich province of the Shire Highlands, and ask why the white men went farther.

Dr. Livingstone went farther because he was that kind of man, because he had heard of a great lake farther north and because he wanted to see where slavery was flourishing and to devise means to combat it.

The later missionaries went farther because Dr. Robert Laws was built after the fashion of Livingstone, determined to go where need was greatest.

The administrators went farther because the trouble from the slaving tribes was centred on the lake, and in the case of Sir Harry Johnston because he foresaw the partition of Africa and he wished to establish British claims, as we have already seen.

The early settler, however, did not follow, partly because the Shire Highlands were wide enough for that mere handful of people, but mainly because the farther one went inland the farther it was from oversea markets and the more costly the carriage of anything they could produce for those markets.

We must go farther because not only is the land beside the lake the greater part of the country but because it is there that it marches with its new partner in the Federation, Northern Rhodesia; it is also becoming the granary of the territory.

We shall have to choose our time of year, or at least avoid the months of January to March, as that is the rainy season and we are leaving tarmac roads behind. It is the peculiarity of most Central African roads that in dry weather they may permit 70 miles an hour yet in the wet season they may degenerate to something like a deeply-ploughed field. There is a stage in between when only the most skilled drivers can avoid nasty skids, and that they do by keeping up a reasonable speed and never touching the brake.

If we have official business up north we take an official car and driver rather than a hired one, as we are sure to need some running repairs and it is very convenient to have access to the

P.W.D. (Public Works Department) depots. If it is a modern saloon car so much the better; if it is a box car or station waggon type with a square end we shall be covered with dust from the suction. We shall have to take also some tinned provisions and jerry-cans for water as we may have to stop the night at a rest-house or even spend a night in the bush, neither of them hardships, but it's as well to be prepared.

We set off from Zomba, the road taking us round the eastern end of the mountain mass and giving a view across the well-settled land towards Lake Chilwa. At first we pass all the signs of European settlement, tung plantations chiefly, but in a few miles we see none but Africans working in their gardens or walking along the road or on bicycles. To attain the dignity of and acquire the mobility derived from owning a bicycle is now the aim of every self-respecting Nyasa boy. One reason for this is that most of the native paths between villages are smooth enough and broad enough for a bicycle so he does not have to wait for a road to be made before he can get full use from one. In the late thirties the cult of bicycles was in full blast. At that time Japanese-made bicycles were flooding the market at half the price of British ones, and Africans invested largely in them. After a year or so they had discovered that they lasted less than half as long as the British and so learned the lesson that now they not only buy British but the most expensive British.

Africans are reckless riders and have many accidents. We came upon one just outside Zomba in which a man had, a few minutes earlier, on a broad road with no obstacles, charged a sapling at the side of the road and had broken a leg in two places. Fortunately, we had just passed an ambulance a little way back so we sent a boy to fetch it, the fractures being far too complicated for our amateur hands. It was, too, an amazing example of the toughness of the African, for he was half-sitting up with his leg zigzagged on the ground in three pieces as far as the bones were concerned and he smiled at us in half-guilty fashion as if he were apologizing for his foolishness or for stopping us on our way.

The road gradually curls under the bare rock face of Mount Zomba till it passes two centres of habitation not far apart. One of them is the village of Domasi where, as late as 1895, the tiny garrison of six Sikhs and a few Atonga from the northern end of

43

the lake held off an attack by 2000 Yaos under their chief Kawinga until its ammunition began to run out. Just then some more Atonga led by two planters turned up. The Atonga sergeant, Bandawe, then made the extraordinary suggestion to his commander, an accountant in the Civil Service, that they should sally out and charge the enemy. This they did with only a few rounds left and the Yao horde broke and fled.

Mr. Sharpe, then in charge of the young Protectorate, was just the man to make full use of such a success and, gathering more men, he followed Kawinga to his mountain fortress, where he completely defeated him in a skilfully-planned engagement. A year later this same chief aided the British in an attack on the major chief who had been behind him in the assault on Domasi, giving as his reason 'that he had been well beaten by the British and it was now time that Zarafi had a licking', an attitude which was repeated often in those early wars.

Our road continues to bend round until we begin to descend towards the Shire River through a pass which here breaks the line of high hills marking the eastern side of the rift valley. There are fewer villages and the route is picturesque with the vegetation changing as the altitude decreases, the baobabs coming in at about 2000 feet above sea-level. The river is reached at the small village of Liwonde, where we cross it on a large steel pontoon. Its size and conformation are somewhat of a surprise until you hear that it was made from the hull of the gunboat *H.M.S. Dove* which the Navy brought out from England in 1890 to help in quelling the slave trade. The slaves were carried in Arab dhows on the lake and so avoided the British troops at Fort Johnston. This pontoon must now be the oldest craft in the territory, though not quite in its original form.

The pontoon gives free passage to all, so it is much patronized by local villagers. A crew of six jolly ferrymen pull it across by cable, chanting a song and cheeking the women passengers thereby. I was most struck by the skill with which they avoided the parts of the cable which had frayed enough to penetrate the toughest African skin. If you have time you go half a mile downstream to see some hot springs, further evidence that you are in a rift valley. They are neatly housed and form a bath of clear steaming water barely a dozen yards from the river itself. Just above it are the pillars of a bridge which was built in 1916 to replace the ferry and was strengthened in 1927. That was just the period when, as we shall see, the lake was beginning to overflow a blockage and the bridge was washed away a year after it was finished. It's as well to be cautious when walking near the hot spring and the old bridge as it is a favoured place for what is locally called the 'buffalo bean', though I have heard better names for it, particularly the 'itch-bean'. It is a climber and its finely-furred pods are attractive to look at, but the 'fur' can be dislodged at the slightest touch or even a breeze and once it has alighted on you the only way you can endure the itch it causes is to strip and do your writhing under water. Your clothes, too, must be boiled before you put them on again.

The level of the Shire River at Liwonde is only six feet below that of the lake, though it is 50 miles away, and the first fast water does not appear till below the old bridge. In the early days of boat traffic on the river they managed to start their passage to the lake from Matope, some 35 miles down. The river being only 200 yards across, there were exciting voyages in those days when the local natives disapproved of strangers and fired from the banks as they passed, so Fort Sharpe was built a little lower down than Liwonde to discourage this pastime of making the white man run the gauntlet. The river here is, like Kipling's Limpopo, 'all set about with fever-trees', which are rather fine trees with a smooth shiny bark of palest green and small leaves giving a somewhat birch-like appearance.

Once we are across, the road forks, the right-hand one going to Fort Johnston 40 miles away, which we must leave for another journey. Our route is over rather uninteresting level bush country for some miles, though you may see a few baboons or even a hartebeest or two. After 15 miles we come to a large village, Balaka, and cross the railway line which has come from Blantyre by a more direct route than our road.

After that the road is more interesting, passing more frequent villages and beginning to climb the west side of the valley. Not till within a few miles of the Portuguese border do we reach the sizeable centre of Ncheu, which has a D.C.'s Boma and five or six European houses. It is also the headquarters of the southern section of the Angoni tribe ruled over, until the unfortunate happenings of 1952, by their paramount chief, Gomani, whom we shall meet again. The Angoni here are on both sides of the international boundary but when I was there last the D.C. was having a very busy time finding room for them all on our over-crowded side of the line, because the Portuguese objected to having them on their side.

No doubt there is some good reason for our accepting their objection but it seems very odd that on the Shire Highlands we have to accommodate their Nguru people, who do not belong to us at all, while they refuse to accommodate the section of the Angoni whose villages always were on their side of the divide.

Whether there is a reason or not it works out as a relief to the Portuguese administrator and a great problem to ours, for this is rocky country and cannot carry the increased population. Nevertheless, it is a pleasant station though, as recent events have shown, somewhat difficult to handle.

A little way out of Ncheu there is a monument of a single large stone, the only one of its kind in Nyasaland, to the memory of Chief Chikusi, the father of Gomani. He had been causing a great deal of trouble, and in 1896 he was pursued by our troops in two parties. The smaller party came up with Chikusi and captured him by a ruse which was certainly not permitted in the rules of war as practised by the Angoni themselves. On the march back to Zomba he was summarily shot under circum-stances which were not understood by his people.

They became peaceable and helpful from that time; never-theless, they nourished a grudge against us over the Chikusi affair. In 1928 the tribe, with our willing help, put up this monument to his memory and it has now both a historical and a religious significance to this section of the Angoni.

Our road from Ncheu now runs along the border for a while, crossing it from time to time, and rises steadily, as we are approaching a knot of hills centred on Mount Dedza, beneath which is the settlement of Dedza, the highest Boma in the territory and probably the healthiest. The height has altered the aspect of the country from bushland to grassland on which is grown wheat and potatoes by the Chewa, a tribe which occupies most of the large westward bulge we are just entering.

The mountain is over 7000 feet above sea-level and it looks down on the scattered township which, with its plantations of eucalypts and pine trees, has an air of being much older than it really is.

In fact, Dedza has a beckoning aspect, and is destined to become much more of a holiday resort as time passes. Its aspirations in that direction began a good while ago with the building of the hotel, its chief focus, of pleasant design, some way from the township itself and under the mountain, up which climbs what might be called a 'jeep-road', as yet not for ordinary cars.

For many years now the hotel has had as its major-domo a picturesque character in the person of Robin, though how he acquired the English name is hard to say. He must have been born in the eighties of last century and his father was then one of the principal slave-dealers at the southern end of the lake. He himself accompanied a slave caravan once or twice to the coast in Portuguese East Africa and tells you in a wheezy chuckle of such incidents by the way as he thinks your stomach will stand. He is simple and kindly and, be it added, wealthy by African standards, so he has somewhat of a proprietary air as he stands for his photograph on the steps of the hexagonal entrance porch to the hotel. The D.C.'s house is even more attractive, almost embowered with high trees and with a garden fit for an English manor house.

The name of Dedza came on to our maps at an early stage because Livingstone on his final journey passed through the district and described it in glowing terms: 'the country is very fine . . . and the patches of cultivation are so large and often squarish in form that but little imagination is requisite to transform the whole into the cultivated fields of England; but no hedgerows exist.' That was in 1866.

Dedza is just half-way between Zomba and the Northern Rhodesian boundary at Fort Jameson. With federation there is likely to be still more movement between the territories and with the flying start of its altitude and pleasant hotel it is bound to profit and become still more of a 'hill station' than it is at present. The district itself goes right down to the lakeside over rather rough country, so it includes rather a mingling of tribes, Yao, Chewa and Angoni. There are perhaps a dozen European settlers on leasehold farms but very few are British in this particular area.

From Dedza we gradually descend on our 60-mile run to Lilongwe, the chief town of the Central Province and residence of the Provincial Commissioner. The road is full of interest, for there are not enough trees here to block the view and there are always abrupt rocky mountains to be seen, each with some character of solidity or shape usually reflected in its native name. We cross bridges over many streams flowing eastward to the lake, but none of any grandeur, as they have their sources only a few miles to the west, and this district has less rainfall than most of Nyasaland. The villages tend to cluster along the streams for this reason since there is a limit to the distance that even an African woman will walk to get water. One might say of this region, and even of many other parts of the continent, that full use of the land cannot be made until the water resources have been more fully developed. The population can be better distributed when there are more wells, more dams and more conservation generally, a state of affairs which is bound to come slowly as it must all be done for them by the white man and is an expensive item.

The major river is the Lilongwe itself, crossed by an impressive but not very beautiful bridge which separates the African part of the town, with its serried ranks of Indian stores, from the administrative section on the north side.

From the bridge itself one may observe the happy-go-lucky attitude of the African towards his water supply, for at most times of the day men, women and children can be seen drinking, washing themselves, washing their clothes and carrying water away for cooking all from the same 50 yards of stream, while the cattle of the district are drinking and wallowing not much higher up.

That kind of promiscuity is being tackled now, for Lilongwe is growing fast and acquiring a civic sense under the wise guidance of its P.C., who has been 30 years in the country and comes into this book very frequently. There is a town planning committee now which has produced a layout observing nearly all the criteria that an English town requires. It will never become a city, perhaps, because it is mainly a collecting centre for the agricultural produce of the country round it, but, taken in hand thus early, it looks like becoming a model township in a few years' time, with ornamental lake, amusement park, civic baths and all the rest of the amenities.

There are drawbacks to gathering Africans too quickly together to make a town and we have only to think of *Cry, the*

Beloved Country for South Africa or the gangsters of Nairobi farther north to define them. Lilongwe is at the stage when those drawbacks are beginning to make themselves apparent, with too many people as hangers-on, too many idlers and too many ready to take advantage of the free speech permitted under British rule; glib orators seeking to create unrest for their own personal gain and trying to establish domination by intimidation in ways already rife in other parts of Africa. It would be wrong to suggest that Lilongwe is unhappy or a focus of danger but there certainly are elements there which have to be watched by the police, elements which cannot exist in the villages but can flourish in a large town. As a minor instance I may quote that while waiting outside the Post Office I took a photograph of a group of Africans in a queue, whereupon three of them walked across and demanded sixpence each for the privilege they had given me of allowing me to photograph them. It was a 'try-on', of course, and easily countered by my saying that on the contrary they each owed me sixpence for the honour I had done them and they quickly melted away to the jeers of those who had understood. A small incident, but one which illustrates the development of 'cheek' (for which the native word is *chipongwe*) which quickly follows liberties given before people have attained the intelligence to appreciate them properly. If we in England are apt to confuse the words 'rights' and 'privileges' we cannot blame the African for doing so.

Perhaps we may regard these as growing pains for a young township and take it that Lilongwe will survive them and grow more orderly in every sense. It will certainly grow, for it is the centre of a rapidly increasing industry of growing grain and tobacco, with one big hindrance, the high cost of transport to the railhead at Salima near the lake. It is not much use calling the Central Province the granary of the territory if it cannot get the products away. When I was last there it had just produced 30,000 tons of mealies which 200 lorries a day were trying in vain to get down to Salima by road before the rains came. Fort Jameson, in a somewhat similar district just over the border in Northern Rhodesia, uses the same route, so we may expect that when the young Federation gets into its stride it will improve the road or bring the railway up from the lake to both towns.

While the pools in the river are the meeting place for the

Africans it is the pleasant golf club that is the rendezvous for the whites and where one may meet most of the few score residents every Sunday. There is a larger proportion of settlers of South African origin here than farther south, possibly because they are more prepared to withstand the hard times of the first few years than those fresh from England. Those of them who speak English settle quickly into the community, but those who talk Afrikaans find it difficult to get Africans to work for them.

At or near Lilongwe the road divides to lead east to the lake, west to Fort Jameson in Northern Rhodesia and north. We take the last route and say good-bye to hotel accommodation and, in fact, to any frequent traffic on the road. Though we have 300 miles yet to go before we get to the north end of the territory there is only one place on the main road, Mzimba, which could be dignified by the name of a township. As we get lower the trees are larger and the view from the road more restricted, nor is there much cultivation to be seen until we cross the Bua River and begin to rise again to Kasungu, which is the centre of an area where tobacco in particular is being encouraged. It has a Boma but only three or four permanent white residents. Near the conical hill which gives the place its name is the headquarters village of Chief Mwase, head of the large Chewa tribe.

The area round Kasungu has always been noted for its game, and the reason may well be that the two respectably-sized rivers, the Bua and the Dwangwa, provide valleys of access to the warmer and richer lands of the lakeside for those animals which migrate at set seasons. There is a large game reserve to the west. At all events even now there is usually a scare or two each year as the more violent types pass near the settlement, and the pleasant house of the D.C., quite unfenced, looks vulnerable enough. Leopards and their concomitants, baboons, inhabit the nearby rocky kopjes.

There are plenty of villages near, however, and there was a large turnout when I was there to see and hear a film, a new experience for most of the villagers. We had seen this same film a few days before at Kota Kota where, as will be seen, it was made an occasion for a minor demonstration against the Government and a full squad of police had to be on duty.

Here at Kasungu, on the other hand, there were no police and the crowd was a model of behaviour.

It is 100 miles farther on to Mzimba, the scenery again becoming rather monotonous, the road hemmed in for the most part by trees which individually have beauty of form or leafage but in the mass tend to tire the eye. This type of forest clothes a vast proportion of Nyasaland and Northern Rhodesia and is called *Brachystegia* forest after the dominant species of tree in it. In this latitude it takes complete charge of the plateau at heights between 2000 and 4000 feet, largely because it is fairly resistant to the annual fires which sweep over much of the country.

About half-way from Kasungu one crosses the boundary between the Central and Northern Provinces and a little later one becomes aware of distant hills on the right hand, and the streams seem to flow towards the west or even north. Hitherto the slope has always been directed toward the lake, the central feature of the whole country. It is even more puzzling when the map tells us we are now in the basins of the Rukuru and Kasitu Rivers which flow due north, in the completely reverse direction to the Luangwa less than 80 miles away to the west. We have, in fact, passed behind the long Vipya plateau which runs parallel to the lake and forces the Rukuru to go northwards before it can reach the lake. This is but one more of the vagaries of rift valleys and there are analogies in other parts of that great series. We are now back in a region of fine scenery, and as soon as we get above the 4000-feet contour the *Brachystegia* forest gives place to open grass downlands, so that views can be had in all directions. In contrast to Mlanje and Zomba it is possible to drive along the crest of the Vipya with views on either side, and in clear weather to see right across the lake. At present the road is of pioneer variety but in time it may well become a tourist route and one of the great attractions of the territory. There are now plans for moving the provincial headquarters from Mzimba to Mzuzu on the plateau.

On my first visit to this region we came to a car drawn up by the side of the road some 20 miles south of Mzimba, and my official driver told me it belonged to the Bwana P.C., who, of course, is the chief administrative officer of the province. So I sought him out where he and his family were having a Sunday picnic and made myself known to him. Then I blundered into a *faux pas* of the grossest kind, though I was, in all innocence, only quoting a headline from a recent Government Commission. I was apologizing for having to hurry through the 'Dead North' and his reception of that phrase showed me too late that it was tantamount to referring in Edinburgh to Scotland as a backward country. He did not forgive me for several years, which shows that P.Cs. take their provinces just as much to their hearts as the D.Cs. take their districts.

Mzimba itself is growing rapidly and so are the prospects for what one may at least be allowed to call the Remote North. It need not always be so remote since a fuller use of the lake as a highway will place it in as good a position for transport as the Central Province, while if the railway from Mikindani in Tanganyika ever reaches the lake by Manda the North will have an all-British rail exit to the ocean, the only one in all Central Africa.

On my second visit we stopped a night at Mzimba with the P.C., who told us that we were just three days too late to witness an invasion from the North, and one that had some of the marks of the Zulu invasions of centuries ago. It was the season for the passing of the migrating swallows from Europe on their way to South Africa and in their thousands they had paused for a day or two at Mzimba. We have many nice ideas about our gentle European swallows besides calling them the harbingers of spring, so it is a little disconcerting to hear of how they behave when they reach Africa. They harried everything they saw, swooping at cats and dogs, turning the young of the local swallows out of their nests, forcing all small birds to keep to the safety of the thickets and mobbing the bigger birds such as the ubiquitous black and white crow of the territory—in fact, it was a mild form of a reign of terror.

In spite of, or perhaps because of, being so distant from the centre of Government at Zomba the administrators of the Northern Province seem to be even more energetic and confident than their colleagues farther south. The North, in fact, is very much alive.

We will take the pioneer road along the Vipya ridge instead of the main north road, thereby missing Mount Hora, 20 miles along the latter, but we shall hear its story in another chapter.

As we climb, quite gently, on to the long wide ridge, which may be likened to the Hog's Back at Guildford grown to thirty times its size, we note a change in the vegetation which will, of course, differ with the season. In November, just before the rains, the outstanding feature is the multitude of 'flame of the forest' trees, each one of them worthy of a botanic garden, their rich scarlet quite outdoing the light green of the leaves, as yet only in bud. Their colour is repeated at ground-level in the extraordinary 'fire ball' plant which is more like a ball of crimson fire than any plant should be, and is, like the flame tree, amenable to garden culture.

As the altitude increases, the trees are seen only in the little sheltered valleys, the broad downs being covered with grass of the coarse thatch variety, and in November this, too, is liable to be aflame in a much more serious way. It is tussocky grass four feet high, as inflammable as tinder when dry and its fires can sweep across country at a most alarming rate. On my last visit we passed in front of such a grass fire for 18 miles of the road, advancing in the then light breeze like battalions of rich red uniforms, occasionally blazing high into the air as it reached a dense patch, at other times creeping stealthily, always with a crackle of the bursting stems which in the distance was a low roar and nearby was like the rattle of independent rifle fire.

This fire-hazard is, perhaps, the greatest hindrance to development on the downlands of Nyasaland, especially if forestry be the aim. There is reason to believe that the fires have produced the grasslands. Africa was fire-ridden long before the white man came but it is possible that in far-off days these uplands were all densely forested till man, in the shape of the Bushmen or the Bantu, brought fire to his aid in hunting game. Then year by year the edges of the forest would succumb, the trees retreating to the valleys where extra moisture helped to check the flames.

Before we encountered the fire we visited a very promising afforestation scheme at Chikangawa, where about one-third of a 3000-acre plantation of pines was already up to five feet in height in three years of growth. It is an example of the work of the Government Forestry Department, not spectacular but very efficient. One young forester took us round, and it was interesting to see the order in which the scheme took shape: first the trees in nurseries which were then planted out while the two young forestry officers lived in mud huts for three years. Then, finally, something better was being put up as accommodation for them but definitely as an afterthought, when the healthy young trees were promising a cash return, in the form of pit props at ten years of age and timber at 30 or 40 years. This was the anxious time of the year and the young Scot from Edinburgh and Oxford not only had 'boys' cutting fire guards all round his two or three square miles but he had scouts posted on the higher hills to watch the progress of such fires as the one we saw. One of the hindrances to schemes at these altitudes is the difficulty of persuading African workers to live where cold weather irks them for nearly half the year, consequently the men have to be housed as warmly if not quite as spaciously as the white supervisors.

With the prevalence of grass and the absence of humans the uplands were always a resort of game and we should have seen far more than we did had it not been for the fire. In fact, to find game we should have followed the tracks of that fire a few days later, when we should have found all the ruminants had out-flanked the fire and were benefiting by the young shoots of grass which at once give a green shade to the blackened landscape. The predators, lions and leopards, would have followed them round.

The road follows divides between steep slopes and climbs occasionally round a high rocky kopje, one of which is nearly 6000 feet high and most aptly named the Camel's Hump, black with scars of fires and blue with its native granite, but too picturesque to be called an ugly lump.

There was some 40 miles of this, with a very occasional native village to be seen lower down, and a gradual descent from the higher part of the plateau to the upper zone of the *Brachystegia* and *Musuku* association of trees. It is in this zone that the great tung scheme is being carried out by the Colonial Development Corporation at Mzuzu. The scheme is still having teething troubles and it is, possibly, hardly fair to describe it while these troubles are in the ascendant. Yet there are, perhaps, lessons to be learnt on the one side and explanations to be heard by the swarm of critics on the other.

Broadly speaking, the Colonial Development Corporation

seems to have started with the opposite sequence of procedure to the Government forestry scheme we have just been reading about, that is to say, it has put accommodation first and trees afterwards. Consequently, there is frequent comparison of the two systems and some harsh criticism, some of which is frankly unfair, for the Colonial Development Corporation.

There are some fundamental differences between the tung scheme and the timber scheme which must be taken into account, the first being that the Mzuzu land is densely timbered and must be cleared by heavy mechanized machinery which requires a large team of skilled European mechanics from outside the country. These have to be attracted to the job by high pay and good housing, so amenities have to be provided early in the sequence of operations.

In the forestry scheme the European officers are technical men keen on their job, accustomed to the country and well aware that there is little money behind the scheme, which would not begin at all if it had to start with an expensive housing programme. The forestry service, like the administrative, has an *esprit de corps* which carries its officers through the early period of hardship which usually falls to their lot.

The bulldozer teams, on the other hand, are not in a service with a high tradition, they are simply men who will take a job in an outlandish place for a year or so if it is made worth their while. The same must be partly true of the more senior officers of the tung scheme unless there is security of tenure, a permanent post in fact, which the Colonial Development Corporation cannot very well promise them, for the Corporation itself is new and busy trying out all its officers.

So one had the impression that the men employed were individually good at their job but somewhat confused by the insecurity of their posts and the frequent changes in personnel.

The same thing applies to attracting African workers. They need high pay and good housing before they will come at all, and it will take a longer time with them than with the Europeans to cultivate anything approaching a team spirit.

For these and other reasons the scheme is having initial difficulties and on paper would appear to be spending a great deal of money for little result in the number of acres planted. It is easy to talk of white elephants if you're not in charge of the elephants, and even elephants have to be trained before you get any work out of them. I would rather wait another few years before criticizing the methods of running these huge ventures in remote places and with hastily collected personnel. They are usually long-term projects and the only thing is to hang on until the scheme is mature.

In the meantime one can certainly give high marks for the excellent office buildings, the comfortable houses of the senior officers, and the housing of the native labour. Mzuzu is very definitely on the map as a place to live in; it has passed the pioneer stage. Of more importance, the personnel has been sorting itself out, those who like the work and have faith in it beginning to take root while the others have passed on to try their hand elsewhere.

It was our good fortune to be shown round by one who had faith, the under-manager, a man who knew the country long before, in itself a great asset, and who had two hobbies which often go together in bachelors on lonely jobs in Africa—a great interest in big game and a passion for reading.

He explained the procedure in planting tung, which in itself is a reason for slow progress. It is necessary to ring-bark all the trees in an area to be cleared and to leave them to die slowly. This is done in order to prevent the starch formed by the leaves from being stored in the roots, where it would nourish a fungus known to be harmful to tung trees. When the trees are dead they are pulled down by two huge tractors dragging a chain almost large enough to anchor the *Queen Mary*. The chain uproots all that comes in its path, after which bulldozers pile the rubbish in windrows for burning. Only then can tractors get to work at 'bunding', that is the formation of contour terraces, between which the holes for the trees are dug by hand. Meanwhile there is skilled work required in the nursery where young tung trees have to be grafted with stems from female plants—otherwise 50 per cent would be males. The tree is about two feet high one year after planting, bears fruit lightly at four years of age and is in full bearing at from 10 to 40 years.

Its land of origin is in South China, where tung oil is a peasant industry, and it is a little ominous that export from that source is increasing. It yields a quick-drying oil with very special uses so that its price has been very high during recent

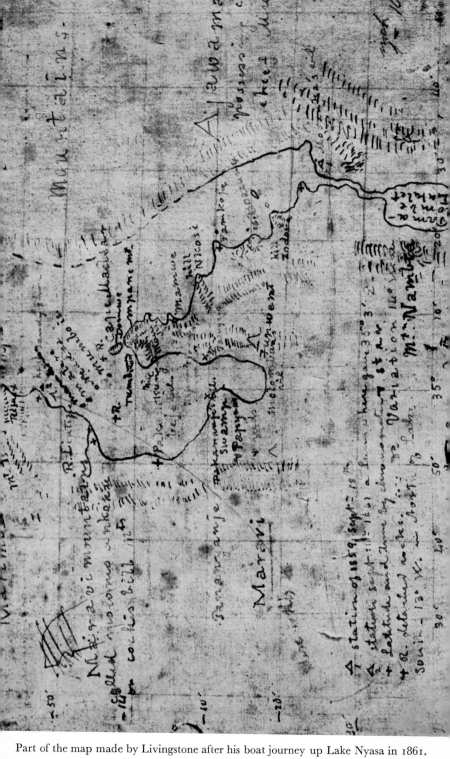

Part of the map made by Livingstone after his boat journey up Lake Nyasa in 1861.

These four men may b
called the builders of Nyasa
land, two great missionarie
followed by two great ad
ministrators. Dr Davi
Livingstone (*left, above*) con
ceived the design when, i
1859, he discovered th
Lake and the curse o
slavery which was ruling th
land around it. He died, i
1873, before his dream ha
taken any practical shape.

He was followed, fou
years later, by Dr Robe
Laws (*left, below*), 'bui
after the fashion of Living
stone, determined to g
where need was greatest
He surmounted enormou
obstacles and established th
great Livingstonia Missio
which became the mora

and educational corner-stone of the young pro-tectorate.

The foundation of orderly government was provided by Sir Harry Johnston (*right, above*), the first Commis-sioner (1890–6) under whom the slave trade was finally extinguished. He was an artist, a linguist and a writer as well as a ruler with great plans for the colony, but it was his lieutenant and suc-cessor, Sir Alfred Sharpe (*right, below*), whose practical common sense carried them out. It is possible to think of Livingstone and Johnston as the architects with Laws and Sharpe as the builders who translated their designs into the solid structure.

The Highlands in the Dedza district of the Central Province.

ROAD AND RAIL
(*Left*) The Road to Monkey Bay. The notice-board remains though the elephants have gone. (*Right*) The new bridge at Chiromo. Pressure of sudd swept the old one away in 1949.

(*Above*) The Old Residency, Zomba. The original roof was of thatch, and some of its features show its secondary purpose as a fortress.
(*Below*) Government House, Zomba, which succeeded it in 1902.

(*Above*) His Excellency the Governor addresses a large meeting of Chiefs and Headmen at the opening of the development scheme at Domasi.
(*Below*) The K.A.R. celebrated their fiftieth anniversary in 1952. Trooping the Colour parade at Zomba.

ZOMBA. (*Above*) The Secretariat. The Legislative Council room is in the upper storey. (*Below*) The type of house being provided for junior officials of the Government on the outskirts of Zomba.

years, but it fluctuates rather violently. In 1952 it was around £250 a ton of oil, which means a gross yield of from £60 per acre, but it dropped severely in 1953, so there are risks which must be faced. The total area now planted in Nyasaland is over 20,000 acres, but in the Southern Province it is grown usually as one of two or three crops by the farmers, who will therefore not be completely at the mercy of the tung-oil market.

Still, that kind of risk is what the Colonial Development Corporation is meant to undertake within reason and it is quite wrong to make cynical remarks about the danger of having all the eggs in one basket.

At the same time there can be no doubt that some of the expenditure has been on a lavish scale, greatly to the advantage of the territory, of course, but not so pleasing to the taxpayer in Britain.

If we continued down this road to Nkata Bay we would see that the Government is hoping for great results from this generous spending, as it is making a magnificent road up from the lake which will serve many other purposes as well as bringing down the few hundred tons of tung-oil that we may hope for in ten years' time.

We should also pass near one of the Colonial Development Corporation's failures, a rice scheme which promised well on paper. The local criticism is that it began without adequate control of the water supply and was therefore at the mercy of rains coming too early or too late. Finally, at Nkata Bay itself we should see a depot of machinery and stores which would be the envy of much bigger schemes than these and represents bad miscalculation on the part of somebody on the managerial side. It reminds one of the story, possibly an apocryphal one, of the giant scraper in the Overseas Food Corporation depot at Kongwa, of 'Groundnuts'' fame. This enormous piece of machinery had duly arrived with many other forms of scraper, but was left lying in the depot because no one knew how to use it. Finally, an engineer, who hailed from Portsmouth, saw this mighty object and exclaimed, 'Good Heavens, what on earth is that doing here?' His companions jumped at him, asking what it was and whether he knew how to use it. 'Of course I know how to use it,' he said, 'we had it at the dockyard for scraping the bottoms of battleships.'

57

This story shows how easy it is to make fun of mistakes made on huge projects such as the Colonial Development Corporation undertakes, and perhaps the only real criticism is that the Corporation in the early days was much too prone to gulp down schemes which really needed careful tasting first.

We shall see Nkata Bay in the next chapter, so from Mzuzu we make our way back to the main north road via Ekwendeni, a village which looks thriving and secure in daylight, yet where, in 1945, I saw no fewer than eight lions at night in a dozen miles of the road. With the long low dome of the Vipya still at our right rear we begin to see a higher and even more massive plateau ahead of us, the Nyika.

As we near it and pass into the junction of the valleys of the Kasitu and the Rukuru the population becomes dense and the villages almost continuous. Just when we have decided that the road must somehow climb the steep slopes ahead of us we open up, at Njakwa, a gorge through the south-west projection of the plateau and find ourselves at the very new and neat settlement of Rumpi, complete with Boma, and in 1952 with a very knowledgeable and efficient D.C. His predecessor had been equally so and it is due to both that we can go up the Nyika plateau with the greatest of ease, whereas a year or so earlier it meant somewhat of an expedition, especially if you chose the winter, when the Africans don't like going up it.

The reason for our wish to go up the Nyika was not merely a passion for out-of-the-way places, and not even because of the poetic description of it by Van der Post in his *Venture to the Interior*. It was because the Colonial Development Corporation was engaged in investigating its possibilities for development chiefly in the forestry line, the timber produced to be turned into pulp for paper. Accordingly, piloted by the D.C., we started from his bungalow at four in the morning and after 30 miles along the main road turned right, up a road made a year earlier by the former D.C. and in the dawn-light began to climb.

By skilful reconnaissance the road had been laid out so as to need only five bridges, until at 5000 feet above sea-level the grassed zone was reached. From there the road was very sinuous, following round each little watershed, but was no less than 60 miles long, going from one end of the plateau to the other. It is a very good instance of how the administrative officers of Nyasaland even now have to turn themselves into civil engineers and how successfully they do it, that this road was laid out by the D.C., who once a week came up from Rumpi to mark out another few miles for the tractor and single grader or light scraper which did the whole of the plateau road. The total cost was quite ridiculously small, about the same as a quarter of a mile of a tarmac road at Blantyre.

As on the Vipya plateau, one passed through a zone of the *kaffirbooms* (flame trees) and fire-balls all in bloom and higher up they were succeeded by a host of other flowers, mostly of the bulb or tuberous kind which can survive the periodic grass fires. A week or so before our coming, a survey party had unwittingly started such a fire—the cook 'boy' was responsible, but the white leader of the party had to pay the £4 fine, and it had burnt over three-quarters of the plateau. The young grass was now coming through and the game, eland, roan antelope, bushbuck, zebra and lesser game were back again roaming, rather sparsely it must be confessed, over these fresh pastures. The grass that had not been burnt looked exactly like fields of corn of that bronze yellow that betokens time for harvesting. Innumerable small valleys pass down on either side of each divide, each of them densely packed with jungle, big trees, lianas and all, looking for all the world like dark green glaciers.

At about Mile 40 from the main road—so far-flung are these landscapes—we came to the infant headquarters of the Colonial Development Corporation party which was to test whether pines would grow on these high grassy moors. They had only been there a few months and their housing was still rather primitive, and their tree nursery very tiny. The young Scots forester who was there was clearly of the type to give it all a very thorough trial. An original idea from someone was to grow beef on this grassland but the forester was in no doubt on that score, for the four cows he had got there were in very poor shape indeed.

It is far too early to say how the forestry venture will go, but the Chief Forestry Officer of the territory had already given the Colonial Development Corporation a lead by setting out a few blocks, each of a hundred seedlings, scattered about at various places a year earlier.

They were purposely unfenced and unguarded in order to test

59

what they could survive in the way of drought, fire or depredations of game. I counted over one of these plots and made out that about 20 per cent had been nibbled badly or pulled up by buck or zebra, about 20 per cent had died of thirst or blight of some kind, leaving about 60 per cent looking as though they meant to survive. This plot was on a bare hillside covered with the small grey mounds raised by a certain kind of white ant which favours sour soils and, except for a belt of bare earth round it to stop fires, it was open to every hazard, including the attentions of a family of wart-hogs watching me from a couple of hundred yards distance.

The fire risk on such a plateau must be tremendous because, although there are no native villages up there, the whole massif is ringed by villages 5000 feet lower down and, in fact, we saw at least two fires climbing up the hillsides from such villages. There is a move afoot to declare the Nyika a game-reserve if the Colonial Development Corporation pilot scheme fails and, as Northern Rhodesia also owns part of it, that may well come about. The game we saw were clearly unaccustomed to seeing humans and the zebra would stand and gaze only a hundred yards away with their toothbrush manes stiffly alert, but not unduly alarmed. The day was made for the D.C. when we saw two giant bustards doing their courting display, gawkily prancing round with wings raised, a performance that he had never witnessed before. Even though the jungle in the heads of the valleys must be ideal for lions and leopards to lurk, the bareness of the grassy slopes must be a safeguard for the wary antelope.

The Nyika is rather unique in its way, partly because of its complete absence of humans, and one can understand why Van der Post wrote his lyric prose about it, 'game moving in the distance—heraldic zebra, roan antelope with horns like Saracens' swords, and giant eland with purple coats and immaculate white dew-laundered socks'.[1]

For those with eyes to see it is rather a magic scene, and no wonder people like my D.C. guide rather hoped the pine-growing would not prosper too well and that the plateau would never become too useful or too populous.

The Nyika then is a vast feature dominating the northern end of Nyasaland but as yet it is little more than that, and if it

[1] *Venture to the Interior*, Chapter 24.

had not been for the Scottish missionaries under Dr. Robert Laws it would have been even more remote and uninhabited. The hard-headed missionaries, after trying two other centres for their work which proved to be rather unhealthy, thought of their homeland moors and decided to go up the mountain, not too far for the Africans to dislike the climate but far enough to make it a healthy station. In 1894 with infinite trouble they built their headquarters overlooking the lake at a height of 4000 feet and it became under Laws a most potent centre for spreading education and the Gospel. At a date not so long ago one might have said that the Livingstonia Mission had done more for Nyasaland than even the great administrators, as we shall see later.

The road from the station down to the lake is famous for its 23 hairpin bends, most of which can only be rounded by reversing the car and making two attempts, but from it there are the most incredible views of the lake itself and of the Livingstone Mountains on the other side. It seems most appropriate that the most individual of the sheer-sided peaks facing the lake should be called Mount Waller, after the companion and lasting friend of Dr. Livingstone. It is on and near Mount Waller that there lies the coal which may yet make the Northern Province the source of fuel for the rest of the territory.

We have not yet reached the northern end of our territory, which is 130 miles on from Rumpi, half of our road running through Northern Rhodesia over outliers of the Nyika which are far below the plateau, and barely touching the most northerly district of Karonga. In fact, you can only get to the district Boma via the lake or by a poor road past the Livingstonia Mission. Yet it is a district with a most interesting people, the Wankonde, and is full of historical associations which are referred to elsewhere. It is one of those stations where the D.C. is very much cut off from his immediate headquarters, at Mzimba, and still more distant from Zomba and yet has a large and most interesting tribe to look after. A responsible station, and not a healthy one, down on the lake shore, yet if you talk to D.Cs. who have done a tour there they will all speak of it with affection.

Here we end our trip through the Land Beside the Lake but we have missed out the lake shore line and the centres there

61

which in effect are more important than those in the uplands we have been traversing. Just as we entered a sort of funnel into the rift valley at Chiromo so our exit, if we had gone by Karonga, would have been by a similar funnel, between the highlands of the Nyika and their counterpart in Tanganyika territory. One cannot journey anywhere in Nyasaland without being conscious of this mighty ditch, along which you may clamber by road or take ship and go by the water which fills so much of it and now claims our attention.

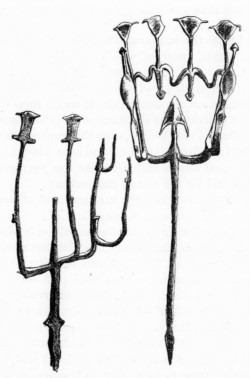

Two branching iron rods or 'tridents' of the type found in the graves of an early Chikuramayerbes dynasty (c. 1780). Associated with kingship, they bear no relation to any existing indigenous iron work. Fragments of 16th and 17th century Chinese pottery found in the same graves were probably brought from Zanzibar

5. THE LAKE

WE have hinted that Nyasaland is, in essentials, the lake and its overflow, the Shire River. The land is, in a curious sense, dominated by the lake, it is shaped by the lake, all water goes to the lake, and all human endeavour faces the lake.

In the visual, physical sense this is true, but in the economic, practical sense it is far from true, for the lake does not support the country; it does not as yet pay dividends.

Lake Nyasa is beautiful but treacherous, it is vast and bottomless, it is abnormal, unaccountable, enigmatic ... mysterious.

Amidst that welter of extravagant adjectives, all of which have some basis, we select the first because it is the one by which every visitor will remember the lake long after he has left it. One may go further and add that, in time to come, it will be the main reason for the vast tourist traffic of the future which is bound to arise.

All lakes are beautiful in their several ways but the beauty is vicarious, it comes from the association of their water with the land, with the sky, with the clouds, the stars, the moon.

To be truly matter of fact, almost banal, one could say that the beauty of a lake is largely a matter of its reflections, but explaining beauty will never detract from the satisfaction it gives.

If that is so then the lake is beautiful because of the land and you may find it beautiful in a different way from wherever you view it on the shore.

The commonest view for the passing visitor is from the coast near Salima, where it is low and sandy and far from impressive, so different from the towering backgrounds in the northern section and from the neat rocky hills of the peninsula behind Cape Maclear.

At Salima, therefore, you have no scenic help from behind you but the lake in front is beautiful nevertheless. As you sit on the narrow verandah of your hotel only a few feet above lake-level you find it hard to believe that it is fresh water that you are looking at.

The beach below has all the marks of a sea beach, the rollers, the surf, the foam-flecked strand, the rocks throwing spume high into the air. Perhaps the extremes are more extreme, the calms more restful with no hint of slow heaving swell, the storms more vicious and frenzied. The sand is as soft and smooth to the feet as on the best of ocean fronts and reminds one of Bishop Heber's hymn, the Greenland's icy mountains stanza, which continues:

> Where Afric's sunny fountains
> Roll down their golden sand.

Pale gold, it is true, perhaps ten carat only, without that coppery tinge of the pure metal but pleasanter to the eyes than the harsh glare of a coral strand. The pale green of the shallow water deepening to an indigo blue farther out is no better than that of any tropic sea, nevertheless it surprises you to find it so when muddiness is so often a characteristic of fresh water in the mass, and because of that expectation, perhaps, you paint it in more vivid contrast than it really deserves.

But these things may be true of any African lake; it is not till you look across the water that you see the real glory that belongs to Nyasa and Tanganyika only of all the lakes of Africa, the towering mountains overhanging them in almost every direction. They may be ghostly as in the bush-fire season, blue with smoke haze, an aquamarine shadow hanging in the distant sky, or, in the rain-washed atmosphere of the wet season, they may be crystal clear, stark in outline and showing every valley and abrupt cliff, the detail so sharp that distance dwindles more than is credible, even to those accustomed to the illusion of the nearness of things seen beyond a sheet of water.

Again it is not the mountains themselves so much as what they do to the lake, the shadows and the colour they impart to its surface which alter from hour to hour in fascinating sequence.

It is hard to say at which time of day the colour scheme is most arresting, and still more difficult to refrain from fantasy in description of what one sees.

Thus at dawn and before sun-up the distant surface of the lake is nothing less than mother-of-pearl, turning to glistening silver as the sun tops the eastern profile of the mountains, and passing with the hours from grey to blue of nearly every tone. Its blue is never as lustrous and vivid as that of the Indian Ocean, which looks as though it had taken colour from the skies of a thousand years till it hurts to view it, but is, at its best, rather the green-blue of the glacier crevasse, which can be so artificial as to be called electric.

It will never do to idealize the lake too much, for it is a reality to the dwellers by it and on it, stark at times if pleasant at others. If for a few days at a time we may use Sir Walter Scott in describing how

> Mildly and soft the western breeze
> Just kiss'd the lake, just stirr'd the trees

we must change our tune and our poet when the southerly *Mwera* blows and in Cowper's words

> . . . howling winds drive devious, tempest-toss'd,
> Sails ript, seams op'ning wide, and compass lost.

And now we had better leave the poets and their fancies and pass on to the facts of this central feature of our territory.

As to its size and shape, Lake Nyasa just gets into the category of the really large freshwater lakes of the world for area of water. For volume of water impounded it is higher still in the list, being second to Lake Tanganyika only, in Africa.

Its surface is about 1500 feet above sea-level but its deepest part is several hundred feet below sea-level. It is about 350 miles long, so if its northern end were at John o' Groats it would reach down to Newark. But it is comparatively narrow; at its broadest part it would stretch only from Catterick to Whitby; at its narrowest from Harrogate to York, that is to say 45 miles and 20 miles respectively.

The deepest part north of Nkata Bay is particularly interesting because it has the highest mountains at its flanks whereas, roughly speaking, the shallower parts have lower mountains at the side.

The figures cannot but rouse curiosity in the least scientifically-minded of readers, but there is more to come when we study the shape of the lake. The merest glance shows that one coast line reflects the other, and if we cut out each (neglecting the actual ends) we can put them together in a rather neat fit as shown overleaf.

To achieve this fit we have had to move the east side of the lake bodily about 50 miles in a north-westerly direction.

We might conceivably pass this off as an amazing coincidence if we were considering Lake Nyasa only. But when we do exactly the same thing with its longer 'twin', Lake Tanganyika, and find a similar rough fit for the two coast lines we have to dismiss coincidence and call in a common cause. Those who know glaciers will admit that most long crevasses would provide no better fit than these two lakes, and will agree at once with the geologists, headed by Professor J. W. Gregory, who called these phenomena 'rift valleys'.

It would be too tantalizing to leave the matter at that point, but this is not a scientific book and we must be brief over any possible explanations.

There are at least two schools of thought on the problem of how rift valleys were formed, one suggesting that they are due to contraction, the 'sunken' part of the rift having dropped below the sides, and the other proposing that under compression the two sides have been pressed upwards leaving a central strip behind and below.

Neither of those theories accounts very clearly for the feature we have just been observing, namely, that the sides of the rift fit rather neatly together as though they had cracked and merely opened outwards, without any sinking of the bottom of the rift.

Let us abandon ourselves for a paragraph or two to a hypothesis of our own, on the principle that where all is unknown anyone may put forward a theory, provided it follows reasonably the known laws of gravity, buoyancy and so on.

We will begin with an extravagant picture in every sense, by imagining a large tank or garden pond filled with treacle, a viscous substance heavier than water, which will slowly obey all the laws of liquids and find its own level.

On this lake of treacle we place a large flat block of pitch, a substance which is lighter than water and which will yield very slowly under pressure if applied gradually, but will crack if it is applied quickly. The pitch will float on the treacle in what physicists call equilibrium except that gravity will tend to spread the pitch and produce a tension outwards from the centre.

If we can contrive a shock, a miniature earthquake in fact, we should get a jagged crack somewhere on the surface of the pitch which will gradually open under this tension.

As the crack opens wider the treacle under the region of the crack will exert pressure upwards, since there is air where formerly there was pitch, and this will tilt the sides of the crack above the general level of the block. The sheer sides of the crack will be unsupported, so minor shocks will be liable to cause slips of pitch inwards like miniature faults.

Some of the treacle may even ooze up these faults, but unless we can introduce some explosive medium it will not imitate volcanic action—we will have to do without the volcanoes, in fact the analogy begins to fade. All we can say is that we have produced a jagged rift in the pitch with sides which would fit and mountains at its side.

If we can manage to make a double crack somewhere, so that an island of pitch is formed, then this island should rise further still and we could claim it as a miniature Ruwenzori, that is to say, a mountain of ancient, lighter rock surrounded by a double rift and higher than the sides of the rift.

And now we had better leave geophysics alone and come back to a normal description of our rift lake. It will be an unstable region, of course, whatever may be the cause, so we are not surprised to find that earthquakes are common in the region (though usually slight), and that there are hot springs in places along the sides of the valley.

The highest mountains flank the deepest part of the lake (as would happen with our pitch and treacle experiment) and the longest rivers produce the most silt and, therefore, the shallow parts are opposite these rivers.

So Nyasaland possesses a mighty lake of a peculiar character, and, to tell the truth, does not know quite what to do with it. It is, in fact, somewhat of a white elephant, which may be a handsome pet to show off to one's visitors but is too unpredictable to serve any other purpose, and is sure to be temperamental. For instance, the steep mountains play the very devil with the weather, and you have only to think how the wind has especial violence in the narrow passage between your house and the next to realize why.

A perfectly normal south-east trade-wind blowing up from the coast suddenly comes on a gap below it, a funnel-shaped gash running north and south. No wonder it dives into it with fury to produce the dreaded *Mwera* or southerly storm which has sunk so many canoes and two or three ships.

One might think that with a narrow lake one could rarely be more than ten miles from land and therefore could take what the Navy calls 'evasive action' in time, but the warning of a *Mwera* approaching is often a matter of minutes rather than hours.

It is the proud habit of naval people to underestimate all storms, but read what the first naval man to sail the lake thought of what he, Lieutenant E. D. Young, R.N., experienced in 1875 when he commanded the first tiny steamer, the *Ilala*, to be launched on its fickle waters:

'The sea was past all conception: indeed it is the peculiar nature of this lake to raise a sea that could only be found off the Agulhas Bank or in the Atlantic.'

On another occasion, a few days later:

'We got into the worst weather we had experienced. It is impossible to describe the awful combination of whirlwinds, thunderclouds and lightning that seemed to throw the lake into the wildest fury . . . At one period we counted no less than twelve waterspouts around us, and we had literally to steam in and out amongst them. Of a sudden there was a dead calm. At once the clouds of the "Kungu" mist hung over the lake, then came the most appalling thunder and lightning.'

What is worse, a safe anchorage for one part of the year is a lee shore in another part, the *Mweras* of the early rainy season tending to be succeeded by fierce westerlies in February and March. When we add to that the statement that there are very few harbours of refuge, it is clear that the lake is no paradise for a sailor.

The *Ilala*, first steamship to sail on Lake Nyasa, brought out by the Livingstonia Mission in 1875. In the foreground is a dug-out canoe from which a fisherman has been using seine nets

The plain fact is that Lake Nyasa is an example of a waste of good water, just because it is so deep. It is the top water, say the upper hundred feet or so, which contains the fish, which we use to sail over, and which can even supply a small amount of irrigation; the rest of the water underneath merely supports the upper layer and that could just as well be done by rock. In other words, mere volume in a lake is no great asset; what we want is area.

Of course it is not quite so bad as that, there are compensations of a kind. Thus the bottom water is cold and, in so far as it ever gets mixed with top water by the storms, it keeps the mass cooler and even slows down the evaporation a little. That is a double-edged argument though, because the cold water below resists mixing as it is heavier and so tends to be somewhat stagnant. Now, stagnant water everywhere is inimical to life; it becomes impregnated with noxious gases, and therefore if it does reach the top it may be harmful to fish.

If and when a fully-equipped 'oceanographical' expedition visits Lake Nyasa it will tell us what is going on in its deeper parts and whether its abyssal waters are of any effect, harmful or beneficial, on the part of the lake accessible to man.

What is of real concern to shore dwellers, of course, is the level of the lake, its variations over the few very important feet which determine whether land is flooded or dry, whether a bay is navigable or not; and on that point the lake has been disappointing, not to say fickle and frivolous.

For the lake level will not stay put. It has ranged up and down over a total of 24 feet since we first began to measure it. Curiously enough, the reasons for the varying levels are not yet fully established, or shall we say not fully agreed upon by experts.

All sorts of factors have been dragged in to account for the cyclical rise and fall, some of them more picturesque than scientific.

There is, of course, an annual rise and fall of level due to the rainy season of inflow from its rivers, and the dry season of evaporation, and the average figure for this seasonal rise and fall is about three feet, with a maximum of four feet eight inches and a minimum of two feet eight inches. The highest level is usually in April and the lowest in December.

This range of level during the year is reasonable enough, and, indeed, rather useful than otherwise, but, unfortunately, there is a cyclical rise and fall, extending over a number of years which, as we shall see, is very serious.

Over the 60 years or so during which we have fairly reliable records we have had what we may suppose is a nearly complete cycle. From 1896 to 1914 the general level was going down, and from 1914 to 1937 it steadily rose to a maximum, since when it has gone down, but there was a second maximum in 1948 which causes doubts of whether we should use the word 'cycle' at all.

To understand the problem of the changing levels of the lake we must have a picture of its outlet, where the Shire River begins.

Almost unconsciously one compares it with the outlet of Lake Victoria, in Uganda, where the Nile, already a large river, takes its first steps down from the African plateau. As you stand on the green banks at Jinja and look down on the Ripon Falls, plunging only a dozen feet or so over a rocky ledge, but with such an impressive commotion, you realize at once why the engineers have jumped at the chance of harnessing it right at the beginning of its course. They have drowned the Ripon Falls and some rapids and raised the level of the whole lake by three or four feet. Jinja will become an industrial city, and the hippos will be shooed off the golf course by sheer numbers of golfers instead of taking nightly possession as they often did in the past.

It is quite different at the outlet of Lake Nyasa. To begin with there are high mountains on either side, rising 3000 feet above the river, there are no rocky rapids and no chance of power for industry. It is true that there are hippos and that is almost the sole point of similarity.

Let us take a little voyage from the lake down the Upper Shire and see where the real outlet, the rapids which must occur somewhere, is to be found. It is a 60-mile journey so we need a boat with an engine in it, which also will serve to keep hippos at a distance.

As you come southward from the main lake you are aware of the funnel effect of the mountains, which overhang the lake on your left hand, and on the right are more distant, seen over a low and forested plain, in which palm trees are the dominant feature.

You have real difficulty in seeing where the outlet is and, when you do approach it, you will find yourself calling it the 'mouth' of the river, as that is precisely what it looks like. It even has a 'bar' of sand at the entrance/exit (call it what you will), which, at times of low lake, has been such an embarrassment to navigation that it has robbed Fort Johnston of its position as chief port and shipbuilding centre for the lake.

71

Most river bars are due to the deposit of sand brought down by a river and dropped where it meets the sea, but in this case the river is flowing out and not in, so we must seek another cause for its being there. It seems probable that the sand is brought there by the longshore drift from the beaches, when the nor'-westerly winds blow.

As we cross the bar the width of river decreases to about 300 yards, the banks being quite hidden by the dense growth of reeds with some papyrus. Over them you see palms in the distance, however, and a few of the characteristic kapok trees, which have such a geometrical pattern in profile, and they are a sign of villages, since kapok, with its useful coarse fibre, has been introduced from Asia in the past. On your right you soon glimpse the village called Mponda's, for here or hereabouts was habitation of the besotted but wily chief Mponda, who gave such trouble to the early administrators in the eighties and nineties. There is now, appropriately enough, a mission station with church and school. On your left hand as you come down the river there is an expanse of swampy land, mosquito ridden, which was the site of the first Fort Johnston, a wooden fort with a high tower which had to be built there to watch Mponda, but was the grave of many men who died from malaria.

In another two miles the swamp vegetation ceases, banks appear, and on your right is the Fort Johnston of today, perched perhaps 20 feet above the river and marked by its clock tower and the pontoon cable and landings on either side.

A few years ago there were half a dozen ships of various ages and sizes to be seen here, and a large Public Works Department depot, but these have now moved up to Monkey Bay and left an air of desuetude behind.

We pass on down-river with little help from the slow current, seeing a few villages on either hand on the higher ground, and passing canoes of native fishermen. At one bend, at the village of Ntundu, the river is only 100 yards in width and this is a possible site for a barrage.

Soon one comes to another 'mouth', a real mouth in this case, where the Shire enters Lake Malombe. The nearer view is not impressive as you see nothing but reeds, some of them on low sandy islands, but in the distance new mountains come into view including the huge lump that is Zomba Mountain.

The water shallows to under ten feet as we enter the lake but increases to 20 feet as we cross it for 20 miles, keeping to the eastern side and heading for the next outlet of the Shire.

The main villages are on the western shore, which also is fringed with reeds, and they are quite difficult to reach without a pilot who can distinguish the channel which will reach a native path from those which end in a hippo-wallow or a blank wall of papyrus.

The Memorial Clock Tower at Fort Johnston

Now, Lake Malombe may be a key feature in time to come because it is so shallow that when Lake Nyasa is low it can become dry, as it did in the early years of this century, or with a high lake it can become a centre for fishing and keep its busy villages along the shore. Its name means, curiously enough, 'the place where maize is grown'.

The journey becomes more intense and interesting again when we find Mwera Point, the exit, and a busy little fishing village just beyond it, bordered by an acre or two of fishing-nets drying on rough frames of poles.

There will also be plenty of black heads appearing above the water surface, since this is a real hippo reach.

The current is now perceptible, but only in one place is it at all fast, and this vanishes as the river becomes broader again all the way down to Liwonde where, as we have seen, the level is only about six feet below that of the lake.

Not till then, opposite the hot springs we visited before, is there rock in the stream bed; in other words, the lip of the lake, or the sill of rock, is all that distance away.

It can be compared to a kitchen sink which has for its over-flow a thin piece of guttering only very slightly tilted, which would be awkward and insanitary as it would tend to get blocked up with vegetable scrapings and soapsuds. If the owner of such a sink were a careless housewife she might not clean the outlet, in which case the rubbish would block it slightly, and raise the level in the sink until the pressure of the water cleared away some of it, when the level would sink again.

The action of that first 50 miles of outlet seems to be very much the same, with the striking difference that the rubbish is not only silt washed in from the side, but the floating sudds which take root in it, so that the blockage can grow nearly as fast as the lake rises year by year. Moreover, when the current begins to overcome the blockage it can only do it gradually since the silt has been firmly established and compacted with the roots of the aquatic plants.

The net result of such a sequence of events would be a rather ill-defined cycle of rising and falling level in the lake, in association with a low discharge in the outlet river while the level is rising, and a higher discharge when the obstruction is being eroded and the level is falling.

This explanation was first suggested by Sir Alfred Sharpe in 1911, when the discharge was at its lowest and was causing real concern to all who had to move their goods by river.

It is easy enough to write of this in a plain matter-of-fact way using kitchen sink analogies and so on, but it is a very vital matter, this variable lake level, and it is that, more than any-thing else, which has so far made it impossible to make full use of the lake, made it unwise to plan hydro-electric schemes down below at the Murchison Cataracts and made it very difficult to keep the native cotton-growing industry going on the great flood-plain of the Lower Shire.

It has been worse than that: it has affected administrative

policy as well as economic development, for how could Governors and Chief Secretaries decide on what was to be done with areas on the river or the lake when the river was discharging less and less water from 1912 to 1936 and, at the same time, the lake was flooding more of the rice lands and such harbour works as had been constructed? The whole thing was mysterious, or could easily be made to appear that way by extravagant theories about subterranean channels and connections with other lakes.

One prevalent theory held when the Shire River seemed to be drying up was that this was a manifestation of a general 'desiccation' of all Africa, a theory which had no scientific basis but was natural enough when people could walk across a river in the dry season that used to carry steamers of six-foot draught 20 years earlier. Again, when the lake-level was steadily rising, and there were plans for pushing the railway north from Blantyre to the lake, the engineers took fright and abandoned their project of taking it to Fort Johnston, as they feared it might be flooded out by the lake. The alteration to its present route increased the cost immensely, though we now know that it taps the grain-growing Central Province better than it would have done at Fort Johnston.

No one listened to Sir Alfred Sharpe's natural explanation, and it was not until after the second World War that his theory was upheld and there appeared to be room for hope that this wavering lake-level could be controlled by engineers. A very careful and rather expensive hydrological survey is now being carried out by eminent engineers, and it may well be that their recommendations may be worth a thousand times their cost to the territory.

We cannot count our chickens before they are hatched, but we may at least be permitted to say what we could do if they are hatched. The hopes of anyone concerned with the whole problem have been threefold. First, that the lake level can be stabilized within a few feet, say a range of eight feet in place of the 24 feet which it has suffered between 1912 and 1950. This, of course, would be done by building a barrage with sluices. That would permit the badly-needed harbour works being undertaken in the few promising sites that the lake shore offers.

The second hope is that the barrage can be planned so as to

hold back sufficient water in the lake to keep the discharge of the Shire reasonably steady, and at such a rate that vegetation blocks can be eroded as soon as they form. That will permit the 1400-feet fall between the upper and lower regions of the river to be used for the production of hydro-electric power, a major necessity for a country which at present has to import all its own coal.

Thirdly, that the control given by the barrage can be arranged to allow the rich flood-plain of the lower river to be fully used, with irrigation if need be, for the fine crops of grain, of sugar cane and of cotton that we already know it can produce.

In that way the three major uses of water can be made available *seriatim* and in the right order, first, for navigation in the lake, secondly, for water power and, lastly, for crops, and there will be no more talk about white elephants.

If this cyclical variation in level has been going on for centuries, there should be evidence on the shores of the lake itself, and this is so to an embarrassing extent. There are remains of beaches and wave-cut shelves high above the present level of the lake, showing that, at a great distance in time, the lake was very much larger, but this has little to do with the kind of variation we are concerned with at present. There are two lines of such features at about 15 and 25 feet above present level which may well be what we require.

There is, however, another type of evidence which is more recent, and that is the existence of dead trunks of palms well below the present high level. These must have grown on low, but dry, land when the lake was low, and their stumps remain to show the fact, and, it must be added, to ruin the nets of fishermen trying to seine the shallow water.

These palm-tree trunks have recently called attention to another kind of variation in level which is exciting the interest of scientists at the present time.

If you have a long bath half-full of water, and you tilt it up and let it down again, you can set up an oscillation of the water, so that, when it is high at one end, it is low at the other, and it will go on swinging for a long time. This is known as a 'seiche' and the period or length of time between two high waters depends almost entirely on the length of the bath.

You cannot tilt a lake 350 miles long, of course, but there are other ways, winds being one of them, earthquake shocks another, by which an oscillatory wave could be started.

About three years ago an elderly gentleman named Mr. W. H. Jollyman, camping on the shore near the south end of the lake, observed that a tree trunk appeared just above water only at a certain time of the day. Though engaged in killing crocodiles, he had been a scientist in his younger days, so he began to measure these daily variations of a few inches. He has now gone further, and has shown that there is a daily seiche or 'tide' which can be as much as six inches at the southern end. Though unlike the ocean tides, it is still possible that this queer effect may be caused by the sun and moon.

It sounds as though this can only be of interest to scientists, but it is mentioned here because there may be repercussions on the control of the flow of the Shire, as the wave must send a surge down that river every time it reaches the outlet.

The shore of Lake Nyasa near Fort Johnston

6. THE LAKE-DWELLERS

WE have seen what a bad reputation the lake has for storms, one shared by Lake Tanganyika, which, in its general features, is just a big brother to Lake Nyasa, not much longer, but nearly twice as high above sea-level and twice as deep, its bottom being 1600 feet below sea-level instead of 700. A point of contrast between the two lakes is that the outlet to Lake Nyasa was obvious from its very first discovery because it is at one end. In Lake Tanganyika, on the other hand, it was not discovered for many years as it is half-way up on the western side, and well camouflaged by swamps at the exit.

One effect of the stormy character of Lake Nyasa was to limit severely its value for transport and fishing in the early days before the Arab and the white man came. There has always been a dug-out canoe industry on the lake, but it was at the mercy of the weather. The type of canoe was rather specialized, being large but not commodious, as the trough cut out of the tree had to be narrow to give as much freeboard as possible. They were often cut out from a tree many miles inland, and moving the finished canoe to water was a major operation. I have twice come across a dug-out being brought down for its launching, and on one occasion the canoe still had ten miles of steep hills to traverse. A tug-of-war team hauls on ropes while small boys run forward with the wooden rollers that are successively uncovered as each standing haul gets the canoe a yard or two farther on its way. There is, of course, much beer drinking and a certain amount of half-religious ceremonial attendant upon this operation, which is not one to be lightly undertaken. The fishermen are good watermen in their clumsy craft, and all have to be good swimmers as the wood of their canoes is usually heavier than water so that when one is swamped by a wave it is the last of that canoe.

The first boat on the lake was the small gig brought up by Dr. Livingstone in 1860, and it was characteristic of the man that in this four-oared row-boat he went more than half-way up the lake, scorning but noting the storms. Shortly before that the

Arab slave-dealers, finding that their way round the southern end was liable to be hindered by these interfering Englishmen, began to build dhows to transport their slaves across the lake from Kota Kota to Losefa, and boasted that in one year they had transferred 10,000 of them in that way.

There was a thrilling incident in 1875 when Dr. Laws and Mr. Young in their little steamer the *Ilala* made their first cruise up the lake. They very soon sighted one of these slave dhows, and gave chase in true naval fashion. It was an awkward moment for the missionaries, as they were pledged to peaceful methods unless attacked. It was, therefore, a relief to find that the dhow, of 15 tons burden, had its slave hold vacant, though guilt was writ large on the face of the Arab captain. From that time the Arabs saw that their trade was threatened by water as well as by land, and to make the lesson still more clear, Young put on steam and ran rings round the dhow before leaving her.

It would take too long to relate the many instances of wreck and disaster caused by the storms. The worst of all was a recent one in which I take an especial interest as my original plan would have made me a victim myself. In 1946 the brand new ship, the *Vipya*, was making her third voyage to the North and had reached the stormiest part of the lake, opposite Florence Bay, where the Livingstone Mountains on one side and the Nyika on the other make a funnel for the *Mwera* when it blows.

She was blown clean over and capsized within a few miles of land and only ten of the best swimmers got ashore. All the Europeans (ten of them) and about 140 Africans were drowned.

These hazards can only be reduced by having more ports of refuge, and these can hardly come until there is more certainty of the lake's future level.

To show that the local people can make efficient sailors when trained, you must meet Chibwana, who was the bos'n of the *Vipya*. Three weeks before the tragedy he was lent to me with a *Vipya* whaleboat to take my party down to Liwonde for a river survey. We at once named him Wallace Beery, after that film star, and we were told by his skipper that he was the best African sailor in his long experience. When next I was in the country I asked the P.C. of Lilongwe if Wallace Beery had been one of the few survivors. It turned out that he had not been on board of her, having just been promoted to skipper of a

79

small tug, in which he again showed his seamanship. He was giving the P.C. a lift down from Nkata Bay to Kota Kota in the tug which was towing two barges and they ran into a *Mwera*. Chibwana carried on against the earnest wishes of all his crew and passengers but could not win through to the shelter of the long spit at Kota Kota. So he turned broadside on to the wind to get into the shallow estuary of the Bua River ten miles short of the port, and by consummate navigation managed to make the entrance. But there the barges fouled some trees which left them still at the mercy of heavy seas. Chibwana cast off the tow ropes, took the tug in farther and anchored. Then he swam down to the barges and, with the help of the crews on board of them he managed to warp them both into safety. Meanwhile, the P.C., due for a conference at Kota Kota, had got ashore and set out to walk the ten miles against the gale to keep his engagement. As he entered the township he looked down at the harbour and there was Chibwana steaming in with his tug and barges all complete. Who shall say then that Nyasa 'boys' cannot use their lake to the full when opportunity comes?

The winds are to some extent seasonal, the southerly *Mwera* being prevalent from April to September, the dry season, while the northerly may be expected from October to March. Both these winds may come from a clear sky, but just as often they are accompanied by thunderstorms, gusts of hurricane force and innumerable waterspouts. These latter have been likened to a map of North America, the slender stalk of whirling water at lake level being the Isthmus of Panama swelling through Mexico up to Canada, which is the broad cloud at the summit of the waterspout some hundreds of feet above the lake.

So far we have not given the lake a very good character except for scenery, and it is time we mentioned some of its assets, either potential or proven. One of these is the fish it yields.

There are many kinds, but the one which, to European tastes, leaves all the others far behind is a species of *tilapia*, mis-called a bream, a name which will endure probably, in spite of its having an intriguing scientific name, as it belongs to the group called the Cichlids. The only way to impress the reader with its excellence is to recite a tale of greed. When first I stayed at Fort Johnston my host gave us fried *tilapia* for breakfast, which I and my companion found so nearly indistinguishable from the best Dover sole that we asked for, and got, it for every meal during our stay. I have since had it from other sources and from other cooks, so I will confess that it was perhaps due to its freshness and my host's cook that it ranked so high with us. Nevertheless, it is a fish of quality, and this is proved by the fact that the Fisheries Adviser of the Colonial Office is rapidly spreading it all over the tropical world. It has good manners too, since its diet is mainly vegetarian, it cherishes its young by sheltering them in its mouth when danger threatens, and it is easily netted, when no dead tree trunks lie in the way.

Some enterprising Greek settlers now have a flourishing fishery near Fort Johnston, and at one time its expansion into a large-scale industry seemed possible. That has been checked by the suspicion in the minds of some skilled investigators that it will be very easy to overfish the lake, and the matter is now under even more thorough examination by a research station at Nkata Bay.

We have only mentioned one kind of fish, but there are over 200 others, most of them peculiar to Lake Nyasa, and all except one are used for food by the Africans. Unfortunately, there are other fishers than men, and the crocodile probably keeps the fish population down from what it might be. Mr. Jollyman, aforementioned, is the greatest authority on fishing in the lake as well as on crocodiles, and his calculations of the amount of fish one requires are impressive. He himself kills crocodiles by poisoning and as he has actually seen nearly a thousand of his victims he has probably accounted for three times that number.

They are fairly vulnerable, and it may be that the value of their skins for ladies' shoes and handbags will be greatly to the advantage of the fishing industry. There are already places in Africa and in South America where the attentions of the hunter for crocodile skins has almost exterminated them. They do not like the open lake nor a steep-to coast so their haunts are limited, and, if shooting and poisoning fail, there are other methods including that of baiting a hook hung underneath a floating petrol drum. The crocodile will take the bait but drown himself trying to avoid the black thing stuck fast over his head.

It is possible that the cormorants are just as great depredators, even though the fish they catch are smaller, since they are present in such numbers. From my verandah at an hotel on the shore 12 miles north of Fort Johnston I counted 2000 flying past between 6 and 6.30 one morning, a host which would presumably need about half a ton of fish per day. Their curious laboured flight, usually just above the water, makes them look awkward but in the water they dart about like large-bodied eels. Nearly every offshore rock is pure white with their guano and stands out sharply against the dark shore line, very useful for navigating a lake with no lighthouses for the early mariners.

A strange manifestation of this and all other great African lakes is the '*kungu* mist'. It appears like a dark mist rising out of the water or even more like the smoke from a hull-down steamer and it drifts slowly along with the wind, covering as much as 20 acres or more. If by chance it comes ashore you soon know all about it as it fills the house and covers the trees. The *nkungu*, to give its full name, is a cloud of tiny midges presumably having their marriage flight, and not intending to come ashore. They are so thick in the cloud that they can be a menace, there being a record of four men in a canoe on Victoria Nyanza being picked up dead with their mouths and noses so full of the tiny flies that they had been suffocated. When they come ashore near a village the inhabitants catch them with cloths and bake a cake out of them which tastes like shrimps.

If the lake has a shady past, as we have seen, with slavery and storms as leading features, what can be said for its future?

It is obvious that its chief value should be for the transport of goods, and, if it had not been for the threat of its changeable level, it would already have fulfilled that function far more than it has done.

A lot depends on two possibilities, both of them fundamental and both rather vital to future development. One is the prospect of controlling the lake level so as to allow good harbours to be made out of the rather poor natural ones. The other is the possibility of coal being mined at the northern end of the lake, either in the red sandstones of towering Mount Waller or else in Songea coalfield some 50 miles from the lake in Tanganyika.

To the passing visitor both these schemes would appear to deserve priority over all others, since if cheap and regular transport via the lake comes, a new day will dawn for the whole of the northern half of Nyasaland.

We have spoken of the inadequate harbours on the lake and

we must visit the most promising ones, beginning with that which has the best claim to history.

Kota Kota was used as a port by the Arab slavers, whence to transfer their live cargo across to the eastern shore, only 30 miles away, in dhows of up to 20 tons burden. It is a few miles south of the mouth of the Bua River and lies on flat sandy land of rather poor fertility, some of the sand being moulded into ancient terraces of a once higher lake level.

It is really a collection of villages of somewhat mixed population since this was a very large slave depot under the Arabs; in fact the Sultan of Zanzibar had some jurisdiction over the chief, called the Jumbe, of this strategic place.

In consequence of this mixing of tribes and of the strong Arab influence the population is Mohammedan in religion, and Swahili, the coastal language, is often heard.

About a mile to the south there is one of the characteristic hot springs of the Rift Valley, and thereby hangs a story concerning a Bwana D.C. In 1945 I visited this spring with the then D.C., who had notions about controlling this hot spring and piping it into the town. The engineers who were asked about it told him it couldn't be done, but he, being the Jack-of-all-trades that a D.C. has to be, set to work in his spare time. By dint of doing the survey work himself, getting some voluntary work out of the Africans, begging cement here and piping there and achieving at last a small grant for a worthy purpose, he provided the town with a pipe bringing the hot water into its centre where it furnishes baths and washing water. Whether its slightly sulphur-ous content will make the people more healthy remains to be seen, but they are certainly very pleased about it, the African being naturally a cleanly person.

The harbour of Kota Kota is really a roadstead, that is to say, a large shallow bay sheltered from the south-easterlies by a long spit running out in a half-circle, but open to north-easterlies. Cargo has to be handled from lighters, the lake steamers having to anchor about a mile from the shore. With a varying level of lake very little can be done to improve the harbour, but there are possibilities when the level is stabilized.

Even then the correct siting of breakwaters will depend upon a careful study of the currents and shifting sand, for I saw the harbour during a *Mwera* and was appalled by the amount of fine sand carried by the waves and being deposited somewhere. At present the chief bulk of cargo handled is rice coming from Karonga to the mill belonging to the Co-operative Society, whose romantic story is told in Chapter 13.

The son of the Chief who was here when Dr. Livingstone landed is now Chief at Kota Kota, but Msusa is now an old man full of gout. He seemed very mistrustful of my purpose in calling on him, as well he might be, because his township is one of the centres of Congress activity. Quite apart from the stand that they were taking on the federation proposals the Congress of young literates are a threat to the authority of the chiefs. In the tired old face of Msusa one could read confusion and suspicion and perhaps a great nostalgia for the days when he was young, when a chief could not be talked at or intimidated by smart young Africans. There was a great sense of dignity about him and his sober, almost benign old face is clearly seen in the portrait in this book. With his former powers as Chief he would have been a rock for the administration but now he felt rather powerless and utterly confused by instructions coming to him from all directions, even from England. Both he and his sub-chief, Chiwaula, are from Tanganyika and not Chewa people at all, a fact which no doubt lessens their authority.

I was able to appreciate this confused political atmosphere of Kota Kota when we attended a film show the same night.

It took place in a temporary enclosure ringed by a fence of hessian and there were at least 1000 there, of whom 500 had paid for entrance (fourpence for a man and one penny for a woman or a child), all sitting packed on the ground. The ushers were native policemen who did their best to keep order. Outside there were another 1000 or so and they were rather noisy.

Very few of them had seen films before so the operator had to explain things to his audience by means of a very loud loud-speaker set on a box in their midst. This alone was of terrific interest to those near it and they did not seem to mind its deafening raucous tones when it uttered instructions like, 'This is "God save the King" being played by a band which is not in the picture', 'Will the man with the large hat on sit down, he's blocking the picture?', 'Will Bwana Debenham's driver go out and bring his car?'

The eight Europeans present and a few of the elders had

deckchairs, but they were hemmed in by Africans and thousands of mosquitoes.

The main picture was the story of their own local school, done in excellent Technicolor only a few months earlier—and therefore it included a large number of the audience—and its purpose was to show the benefits of community feeling and co-operation. The central figures were those of the Chief Msusa and a tall grave man named Hamisi, of an Arab cast of countenance, who had been the chief promoter of the scheme which was to raise money for the building of a school.

So there were scenes of Hamisi and the elders talking to the people, of the people coming forward and handing in their shillings, of Hamisi handing the total (£300) to the Bwana D.C., who acted as treasurer. Then there were scenes of the brick-making and the building of the school, the arrival of the P.C. in an aeroplane to open the school and so on.

The commentary was given over the loudspeaker by the very able operator, but he had to be rather carefully listened to by the D.C., who was sitting next to me. For instance, at the end of the school film the commentator summed up the matter with a sentence somewhat as follows, 'So now we have shown the white people that we can do things for ourselves.' The D.C. went across to him for a little chat, after which the operator had to announce, with obvious reluctance, that to supplement the £300 they had contributed themselves the Government had given £6000 for the school.

During the film an African police sergeant came and spoke to the D.C., who had to go out and deal with a rather noisy propaganda meeting being held by Congress speakers. His appearance was enough to calm the audience and the speakers at once became less inflammatory. The atmosphere of suppressed emotion with a political flavour was very evident the whole evening and one realized how very easy it is for a speaker to sway an African audience either for good, as in the case of subscriptions for the school, or for ill, as in the case of the speeches outside the enclosure, suggesting that the white man must go, as Africans could run the government better.

The background of superstition, always present in Africa, came out in the showing of the film. The audience yelled with delight at the brickmaking scenes or when they recognized themselves, but fell rather silent whenever their real benefactor, Hamisi, appeared in the picture. This was because that wise counsellor had died since the film was taken. Some of the audience, rather naturally perhaps, did not like seeing a dead man come to life again on the screen, while others of them, by their remarks, showed that they believed that the white man's cameras had in some way caused the death of Hamisi.

Other remarks, interpreted to me by the D.C., were interesting. They were slow to recognize the picture of H.M. the Queen and looked puzzled at our standing up when the National Anthem was played. That, too, was natural enough, but knots of the audience went on to wonder why the Queen Mother did not succeed the late King, and they could not quite place H.R.H. the Duke of Edinburgh.

As mentioned before, we saw the same film at Kasungu, where the audience was orderly and still more unsophisticated.

It was very clear that the film is a very powerful agent for good or evil, but that it needs very careful handling. There is much more experience in its use in Northern Rhodesia, where the very progressive Office of Information makes its own films and has mobile cinema vans touring round the more accessible parts of the country. The former Director of Information, Mr Vernon Brelsford, an ex-D.C. with an anthropological training, has described the reactions of Africans to films of different kinds and the risks of misuse.

He says, for instance, that the enjoyment of a film by a native audience is 'a full-throated physical release of emotion such as we only see normally at football matches . . . a fight on the screen brings the whole audience to its feet shouting and laughing . . . the machinations of the villain, if they are obvious enough as in Wild West films, cause clicks of astonishment and unbelieving grunts at the sight of such evil.'

It is no wonder then that the European is apt to regard the full-grown African as a child with childish emotions, an attitude which is not a very useful one on which to base understanding.

In the vicinity of Kota Kota there is a secret society called *Nyau* which is of some interest. It has been studied by Mr. W. H. J. Rangeley, from whom we learned some of its characteristics, and they are interesting as showing the influence of such societies.

Originally *Nyau* was an important element in village life and its dancers, with masks and traditional paraphernalia, were connected mainly with funeral ceremonies. It was also confined to men only and was highly selective; it therefore had a certain disciplinary value.

It has now degenerated greatly and though confined mostly to the backward elements of the population it is none the less effective. Rangeley writes, 'Nowadays, in the hills, gangs of

Masks used by a former secret society

Nyau travel about the countryside openly, terrifying people and committing all sorts of excesses, such as demanding food and beer, seizing fowls and goats, assaulting persons, etc.'

There are indications that in some degree *Nyau* is a counter-blast to the influence of the missionaries, and an attempt to keep alive the traditions of the tribe and respect for its leaders.

One would say that a secret society perverted from its original purpose is bound to die out in an atmosphere of education and economic progress, yet that has not happened in other parts of Africa.

We must go now from the oldest lake port, with its complications due to an urban population, to the youngest, Monkey Bay, which until recently had no population at all. For 50 years Fort Johnston had been the centre of all the shipbuilding but it was always at the mercy of the lake-level and the sand bar at the outlet from the lake. The railway authorities, who also run the lake transport, therefore looked round for an alternative place for this industry and they decided on Monkey Bay, about 40 miles north of Fort Johnston. When the *Vipya* was lost and another vessel had to be laid on the stocks, the whole set-up of workshops, machinery, etc., was moved up to this bay in a commendably short space of time. Monkey Bay is even more remote from the nearest railway than was Fort Johnston and is reached by a very interesting road from that township. Part of its interest has evaporated now because, although the original large notice board still stands requesting all travellers to beware of elephants on that road, those unbiddable beasts have now been destroyed as being a rather unnecessary hazard to shipbuilding. They were particularly fierce and inquisitive on that route and there is a story which illustrates both traits. An elderly reverend and a matron of a mission hospital were being driven along the road in a truck when elephants were sighted ahead. The driver and other 'boys' immediately sought trees while the Europeans took refuge under the truck. The elephants came up to put in their usual tactic with these noisome human inventions, of turning it over. Fortunately, one particular elephant butted it from the rear instead of from the side and, no doubt, was intrigued to find that it moved along instead of turning over, so he kept it up for a little distance while the elderly couple underneath it had to wriggle along to keep pace with their refuge.

Though the elephant interest has departed there are still lion and leopard in the offing, though they are only to be seen at night; my only game incident was to be held up by a father wart-hog, determined to see his wife and progeny safely across the track, after which they all trotted off with tails rigidly erect and an air of having 'seen off' the human from their premises.

Fort Johnston has the reputation of being hot and uncomfortable to live in, yet it is the chosen home for retirement of a number of people, nearly all of whom have some claim to fame in the history of the territory. In 1945, for instance, the white population consisted of two retired doctors, both eminent in their day, two retired captains, and two serving ones, of the lake ships. The D.C. was a son of Captain F. C. Selous, the great hunter and there was an agricultural officer. There were only two wives, one of whom was a skilled artist.

Monkey Bay is quite a charming little scenic gem, rather deeper and wider than Nkata Bay and, like it, flanked by rocky hills, with a broad sandy beach at the end, and a low isthmus behind that again. Its beauty has had a rude shock with its sudden change to industry but there is no need for it to be permanently spoiled. At present, it is true, it is a tiny and untidy settlement of temporary huts and warehouses run up in a hurry, and the lovely little beach is a clutter of barges in-the-building, cheek by jowl with native dug-outs, temporary jetties and pontoons. The bay is sheltered from the worst of the winds, the south-easter, and is further protected by a small islet off its southern headland. It was here that the latest ship was built, the *Ilala II*. No doubt the exigencies of safety and hold space are responsible for its queer shape and certainly its appointments are first class; nevertheless, seen alongside the beautiful 50-year-old *Chauncy Maples*, it comes as rather a shock and is only one degree more graceful than the floating dock moored off the beach.

Yet it will be hard to spoil the natural beauty of the locality and when the engineers have time to consider the amenities perhaps it will once more become a place for week-end yachting and for tourists.

For our third and last port we will go to Nkata Bay, 90 miles north of Kota Kota and a great contrast to it. Instead of being a large and shallow roadstead, it is a small and deep bay overlooked, like Monkey Bay, by high hills which reach out into the lake as short promontories.

The road down from the interior has some difficulty in reaching Nkata Bay, so sudden are the hills, but it is an important one as it taps the whole of the promising Vipya plateau. It is therefore, being realigned at great expense and with the aim of permitting mean speeds of 50 m.p.h. over the 30 miles to Mzuzu and the tung estate. At the harbour end the road sweeps round the northern promontory past the residence of the D.C., dives down to the tiny beach and then turns again along the southern

promontory to the Boma, the gaol and the rest-house. All very
bijou at present and future expansion must be to the south along
a hilly coast, but here, too, town planning is to the fore and
there is no reason why Nkata Bay should not retain its proud
position as the most beautiful of the lake ports. It has a fine-
weather road down to the next administrative centre, Chinteche, and on to Bandawe, famous as being the second station
of the Livingstonia Mission. The bay is fairly well sheltered
from the south but open to the east and, as the water is deep
inshore, it will not be easy to improve the shelter with breakwaters. There are at present no harbour facilities whatever, as
the changing level of the lake has made it idle to provide them.
All stores are, therefore, unloaded from lighters straight on to
the beach. In the bay there tosses the neat little cabin launch of
the D.C. in which he can have exciting times going across to
the mission islands of Chisamula and Likoma, over the deepest
and almost the stormiest part of the lake.

It was the D.C. who gave me the interesting information that
he had once lowered a bucket to a depth of 120 fathoms and
brought up water which had a 'bad smell'. The fishing here is
poor because of the deep water and the township itself has little
ground for cultivation. A few miles back from the coast, however, there is the low ground of the Limpasa swamps, the scene
of the rice scheme which failed. Rice will certainly come again
here, but without the over-mechanization and general hurry
that proved its downfall under Colonial Development Corporation management.

Nkata Bay and Chinteche are the administrative centres for
the Atonga tribe, who stand out from the other tribes of the
territory for their high intelligence and, less happily, for their
high proportion of migrating labour. Consequently the dearth
of able-bodied males is an embarrassment to the tribal economy
and those who are left behind have the reputation of requiring
very careful handling by the Administration. More will be
heard of them in the chapters on missionaries and the people.

In the eyes of the D.Cs. who have been there, the most
northern tribe, the Wankonde, are even more interesting than
the Atonga, but there is no real port beyond Florence Bay,
overlooked by Mount Waller and other outliers of the great
Nyika plateau. The open roadstead off Karonga is usually a

lee shore for the worst winds and all stores have to be landed in barges; these with their slight draft can find shelter in a shallow bay which is part of the estuary of the river draining the northern side of the Nyika.

From these few pages it will be seen that the lake is distinctly ill-served by its harbours, and until these can be radically improved the transport of goods by water, the most natural service a lake can give, cannot come into its own.

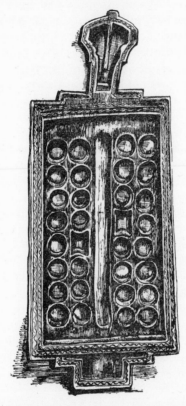

'Mancala' or 'Ubao' board. Length about 4 ft.

7. THE SETTLERS

THIS is a strange name for those white people who are in effect true Nyasalanders, and to whom the territory owed most of its economic progress in the early days of the Administration.

They are the people who intend to remain in Nyasaland, who have interests, not only in land perhaps, which will ensure their permanent residence. They are, therefore, far more important than their small number indicates.

It is difficult to say just how many permanent residents there are, because many are not landowners and not a few are retired civil servants. If one is to reckon only those who hold freehold land the number is extraordinarily small, perhaps less than 100, not counting wives and children, and we must inquire how that has come about, and what its effect is on the country.

When Livingstone so wisely advised that the best way to combat the slave trade was to undersell it by introducing trade, and a settlement of traders-cum-colonists, he hoped it would be under the control of the missionaries themselves, and, no doubt, he hoped that the British Government would provide some sort of administration. The first part of his plan bore fruit when a pioneer party of Scottish missionaries came out in 1874 and based itself on the lake. They were followed two years later by the Church of Scotland Mission, based on Blantyre. They endeavoured to combine trade with religious teaching but various circumstances, including the lack of personnel, rendered this plan impossible, so a trading company, 'The African Lakes Company', was promoted in Scotland, affiliated to the missions but conducted on an independent commercial basis.

The story of its success is largely that of the lives of its two first managers, John and Frederick Moir, who played such a notable part in the affairs of the territory, including its wars. But it was impossible, even if it had been advisable, to prevent other and individual traders coming into the country and establishing themselves by various means.

Few of them went beyond the Shire Highlands, which were then comparatively sparsely populated, and it was not difficult for them to acquire land from chiefs or headmen by purchase.

These transactions have come in for violent criticism in later years, the points being made that the land was communal, and not the property of the chiefs to sell, and that the prices were ridiculously low.

In the majority of cases, though there were some glaring exceptions, neither of these criticisms was valid. The chiefs made these bargains with the acceptance if not the approval of their people, and the land they parted with was, to them, waste land, unoccupied by anyone. Moreover, their own coming to the land was in many cases quite recent, and, if they were owners at all, it was by conquest and enslaving their forerunners.

By the time that Mr. Harry Johnston arrived in 1889 to establish some sort of administration there was a small but energetic number of such traders and planters, many of them following the lead of Mr. John Buchanan in beginning the cultivation of coffee. As time went on, the trading tended to fall into the hands of two or three companies, which could afford the outlay of capital required for transport of goods, and the individual settlers became primarily planters or farmers. They were not necessarily lawless, but, in the absence of any administration, some of them made plans of their own for governing the country. One in particular, a British citizen of German origin, was planning to become a sovereign ruler himself, and the knowledge of his plottings was a not inconsiderable factor in hastening political action by Buchanan, later supported by the Consul himself, and confirmed by the Home Government.

Once the Protectorate was proclaimed the number of settlers increased, and by 1892 Johnston set about registering their rights to the land they were on. For this purpose every claim was visited by the Consul himself or his deputy, Mr. Alfred Sharpe, or Captain Sclater, an R.E. officer attached for roads and surveys.

These adjudicators were very stiff indeed about granting titles to the land. The claims had to be supported by properly executed documents and the chief was asked if he wished to repudiate his bargain. In some cases where the price originally paid was considered low the claimant had either to pay more or have his area reduced.

Naturally there was a good deal of feeling displayed over these 'Certificates of Claim' by the settlers themselves, especially as the certificates included conditions concerning the right of Africans to occupancy of the villages and gardens already on the estate, and safeguarding rights of access to the Crown for roads, water, etc.

It is really rather astonishing that this careful and just registration was carried out while there were robberies and minor wars going on all the time in one part or another of the country. The most telling sentence on this matter in Johnston's *British Central Africa*: is, 'On the whole the settlement was well accepted by the Europeans, while it gave distinct satisfaction to the natives, and was approved without modification by Her Majesty's Government.'

The total area of land in the southern part of Nyasaland held under Certificates of Claim, that is as freehold, is rather over 1,000,000 acres. Nearly all of it is on the Shire Highlands, including the Zomba area, and forms roughly four per cent of the whole of the territory's land surface.

A high proportion of this freehold is now in the hands of large plantation companies, so that the amount available for private ownership is more like one per cent. It may be said, therefore, that from the date of proclamation of the Protectorate the acquisition of land by settlers has been closely regulated and is now practically at an end as far as freehold is concerned.

It would be too complicated to go into the several forms of land tenure in the territory, by which leaseholds can be acquired, a percentage of the rent being paid into the Native Trust Funds. The effect is, on the whole, that settlers risk a good deal in renting land as individuals and consequently their number will always tend to remain low and steady.

Perhaps enough has been said on this important but dull topic to show that no land has been taken from the former occupants without their consent and at a fair price. There was no actual dispossession or moving of population from the land which was purchased.

What has happened to make those two statements appear to be untrue is that there has since been an immense increase of the native population on the Shire Highlands, much of it due to an influx from Portuguese territory.

It was, then, in an atmosphere of some reluctance on the part of authority in the young Protectorate that the pioneers of the first twenty years or so acquired some footing in the territory.

There was a good reason for this in the eyes of the first consuls who were appointed, in that the incoming white men included some very undesirable types. Johnston himself puts it succinctly and sorrowfully in his book, 'In reviewing all that has happened since Europeans settled in this part of Africa, I have been increasingly struck with the rapidity with which such members of the white race as are not of the best class, can throw over the restraints of civilization and develop into savages of unbridled lust and abominable cruelty.' Many of these bad characters had got into the country in the guise of lay-helpers for the missions. There were horrible crimes committed, which were finally reported by two visiting big game hunters, and, after an inquiry had been held by commissioners sent out from Scotland, the personnel was carefully screened and the Foreign Office in 1883 appointed the first Consul for Nyasa, Captain Foot, R.N.

On the other hand there was a core of very worthy men, of the quality of the Buchanan brothers, for instance, who not only kept the standard fairly high but stayed on when hard times came and the men who were there for quick profits went. All accounts seem to show that the early settlers were of the best type for the unsettled country that it then was, and indeed a few of them are alive to this day. Many of them were attached to the Administration or the missions in the first place, and became settlers after they retired, and it was from one such that I got some idea of the conditions of fifty years ago and more, when there were under 500 whites in the country.

Mr. Cardew must be regarded as the Grand Old Man of Nyasaland, as he goes back to Sir Harry Johnston's day. He was 86 when I met him at his house near Ncheu in 1952 and, though he was too modest to give me much information of his own doings, his anecdotes of events in the nineties of last century are worth recalling here.

He was a trooper on the march into Southern Rhodesia in 1890 when that colony was proclaimed, but he confessed that he had never attended the annual reunion of the pioneers held every year in Salisbury, their numbers having dwindled now to very few indeed. Then in 1891 he was given a job by Johnston at the new-found mouth of the Zambezi, Chinde, and then he became a 'Collector' (forerunner of District Commissioner) at Fort Johnston, which was a very hot spot for many years. He had some 28 years in the service as Commissioner, retiring about 1918, when he paid his last visit to England and hurriedly returned to Nyasaland. He was at Westward Ho! school five years after Kipling and is, I believe, cousin to Field-Marshal Montgomery's mother. He is still upright of carriage, though somewhat stiff in the knees, has a very good memory and is modest and sensible in all he says. A bachelor all his life, he seems quite content to live out his remaining years in a rather draughty house at 4000 feet above sea-level. Needless to say, the local D.C. and his wife do their best to make things easy for him, but are often worried over his health. He was a great hunter in his day, as were most of the pioneers, but though he showed me some of his record horns I could get nothing out of him concerning the several narrow escapes he had with big game.

When asked whether his long time at Fort Johnston was not rather lonely, he at once said, 'Oh no, there was always something happening, someone coming or going; why on Christmas Day in 1896 I had 19 white people to dinner.'

He did admit that he had a lot of trouble with man-eating lions in his district, and mentioned in particular a lioness near Liwonde which had killed and eaten eight people.

In fact one can see from the early issues of the *British Central Africa Gazette*, which began in 1894, that as a topic of conversation lions were very useful, and there are curt remarks like the following: 'There is another visitation of man-eating lions at Liwonde. Two women were taken. The lions were mangy.'

There is a brevity in these and similar items of news for local consumption which is picturesque in itself.

For instances, quoting from the issue of January 1895,

'Mr. Cardew has sent down 54 fine-looking *Yaos* for the Armed Forces.'
'Rice at Kota Kota will be $\frac{3}{4}$d per lb. delivered at the beach.'
'Rhino and elephant have been troublesome round Zomba lately.'
'Output of ivory for the year past was 26,485 lbs., an increase of 500 per cent. The output of coffee was 146 tons, an increase of 50 per cent.'

In the previous month there was an advertisement:

'Look out! Grand Raffle of a splendid new piano at 1.30 prompt. Tickets £1 each. Number limited.'

This was followed by a detailed account of the war against the chief Zarafi which was going on within 30 miles of the printing press, also the item—

'Number of slaves released in the recent fighting—1184.'

So no one could complain of life being dull in Nyasaland at the turn of the century. On the other hand the only crops that were profitable were coffee, and later, tea, for which one had to have capital and be able to wait some years before getting any return. There were no minerals for quick returns as there were in South Africa, so the European population grew slowly and few came with the intention of staying as permanent colonists. Those who came to trade rather than to plant crops found themselves being undercut by the Indians, who equalled the Europeans by the thirties and now exceed them.

As the country was opened up by roads and a railway there was an extension of white planters to the Lilongwe district on leasehold land, but the tendency has been for syndicates rather than individuals to undertake the plantations, with Europeans as staff rather than owners, though many of these became permanent residents, sons following fathers on salaried jobs.

There is, of course, no way of finding out who are permanent in the full sense, since they do not know themselves whether they intend to stay, but one might guess at reckoning about half of the white population, that is to say about 2000 persons including women and children. Many would say that that was too high a figure.

It is not until one moves about the country and lives with these few permanent residents that one realizes how very little attention should be paid to statistics of this kind. Mere arithmetic or counting of European heads means very little. The same would be true if we worked out the average income of these permanent residents; it would not be at all impressive, probably far less than that of the Indian traders.

The important point is that the key people of Nyasaland are the Europeans; they have made the country secure and changed it beyond belief in the 60 years or so that they have been there. Some of the changes have been very embarrassing to themselves, such as the fact that they have turned the Shire

Highlands from almost the least-populated area into the most densely-populated, over half of the newcomers having come from Portuguese territory.

The settlers would say that, though they helped in making the country secure, they did not, until recent years, feel very secure themselves, for they were governed and regulated by the Colonial Office through the local Administration. Now we can say at once, and underline it, that the personal relations between the D.Cs. and the settlers have, with rare exceptions, been most friendly and understanding. But it is obvious that their points of view must be very dissimilar. The Administration is, broadly speaking, there to protect the African, while the settler is there to make his living alongside the African. Or, if you like to look at it that way, the settler is self-employed while the civil servant is salaried. The latter can move elsewhere if he likes and he has a pension due to him; the settler must stay where he is and provide his own pension out of savings. A slump or a bad season may ruin the settler, while it can only embarrass the civil servant.

Neither of them makes these comparisons perhaps, but those are fundamental differences, and go some way to account for a certain undercurrent of feeling as between the governing and the governed.

Is it any wonder, then, that in Nyasaland, as elsewhere in British Africa, there has been pressure by the settlers to get full representation on the legislative bodies?

The fact is that it is fear, the feeling of insecurity which is always behind this pressure, and it is not fear of the local administration itself so much as fear of what the Home Government may do. The Colonial Office is the body that is named, but only as a stalking horse; it is the politicians who, ultimately, direct the policy of the Colonial Office and are, in the settlers' view, to blame for their sense of insecurity.

It is an old, old tale, this lack of understanding between a Home Government and its colonists overseas. The latter feel, with good reason, that they understand the position of the home country but that the home country does not understand the position of the colony. Particularly do they fear the isms of different kinds that sway the politics and the sentiments of the people at home and have such a vocal press behind them, whether the ism comes from Bloomsbury Square or from behind the Iron Curtain.

One might go further still and say that the so-called blessings of democracy lose much of their lustre when viewed at the distance of thousands of miles from their centre. It is from there that the great weakness of using the counting of heads as a guide to legislation becomes so glaring. To tell the settler, as some extremists in England have done, that his most unskilled African labourer should have just as much voting power as himself sounds to him rather like telling a ship's captain that his passengers must be consulted equally about the ship's course.

It's worse than that because the people at home can, under certain circumstances, make it the law of the land, whereas no one has yet the power to compel captains to defer to passengers.

Nor is the settler himself blameless, of course; he is liable to forget that his closer view of his territory may also be too narrow a view, that he cannot always see the whole wood because the near-by trees are in the way; to which he can retort, aptly enough, that the home people don't seem to recognize the existence of the trees which, after all, are part of the wood.

And so it goes on, century after century, a lack of understanding on both sides, but the greatest lack must always be on the side of those who cannot visit the colony, whereas the colony always visits the homeland or keeps in touch with it in other ways. *117321*

Perhaps we have taken up too much space over this matter, but for home readers it should explain some of what they are liable to call obduracy on the part of their cousins overseas.

There is, however, a very bright side to the picture, the fact that the settlers of Nyasaland, partly because they are so few, are nearly as British as the temporary administrators; the links with home are sedulously preserved, and when funds permit the leave is taken in the homeland.

Another bright side is that, until the Africans were disturbed by recent politics, the relations between black and white were nearly perfect, and there was complete trust on either side. It is worth saying here that on federation the verdict of those who best know the nature of Nyasaland natives was that if they had been told that the Crown thought federation would be a good thing for them they would have accepted it without a murmur, just as they accepted poll tax, latrines, native councils and all the other strange devices of the white man which gradually proved themselves beneficial.

The two things which upset the African were that he was asked to choose on a matter he couldn't understand and that when he went to the man he trusted for advice, his Bwana D.C., he got the surprising answer, an answer which he had never had before, that the Bwana must not advise him, that he wasn't allowed to advise him.

There is, of course, no real quarrel between administrators and administered; it cannot be called anything worse than a difference of point of view and always the basis is the fear of insecurity on the part of the settlers.

It is the privilege of the visitor to the country, provided the visit lasts long enough, to see both sides of the case, and even to sympathize with both.

A very good example is this matter of accommodating the many thousands of Nguru who have flocked into Nyasaland from their former homes in Portuguese territory. Between Mount Zomba and Mount Mlanje there are now 300,000 Africans where formerly there were only ten thousand.

The point of view of the D.C. is that since he must look after that surplus thrust upon him he wants to convert them into steady and permanent residents, living as tenants on a peasant basis, with the side-line of offering their labour to the tea estates when they want a new bicycle or a new wife. He wants to tidy up his district in fact. He, therefore, worries away at his Provincial Commissioner or other officers concerned with that omnibus word 'development' until he gets control of some of the land. Or, and perhaps more often, the schemes come down to him from higher authority. The Government buys land for development from the very large estates, land originally held under the Certificates of Claim, and puts the people on to it. The people are content, and the D.C. is satisfied; he has tidied up one small section of his community, and it must be understood that once back under native use, even as Crown land, not Native Trust land, it is never likely to become available for white farms again.

The settler, therefore, must view such development with dismay, not necessarily from his personal point of view but because it means that so many potential European farmers, the colleagues and companions of his future, can never use that land. The small numbers of true Nyasaland residents can, in fact, never increase, so far as working the land is concerned. No wonder he says that, whatever the modern shape of the formula may be, it still holds good in Nyasaland that, in cases of priority rights, the interests of the African are paramount. In other words he, as a private individual, will always take second place in land matters to the African.

Worthy people far away in England will say that it is right that it should be so, that Africa should be for the Africans, even if they were not in that district till the European came, but they must not wonder that the white Nyasalanders see the case through a very different pair of spectacles.

The word 'partnership', which has come to the fore since the discussions began on federation, has been acclaimed by some and reviled by others. I believe myself that it is not only a valuable word for the future but also has been operating from the beginning, certainly in Nyasaland, where agriculture and not mining of minerals is the mainstay.

No one but the white man could have brought coffee, tea, tobacco and cotton to the country for its own prosperity, but neither could he have done it without the partnership (of a very junior grade it is true) of the African labourer and foreman. The latter has his share of the profits as wages rather than dividends, but that is ultimately a difference only of name. Partnership with the junior partners rising very slowly in status has been at work for fifty years, and the rise is now taking on a quicker tempo. Only in a few cases as yet, perhaps, the African in Nyasaland has proved that he can develop energy and initiative in business, and as he can live at very much less expense than the white man, he can and will undersell the white man in time in certain lines, just as the Indian has long since captured all the trade. He will, in fact, become the competitor of the white man in quantity, but it will probably be a very long time before he can compete in quality of his produce.

The disturbances in Nyasaland in 1953 were, in part, concerned with the problem of the freehold land belonging to the settlers, and having been publicized then it has since been the subject of questions in Parliament. A visiting author can do no more than try to present the case, without bias, from the point of view of each of the parties. There are three—the Africans, the European settlers and the Administration, each of which sees the matter from a different angle.

The African case is that there is now a congestion of population in the Southern Province, and especially in the Shire Highlands, allowing on an average only six acres per head or, say, about 15 acres per family. It is worse than that, because the Government will not allow them to cultivate steep slopes so the average may be only ten acres per family.

Their spokesmen declare, quite truthfully, that over ten per cent of that land was, by the Certificates of Claim, made over to European settlers and they complain that the Government has not gone far enough, in buying back only one-third of that land for the resettlement of Africans. They admit, perhaps with some reluctance, that when those certificates were awarded there were very few Africans there and that several hundred thousand of them have come in since from other regions. Still, they would add, no one took very definite steps to stop them coming, and why should they not leave a territory where there was forced labour and go to one where there was a kindly government and a chance of working for pay.

One must admit that the argument of *j'y suis et j'y reste* is a natural one and has a certain amount of force, but of course it may be used from both sides.

This flocking of Africans to the vicinity of the Europeans is not unlike the recent trend of movement from the country to the cities in our own land, and in each case the better amenities are the attraction. The analogy stops abruptly at that point of course, since in Britain the Government is trying to relieve the congestion by building satellite towns and not by telling the original citizens that they must give way to the late comers.

The settlers' case is naturally stated more ably and with less exaggeration. They can claim that they were there first, that the land was legally handed over to them and paid for, and that it was their use of it which attracted the Africans to reside in a district which they had not liked before. The non-native population can say that theirs has been the burden of the finance of the country since they contribute about £100 per head in direct taxation whereas the African share works out at about 2/6 per head per year. It is their money and that of the British taxpayer, which is buying back the land for the new-comer Africans.

These are strong arguments but there are some weak ones as well. In the past it was the settlers themselves who, in their eagerness for labour, helped to attract the alien African. A good part of the land under discussion belongs to companies rather than individuals and is not under full development and that in itself is an incitement to envy. Then there is a system by which Africans living on an estate pay a rent for the ground they use as gardens, either in cash or by contracting to work on the estate for five months at full pay. This system of *tangata*, as it is called, may have worked in the past but it is awkward to operate and not easily understood by the African.

The Government, too, has a case. It is its bounden duty to do right by the Africans and also to ensure peace and ordered development among them. With the Government must rest the last word on what is expedient. It can claim that there is no case of injustice here, since they are buying the land; it is rather a question of policy, and that is to a large extent the prerogative of the Government.

To an outsider the weakness of the case is that the policy is framed by people who do not belong to the country, who have but a temporary interest in it, and cannot have the same devotion to its future as those who have made it their permanent home. Consequently it is easy for an Administration to be swayed by expediency and to pursue a short term policy of compromise rather than stand firm on a long term policy of what is best in the interests of all the people.

If the foregoing statements are correct and fair to all parties, it would appear to boil down to which is the soundest policy, whether to reduce the possibility of more Europeans coming to the country as freeholders, to become permanent Nyasalanders, or to follow the policy of the leaders in Northern Rhodesia and attract more Europeans.

To the visitor passing through the country it is fairly obvious that the lot of the African is better where he is close to the Europeans, which unfortunately does not mean that he is more contented there. What is even more obvious is the almost complete lack of economic pressure on the Nyasaland African compared with his opposite number in India or China or Egypt. A traveller to those places is liable to get the impression that the peasants there are not really happy unless they are at work in the fields, whereas in most parts of Africa they are not happy unless they are at ease. We need not call the African lazy, since there is little obligation to work hard, but we must most certainly call him lucky.

There we must leave this question of freehold land for Europeans, having stated it as fairly as we can, with the final remark that if a policy of restriction of settlers is followed rigorously it will be rather sadly out of step with the other partners in the Federation, and that would seem to be a pity.

And now let us take a look at the mode of life of the settler-farmer, and more particularly of his wife and children. We have seen already that in every way humanly possible it is based on British tradition, but with wide differences in practice.

Let us, therefore, take a glance at some of these freeholders and leaseholders and their properties.

We have already seen a small one in the Cholo district, which has just passed the critical stage when a single bad season might have meant the end. Both the owner and his wife have laboured hard to reach that position, and, since their holding is small they could not have done it without taking on other activities as well, especially as both of them were away on war jobs, and had to leave their 'estate' to tick over as best it might for two or three years. Each year saw a little more security, a little more reserve against ill fortune, a little more acreage of tung planted to await five years before there would be any return. The last thing to come was increased personal comfort; the only one I can recall over three separate visits there is the accession of a small dairy herd, so that for milk they are no longer dependent on a neighbour some four miles away. For instance, I asked why they had no frigidaire, that stand-by for house-wives in Africa, a *sine qua non* for most of them. The reply from my hostess was that she could think of half-a-dozen other things she wanted more urgently and that you could make-do with porous jugs and wet towels to keep the milk and the meat from going bad. Instead they add items such as a small dam on the farm one year, treatment with cement for their spring below the house another year, a guest room for visitors in a third, and a good deal of expense on amenities for their African staff all the time. Their

(*Above*) The old *Ilala*, first steamship to sail on Lake Nyasa, in a Thames dock, 1875, with all her plates numbered ready for shipping to the Zambezi.
(*Below*) A stern-wheeler at Chiromo Bridge on the Lower Shire River.

(*Above*) Nkata Bay, 'the most beautiful of the Lake ports'.
(*Below*) The *Ilala II* at Monkey Bay, where she was built.

(*Above*) A typical lakeside dug-out canoe, showing the high freeboard and narrow opening required for the stormy lake. (*Below*) The U.M.C.A. Mission Steamer *Chauncy Maples* in her jubilee year (1940). She is now laid up, pending sale.

...ba mountain from the north road. The capital is round the **corner** beyond the peak.

(*Above*) The Lake shore at Salima—a common view for the visitor, but not the most impressive.

(*Below*) The French Consul's flag flies over his office in Victoria Avenue, Blantyre.

(*Above*) Liwonde Ferry, fashioned from the hull of an old gunboat.
(*Below*) Part of Zomba's main street, where lions have been known to parade at night, a singular distinction for a capital.

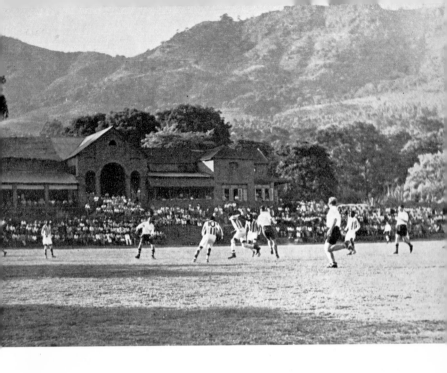

(*Above*) The Club, overlooked by the mountain, is Zomba's social and sporting centre. (*Below*) The Nyika plateau is remarkable for the complete absence of humans, being too cold for Africans to live there.

rare holidays are devoted to their special hobby, the improvement of game reserves on the lower river and that is indeed a busman's holiday—going on *ulendo* in that hot steamy district, mostly on foot with carriers, till they reach the remote reserve where they try to improve waterholes for the game or build platforms up trees from which to watch elephant and lion. The relations between them and their 'boys' seem to be perfect, and their head boys never change, unless it be to possess better clothing and more solicitude for their 'Bwana' and 'Dona', and something approaching an *esprit de corps* or partnership.

That is an example of a pair of settlers who have only just proved to themselves that they can remain what they want to be, Nyasalanders to the core. Now let us go to a pair who got to that stage long ago. We only have to drive down the same track for a few miles to reach a rambling estate of some 1600 acres, with a rambling old house and still more rambling sheds behind it.

I have been there many times and the last visit was typical of the others. I was greeted with a bevy of peacocks all making their execrable noise at once and a leash of dogs whose frenzied barking was doing its best to tell the deaf owner that a visitor had come. But the owner wasn't there, so I made my way up to the workshops, shedding dogs and peacocks on the way and passing an open-air rope factory and turning a corner to see a motor launch of several tons getting its finishing touches some forty miles from and at 3000 feet above any water that would float it.

I had not seen the owner for three years and he couldn't have known I was in the country, so I tapped him on the shoulder as he was bending over a piece of machinery in that hot sun without a hat to protect his snow-white head. He turned and his wrinkled face broke into the winning smile that he must have inherited from his famous father, the best of all the early administrators.

His first action was to disdain the hearty handshake that was waiting for him, instead of which he put both hands to my cheeks patting them and saying,

'You're putting on flesh, like I am: nice to see you: wait till I get Albert,' and off he stumped into the shed to get his hearing apparatus known to all as 'Albert'.

Such a set of improbables is worthy of fiction yet it is a plain and well-known fact that he is the only man in the territory who makes rope from sisal fibre, he is the best if not the only boat-builder and he does it all singlehanded but for his African mechanics and a swarm of *totos* for the rope-making. Also he loves peacocks as he never hears their vile cacophony and he has the nicest smile in all Nyasaland. He leaves most of the management of his tobacco and mealie fields to his able wife, who also represented their district in Legislative Council till recently.

They are really far too old to be doing such strenuous things, yet no one can persuade them of that, and you can hardly believe their tale of years when you see him blinding along the road in his old car oblivious of everything but what he sees in front of him, or his wife tramping the tobacco fields supervising her labour and, at the same time, composing a political speech for the next public meeting in her engagement book.

A remarkable pair anywhere, you would say, but doubly so when you realize what they have gone through in getting where they are now. I do not know for certain but I imagine that they could have retired to comfort and ease in England any time these last twenty years: that they have not done so is the reason for their appearing here, namely, they haven't wanted to, they are bred-in-the-bone Nyasalanders. Of course, there are occasional backward glances to England and their married daughter and even the occasional trip home, but not for long. Curiously enough, I have met him in high circles in London and he looks just as much at ease there, complete with Albert, as he does in his old suit of white duck, drawing designs in chalk on the workshop wall for the next boat.

We differ diametrically on most of the topics we discuss, particularly as to why the lake level varies, yet I would rather differ violently with him than agree with almost anyone else in the territory; best of all is his gesture when he is worsted in the argument as he says, 'I'm going off the air now,' and switches Albert off to resume the life of utter silence which would have ruined the temper of any lesser man.

Lastly we will take a couple who are not even landowners, but manage a large estate up in the Lilongwe district, and they come in age betwixt the two examples we have had, as they

have one grown-up son and younger children as well. They are
settlers in the sense we have in mind since whatever they do
they feel they belong to Nyasaland; indeed the husband is now
representing the country in the Federal Parliament.

We spent a day with them on that estate and some of its
incidents will possibly surprise those readers who think of
Nyasaland as a place for brawn and energy but a little short on
culture. My own purpose on the visit was to give advice concerning a reservoir on the estate which had been giving trouble,
a dam of 15 acres of water constructed for the sole purpose of
breeding fish for the African labour on the estate.

Mid-afternoon found the party at the dam where I was seated
on the grassy bank with the gentle little lady who owned the
estate. After discussing what might be done with the dam so as
to get a better yield of protein food for her Africans we got on to
her future plans. She told me of the social hall she had built for
them the year before, and of the cinema hall she had just finished
for them in the current year, and other projects till I felt I had
been whisked back some centuries to feudal times and here was
the châtelaine, the lady of the château, telling me of her people
and what they needed and more particularly that they must not
be spoiled with open largess, the gifts had to be earned or come
to them under the guise of education or health.

Meanwhile beneath us on the bank her manager, J., was
fishing with a deputy P.C. who was a cousin of Sir Laurence
Olivier, and they managed to catch eight *tilapia*, the fish we
have heard about already. Out on the water in a crude punt was
a party of children with the wife of the P.C., a daughter of the
late Sir William Orpen. The joke of the afternoon was that
she did some rapid sketches of me and the lady of the manor
because I was sitting very close to her and, believe it or not, the
reason for that was that I had just discovered an ants' nest on
the opposite side and edged closer to my hostess rather than
break into her conversation.

Then back to sundowners at the manager's house and conversation with his brilliant and beautiful wife, and finally to
attend a play given entirely by Africans in the cinema hall. This,
then, is an example of a large estate owned individually, which
is rare in the country, and of how it is ploughing back much of
its profits into the welfare of the people. The ploughman was the

manager, who, without owning land, is just as much a settler-for-keeps as his lady-boss.

It would be idle to pretend that these are not picked examples though the list could be a much larger one. Not all the settlers have good relations with their Africans; some of them are entirely lacking in culture and a few are definitely unpleasant people, but all these are in the minority and there is reason for Nyasaland to be proud of her settler-standard.

Scattered widely over the country and few in number, the settlers have difficulty in organizing community activities, whether for pleasure or business, but there are various thriving associations of which two may be mentioned. The first is the Nyasaland Society, only founded in 1946, but already over 400 strong. It has regular meetings, publishes a journal and is collecting a library, all with the object of fostering interest in literary and scientific matters with special emphasis on the history of the country and its peoples.

The women of Nyasaland are little behind the men in their organization and they have a very active society which is almost always known by its cherished nickname of 'The Naggers', and which carries considerable weight in high circles.

Printing had an early start in the country, the first journal appearing in 1878 from the press belonging to the Blantyre Mission. In 1894 the official *Gazette* appeared, and for a while it was a news-sheet as well as a vehicle for official announcements. A facsimile of its print is to be seen on the end paper, together with that of an independent paper, still known as *The CAT*, now the *Nyasaland Times*.

The main source of news for the settlers is the *Rhodesian Herald* published daily in Salisbury and sent by mail, but there is also the *Nyasaland Times*, published twice a week in Blantyre. The rapidly growing literacy of the people is catered for by a weekly in the vernacular called *Msimbi* under the supervision of that very important person in the Administration, the Public Relations Officer at Zomba.

This and later news-sheets in the local language are cheap and probably reach at least 50,000 of the African population.

The cost of living in such a remote corner of Africa is naturally somewhat high and the rate of taxation is not low, though tempered to the shorn lamb. It is interesting to note that the total of taxes from the non-African people, who number about 10,000, is about £750,000 per annum, whereas that from the Africans, numbering two and a half million, is about £300,000, so it can be said that the burden of running the country is still resting fairly lightly on the shoulders of the 'junior partners'.

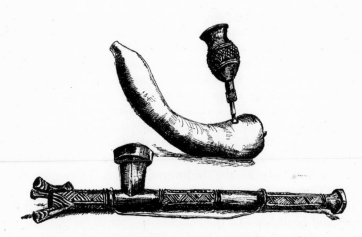

Two tobacco pipes. The lower one is from the H. H. Johnston collection and is carved from one piece of wood. The upper has a gourd mouthpiece and carved wooden bowl.

109

8. THE BWANA D.Cs.

THERE is one set of initials which, all over British Africa, means more to the African than all others, and that is D.C., which is short for District Commissioner.

If one can point to any one set of men to explain why British Africa in general and Nyasaland in particular have settled down in fifty years from slavery, wars and unrest of every kind to general content and well-being it must be the D.Cs.

In all Africa there are only a few hundred of them, and in Nyasaland less than a score so one can hardly speak of them as a body of men or a 'corps', yet they are our real agents in governing the territories. Unless we understand their duties and realize their status we shall never understand Nyasaland.

In the hierarchy of authority from the Colonial Office down to the native African the D.Cs. are the lowest grade but one, being senior only to the beginners, the A.D.Cs. (Assistant District Commissioners), but they are the men who are in direct touch with their people and can be known personally by all the chiefs and headmen. To the common people in the villages the Governor is some supreme being whom they may see only once or twice in a lifetime, and the Bwana P.C. (Provincial Commissioner) is only slightly lower in supremacy. But the Bwana D.C. they know, for does he not come amongst them, camp near their villages, and shoot their marauding elephants or man-eater lions? It is true that he also commands them to construct those queer pits called latrines, he stops them making gardens on steep slopes, he is, in fact, full of 'Thou shalt nots', but he jokes with them, and he is ready to listen to their woes. He is, in short, a real person to them.

Even the malefactors amongst them will have a good word for him though it be only the local equivalent of 'a beast, but a just beast'.

Only those who know their language and can eavesdrop at a village gathering can quite realize what the people think of their rulers, and in default of being able to do that I can only give a second-hand statement from the men of the Nyasaland battalion of the King's African Rifles when they were in Burma. A young army officer who had never been in Africa was seconded to them as platoon commander and won their confidence in some way. They spoke so warmly of their 'Bwana D.Cs.' even to arguments about how much finer their own D.C. was than any other mentioned, that he determined to join that service after the war was over. That officer was unhappily killed in the jungle warfare, but there were others who were of the same mind, and are now in Nyasaland as D.Cs. largely because they liked their Nyasa boys in uniform and because they spoke so often and so proudly of their 'Bwana D.C.'

That is, of course, a rather abnormal way of recruiting for H.M. Oversea Civil Service, to give its new title. It has had no Kipling to record its trials and its triumphs as had the I.C.S. It is no use making comparisons however, since, apart from these being odious, the two services have not enough common ground to form a basis for discussion. A number of I.C.S. men were, in fact, transferred to the African service and were at first dismayed at the contrast.

They were apt to speak a little slightingly of the small areas, and scattered population they were asked to govern, after the teeming millions and vast scope of the Indian Provinces they had come from. The next stage was one of frustration at the scarcity, in fact almost complete absence, of skilled native assistants, clerks who knew the law as well as they did, junior native officers who could take courts, and an army of 'wallahs' of every kind who made life reasonable. Worst of all, one could no longer wave a wand and call up money to start this irrigation scheme, or remedy that famine, or make bridges over the other river. Here, in fact, there were no wands, and one had to be all things to all men, engineer, agricultural expert, even doctor, to people who couldn't understand things like wheels, and anti-erosion bunds, and conservation of grain, and who had never learned the habit of industry as their Indian folk knew it.

No, the Colonial Service administrators in Africa are not at all analogous to those in Asia, simply because Africans are so very different from Asians.

Time was, in Nyasaland, when administrators were picked up by the wayside and appointed on the spot by the chief administrator who at various times was called Consul, or

Commissioner and finally Governor of the Territory. John Buchanan, the aforetime missionary gardener was one such, but he at least was settled in the country. Sir Alfred Sharpe was another remarkable one with an even more haphazard beginning, since the reason for his presence in Nyasaland was his love for big game hunting. He was drawn into the fighting at the northern end of the Lake, but when Mr. Johnston arrived as Consul he took Sharpe on the strength within half an hour of meeting him, from which moment he turned out to be his right-hand man for the whole six years of his time in the country, and succeeded him as Commissioner, and finally Governor.

The early D.Cs. were called Collectors, for their most important and most unpleasant duty was the collection of taxes from the people who either didn't know the meaning of the word, or else didn't expect to see any of it back again. As time went on the recruiting became more formal, especially when British Central Africa, changing its title to Nyasaland (in 1907) came under the Colonial Office instead of the Foreign Office.

There was, for a long time, little preparation or training for the service, and men were hurried out to their posts after a few courses, generally held in London, the idea being, apparently, that they would best learn what they had to do by doing it. In practice it meant that they had to get their training from the D.Cs. to whom they were allotted. That this was not always to the liking of the D.Cs. themselves is apparent from a story which could be paralleled in several other territories besides Nyasaland. A friend of mine, recently retired from being a Provincial Commissioner, arrived in the middle twenties at the Boma of his D.C. He was greeted most gruffly by his superior officer, and told very plainly that the new recruit's whole duty was to keep out of the sight of his senior, and I believe that that five-minute interview was all they saw of each other for three months. One would think that a lonely bachelor, far away in the African bush, would welcome the company of another white man, even if he were raw and somewhat useless. But it doesn't always work out that way, and even now you may come across plenty of lonely bachelors in Africa who resent company rather than welcome it, unless it is that of some equally crusted old-timer of their acquaintance.

The new boy in the service had, in fact, just as thin a time as the new boy at a big school, and it did not necessarily mean that the senior officer was hostile or even ill-mannered.

Things are different now, and cadets or probationers for the service are given a whole year at a University, learning a variety of subjects in preparation for their job, and taking examinations in them. Before that they have been carefully interviewed and in fact they are so much under surveillance long before they go to their territory that some almost get nerves about it, while a few, but very few, begin to feel that they know all about the job, and have perforce to receive a few snubs before they turn into the pattern that is extraordinarily uniform considering the different types of men they were originally.

Committees are still at work discussing and altering these training courses, and having served on some of them, I know how hard it is to come to any firm decision on what best to teach, and for how long to teach it, to a probationer destined for Africa.

What matters far more, of course, is the choosing of the man before he goes to his training, and there all Africa, as well as other parts of the world, owes an immense debt to one particular man, now retired, who brought to the business of recruiting not only an uncanny perception of a youngster's character, but a real personal interest in him as soon as he was selected. After all, Wasbees and other more or less intimate methods of finding out the worth of a man are not much use unless there is real interest in the candidates and unless the final selection is guided by a man who has wisdom and balance and, in addition, a wide experience of men and the world.

But, however he has been selected, and however trained, the District Officer finally takes on the same pattern wherever he goes, and it is interesting to inquire why that should be.

My own explanation is that it is because he develops an interest in the people he is looking after, and a responsibility towards them, based partly upon the great gap between their standards and his own. He will alternately admire their patience in adversity, and curse their stupidity in not adopting the remedial measures that he himself knows will modify their ills and necessities. If he is left long enough in one place, he will even develop a real affection for them, though he will probably

113

disown any such weakness one minute while fiercely defending his people the next.

Almost without knowing it he will constitute himself a buffer between his people and higher authority as represented by his senior officers of every grade up to the Secretary of State himself. He is liable to consider that no one but he understands what is needed for his people, and it is quite delightful to hear him ranting against the latest orders that have come down to him from the Secretariat, which he says do not apply and, at the same time, plotting how he can modify them so as to ease the burden. He has to carry out the orders, of course, but he can do so with tact, and even with guile, so that they lose any note of harshness. Take, for instance, the question of seeing that his people shall send more girls to the local school. Orders come down from H.Q. that somehow the percentage must be raised. He probably sees that it ought to be done, but his sympathies may well be with his people who cannot understand that little girls should be taught to read and write, and he deplores the impatience of the Higher Authority. Nevertheless, he transmits the orders to the headmen and parents, though in ways not always to the liking of that Authority, which prefers its commands to be given in its own words. For instance, one headman and his elders will say that they want a new thatching on their school, will the Bwana D.C. do something about it? Yes, the Bwana D.C. will consider the matter, but only if he sees more little girls amongst the pupils. Bribery and corruption, you would say, but the money is found for the thatching and the little girls go to school. Moreover, it has all been done on the basis of barter, the immemorial custom of all Africa, so no one's corns are any the worse.

Of course the headmen get to know their Bwana D.C. and his foibles, the understanding is mutual and it is in fact part of the game. The D.C.'s messenger arrives at a village to say his Bwana will be coming next week and immediately plans are made. Last time he came the Bwana D.C. said the village paths were untidy, make haste, all the women, to clear the paths he is likely to look at! This Bwana D.C. has the strange idea that every village should have latrines, let us hurriedly patch up the ones he said were useless. On the other hand, we have requests, we have complaints, we want a long *milando* (debate) and if we fulfil this command he may grant that request. Perhaps he will even tell us why we got less for our cotton this year than last, perhaps he will explain why the Shire floods are worse now, for he knows everything. Our Bwana D.C. is sometimes very severe, but he smiles often. He even makes shameless accusations about the amount of beer we elders drink, but he does see that our authority is upheld. He is a mystery, our Bwana D.C., for he works harder than any one else and not for himself, he plans things for our welfare but never shares them, truly the Bwanas are strange people and beyond all understanding.

Things are not so simple for the D.C. in the towns as in the country villages. In the towns there are Indian traders, other Europeans, and there too are Africans who have been to school, who can read and write and do things the Bwana can do, and they can complain and conspire and reject some of his authority.

Life for the urban D.C. is very much more complicated. He is still in the position of guardian for the African, but here he has to stand up as buffer for him against new impacts, not only the Asians and the Europeans, but such things as the effect of property in land, town planning, political groups and so on. It is true that his house will probably be a better one, his wife will have more friends and they will be nearer to civilization, newspapers, telephones, even golf and tennis, but he will usually sigh for the days when he was at an out-station, when he could go on tour (*ulendo*) when he wished and when his office work was not his daily tyrant and taskmaster.

It must be obvious by now that I have the greatest admiration for the D.Cs. of Africa and especially of Nyasaland, but I am ready to admit that there are exceptions and that many make mistakes, or in some measure fall by the wayside. I happen to have been in touch with the administrative service in Africa for nearly 30 years and in all that time I have only met one D.C. who was a complete misfit. Others have been odd or awkward, a few have been short-tempered and some have been complacent, but as a service I would say that theirs is one of which the country should be proud. It may be partly the survival of the fittest, it may be that the impact of responsibility refines the less promising material, but the fact remains that the ordinary D.C. one meets in Africa is a fine man. If that is true of the D.C. it is even more true of the P.C. (Provincial Commissioner) who rules a province made up of several districts, since he has been picked from the best of the D.Cs.

What has been most interesting to me personally is the way in which the careless schoolboy and casual undergrad develops into the responsible and wise and even devoted district commissioner.

I was recently taken round his district by one such, whom I had known from his schooldays, and at every stage I had wondered whether he had chosen the right career, whether his lighthearted attitude to life would ever marry the responsibility that came upon him. Yet it did and after this tour with him I mentioned to his P.C. how pleased and yet surprised I was that this man had become such a highly promising member of the administration. The P.C., being that kind of man, immediately said, 'Would you mind telling that to the Governor when you meet him? I'm too official to speak so warmly about a junior officer.'

During the day this D.C. had taken me to a mission where I spoke through an interpreter to the boys, saw the older men at work on handicraft and then had morning tea with one of the lay brothers. Up to that moment my friend had been the D.C. inspecting, but at tea we simply talked Rugby football and returned to our undergraduate days in reminiscence.

Then he took me to a chief holding his court in a large village. The case was suspended till we had shaken hands and seated ourselves alongside the chief, when it was resumed, and judgment given. As we were escorted back to our car by the chief the D.C. was rallying him about drinking too much beer, asking him why the village was so untidy and yet giving him a good word for the amount of tobacco the village produced; in other words, using that mixture of raillery and severity which, in the hands of the Bwana D.C. seems to be so effective with the African. When I asked him, as we drove on, what sort of a chief he was, he said, 'He's a drunken old devil, but he has authority and if only I can see him often enough he delivers the goods. He's a nice old rogue and he knows I'm watching him.' A little later we passed a new and very tidy side-road and his administrative pride for once came to the fore as he said, 'That road was made by the headman and his people gratis and for nothing, a record in this district and I'm rather pleased with him.' And so for the rest of the day, smiles for one headman, frowns for another and boyish enthusiasm bubbling through every now and then. Yet ten years earlier he had been the bane of the proctors' lives for his rags and night climbings and other ebullitions at his university.

Most of these remarks on the Bwana D.Cs. are applicable to all the territories of Central and East Africa, but there are certain peculiarities in the Nyasaland picture. An obvious one is that there is more contrast between the different tribes of Nyasaland than elsewhere and on the whole a higher standard of intelligence. This is partly because the missionaries have been effective in the territory for a longer time, and because the standard of education is higher. In contrast to that advantage, there is the fact that Nyasaland is poor and the D.C. has to make do with less money to spend on his people than in almost any other British protectorate. To set against that again, the country is smaller and the D.Cs. are fewer, so there is more frequent personal contact with senior officers. Some stations are definitely unhealthy but, as we have seen, it is never far to get to a higher altitude even if only for a picnic at the weekend.

For every pro there is a contra, of course, and there is little profit in trying to draw up a balance sheet in detail. Thus Karonga in the far north of the territory may be remote and not very healthy, but the tribe there, the Wankonde, is a particularly interesting one, and the country behind the station is varied in relief and in products.

Chinteche, on the lake, makes up for its bad reputation for fever by being amongst the Atonga, the most prominent of all the tribes both for intelligence and for disputes.

So the tale of stations goes on, but I cannot say I ever met a D.C. who hated his station, though all will have preference for personal reasons of taste, experience and hobby.

The personal hobby is very important, and in the past when stations were more isolated and wives were conspicuous by their rarity it was wellnigh vital to the administrator. The most natural one was hunting in some form or another, preferably big game. Even those who didn't appreciate the slaying of animals were forced to help in the destruction of man-eating predators or garden-wrecking elephants. Garden-making was another natural hobby and with the coming of wives it has reached a high standard.

I called on one D.C. whom I knew as a student when he had less than no regard for a garden, and when I teased him about becoming an ardent grower of flowers he almost ruefully scratched his head and said, 'Yes, I'm mad on it now but I never thought I should sink so low.'

Others become authorities on birds or butterflies in the nature study line, on folk lore or tribal music in the anthropological field, while a few spend their spare time in reading. Nearly all find interest in the history of their district, and the notes they put in the Boma journals, if carefully kept, will one day be a treasure trove to the historians and the archivists.

After all they are themselves making history, even if only on a minor scale, and every year the local scene changes slightly, largely owing to their own efforts; the sense of evolution amongst their people is always evident and under their eyes.

We have been suggesting that we people in Britain should take off our hats to the Bwana D.C., but if we do we should also bow even lower to the Dona, the D.C.'s wife, the unpaid collaborator in much of his work, who has gone there for his sake alone, not for honour or career, and least of all for comfort.

There was a time, as we have hinted, when wives were at a premium, when they were welcomed neither by the Administration, who felt responsible for their safety, nor by the D.Cs. themselves, who hardly dared to ask a girl to share their trials and hazards in the bush. Yet come they did, even in the early days and I have been privileged to meet many such who look back with amusement, tempered with an occasional shudder, at their experiences of twenty or thirty years ago. It was then almost a necessity, and certainly a fashion, for the wife to accompany the D.C. on his *ulendo*, or tour, and perforce the children, of whatever age, had to go with them. Even as recently as the middle thirties life in Nyasaland for the wife fresh from England was exciting and needed all the sense of humour she could command.

To prove that point, here are some extracts from a letter to me from a friend who went out to marry an Agricultural Officer who was on the lower Shire River at that time. They were married by a D.C. at Cholo, of which she wrote, '. . . being

married by a D.C. is an amusing business with none of the grim
official atmosphere of a registry office. No mention of a wedding
ring comes in anywhere, and it was one of the witnesses who
suddenly said, "I say, oughtn't you to put a ring on her finger
about now? I can lend you a makeshift I think." ' There was
no honeymoon because 'James had work to do down on the
lower Shire and I was full of curiosity to see my mud house.'

So off they set in a borrowed car down the road from
Blantyre to Chikwawa, of which 'thirteen miles is a very steep
hill, most of which one takes in bottom gear. Near the bottom
we came upon a landslide of great rocks blocking the way. I
laughed because I had just been thinking it was time something
happened to us. There was nothing for it but to get out and
walk the remaining seven miles to our house, sending back boys
to collect our luggage and arranging, with some difficulty,
because of lions, for someone to stay with the car and guard it.'

'The D.C. had kindly sent his *gareta* or bush car to a nearby
village and thus we continued our journey.'

'A bush car is really a bath chair on one wheel underneath
the seat. One man pushes behind and another pulls in front.
Sitting in the chair one feels a complete fool; and looks one too;
at least everyone else I've seen in a bush car looked foolish
enough. The men prefer running to walking unless there are
too many snags on the path, and they carry on odd bits of
conversation, which James tells me is mostly rubbish.

> *Front man:* 'Where are we going?'
> *Rear man:* 'I don't know.'
> *Front man:* 'Aren't we going to Maperera?'
> *Rear man:* 'Oh yes! I believe we are.'
> *Front man:* 'Do you think we'll ever come back again?'
> *Rear man:* 'I don't suppose so.'

and so on. They also make funny noises to each other, rather
like horses neighing. All that journey I wanted to laugh continuously, the whole affair seemed so ridiculous.'

But reaching their 'mud house' was always liable to be
exciting as I found for myself many years later, owing to temperamental rivers having to be crossed.

The letter proceeds: 'We came to a rushing torrent quite impossible to cross, but James said, "I'd rather risk the crossing
than spend the night here." Men came from the nearby village

to help and I climbed upon the shoulders of Alexander, James' head native boy, and a man came on each side supporting Alexander.'

'All went well until we reached the main current, and it's a bit difficult to know just what went wrong. What actually happened and what I thought was happening were two different things. Everywhere there were hundreds and hundreds of brilliant fireflies looking perfectly beautiful, I shall never forget them. Alexander was washed off his feet and couldn't regain his footing. So he swayed about in the water with the other men trying to hold him up and me slipping about on his shoulders. James turned back to help and, of course I couldn't understand what the men were telling me to do, and I thought we'd all be drowned by the light of the fireflies.'

But their luck stayed with them and 'the rest of the journey was of no particular interest.'

She goes on to describe her house 'built of wattle and daub, whitewashed inside and out to keep it from disintegrating too fast in the wet season.' But she has to concentrate on the view from the house rather than the house itself.

'The chief excitement of the day comes after dinner when we are in our sitting room with all doors and windows open for the sake of the draught, for it is then that we receive visitors. The usual crowd of insects that gather round the lamp and die in heaps, of course, but its the larger animals that are such fun. About half-a-dozen frogs, turn up regularly and station themselves about the room eating up all the flies and moths that come their way, including a really enormous frog whom we call G.K.C. Then there are lizards, there are generally two or three on the walls where they look rather artistic, giving a sort of Chinese pseudo-dragon effect.'

'One or two enormous "rain spiders" have come in and rushed wildly round the room and out again; I don't like them but they haven't bitten us so far. A snake got as far as the front door once but there he died a sudden death.'

Perhaps we have quoted enough of one Nyasaland honeymoon to indicate that certain qualities are essential in the official's wife, but if they are there then she will become a Nyasalander for keeps as has this particular wife.

It is true that many cannot stand the strain, but it is significant that those who fail generally do so because they haven't the mental calibre to stand the mixture of too much loneliness interspersed with too much frivolity at the occasional but intensive sundowner parties.

Nyasaland, any more than other African territories, cannot hide the fact that many marriages go wrong, that the choice made in civilized Capetown or England doesn't always stand up to the stresses of bush life. If the men need a hobby then it is doubly true of their wives and unless they have the interest of children they are apt to have too much time on their hands. In fact, they will inevitably get the hump that is black and blue if they haven't enough to do-oo-oo, and once the hump has formed then mischief is liable to follow.

In the case of the D.C.'s wife there are a host of duties which descend upon her, never written in the constitution but very definite nevertheless. First and foremost she has to be hostess for her husband for almost every traveller that turns up, because most stations are far from hotels and many have no rest-houses near. In times gone by their income always had to stand the strain of supplying provender, especially drinks, to hungry and thirsty visitors, but now that hardship has been met by a more understanding Government allowing a claim for expenses for such hospitality.

In the larger centres her contact with the Africans is not so close but she is expected to take the lead in such social life as the resident Europeans can arrange; she is, in fact, automatically the 'first lady' in the community, though she may not like to exercise her authority in that status.

The wives of the Bwana D.Cs. are, therefore, important people who, quite unofficially and slightly in the background, can make a great difference to the atmosphere of a district. Quite a number of them in Nyasaland are, like most of the D.Cs., graduates of some university and my own impression was that these usually had plenty of mental resources to fall back upon in the way of interest and hobbies. On the other hand, those wives who come from South Africa were able to pick up the practical side of life in the bush more quickly than those from Britain. Even they could be somewhat astonished on occasion, as in the case of one whom I met who had never been away from the electric lights and other amenities of

Johannesburg but arrived at her husband's station on the lower Shire to find two lions lying on the lawn outside her house.

With all the wives there is a constant source of exasperation mixed with amusement in the management of their staff of native 'boys', especially the cooks, and their experience in this field would fill a whole chapter. One wife told me that her first cook had reduced dishes for the Europeans to the simplest of formulas. If it contained meat it became 'hash', if of vegetables it became 'mash'. Personally, I regard the Nyasaland cook as amazingly competent considering that he himself eats practically nothing but maize meal made into a thick porridge, eaten with the fingers. What wonder then that when he is told to make a white sauce for the Christmas pudding he proudly puts salt and capers into it, as the Dona showed him when he served it for boiled mutton.

These, however, are minor problems and can be borne fairly lightly but the case is different when the family begins to arrive. Then indeed does motherhood become a full time job, because no station can be regarded as quite free of African germs of one kind or another—if they're not in the air via mosquitoes they're on the ground via ticks or in the water as bacilli or viruses. Infant mortality amongst Africans is high, but amongst Europeans it is low, which says a good deal either for the European mothers' care or perhaps for the toughness of European babies. I am quite sure the latter is true for I once saw a baby at the crawling stage picking up crumbs from the floor in competition with the pet dog and when I hastened to the rescue the mother assured me all her children had done that kind of thing without harm.

Another problem for some mothers arises at the three-year-old stage concerning how much contact should be allowed with the African children. But at that age there is really no feeling of colour difference on either side and not much difference in degree of intelligence, and for a year or so they can become good playmates, probably to the advantage of each. Even at that age one notices that the European child is more persistent and serious in the baby games than his black brother, who is much more ready to laugh but also to throw away the game for another one.

The real trial for parents in Nyasaland comes when the

children reach school age, for that inevitably means parting with them. For various reasons, which were good ones in the past, but are steadily losing their force, the Government decided against having senior schools for European children in the territory. To make up for that a grant is made for the expenses of sending each child away to school in Southern Rhodesia or in South Africa.

There is the awkward stage when the children are not old enough for a distant boarding-school, but are well able to begin schooling, and for these the larger centres have small preparatory schools. In the distant stations there can be no such aid and it falls to the parents, usually only the mother, to begin the schooling. This may have magnificent results, or in other hands the reverse. Certainly the best-mannered and most intelligent little girl of eight years of age that I have ever met was the daughter of a D.C. and she was being taught by her mother by means of a P.N.E.U. correspondence course. She and I became greatly interested in some chameleons we found in her garden and I confess that her contribution to our study of their colour changes was much more grave and quite as illuminating as my own. Lest every one should conclude that P.N.E.U. courses solve the problem I must add that the parents themselves are rather remarkable people, both of them graduates. Their sitting room alone was evidence of that in its books and pictures and arrangement, reflecting their English homes, even to an heirloom of a Saracen helmet and a suit of chain-mail which had graced their several stations in turn in Central Africa. As so often with the wives of the D.Cs. there was clearly a calm acceptance of all the duties and trials of the state of life in which she found herself but a deep longing, never uttered but yet obvious, for home leave and final retirement to England.

There are now many scores of children of school age in Nyasaland so their transport to and from their boarding-schools is a major operation. It used to be entirely done by rail and the school trains I happened to travel by were quite an experience. Two grown-ups are chosen by the parents to accompany the train and their task is not a simple one, African trains being what they are; the doyens certainly earn their free trip to centres of civilization. At each of the many stops the boys in particular are liable to descend and get up to some kind of trick, the favourite one being that of not getting on to the train until it is moving fast and the more awkward one of preventing the last comer getting on at all. The breaks in the journey at Beira, Umtali, Salisbury and farther south must all be provident of various crises varying from lost luggage to lost children. The European child of Nyasaland is usually full of assurance, however, and seems to take a journey to school lasting several days very light-heartedly, in fact as a great lark.

Many now go by aeroplane quite unattended and I remember the surprise of a schoolmistress in Johannesburg who had just met a nine-year-old acquaintance of mine at the aerodrome on her first term to school. The tiny girl, looking at least two years younger than her age, thanked the mistress nicely but said that she need not have troubled, she would have found her way all right to the school. Her father being a Provincial Commissioner who had himself coped with many a more difficult situation in his life, no doubt the daughter would have been able to look after herself unaided, as she said.

It was from this little girl's father that I gathered what the D.C.'s life was like 20 years ago in Nyasaland long before I knew the country, and particularly the queer problems he was liable to meet in the Central Province, which was only just emerging from a very primitive stage.

One of these was in connection with money. Curiously enough the African took to money quickly, though he thought it rather a silly roundabout way of doing business, to get some pieces of metal for his rice or tobacco which he then gave back again to a European for a hoe or cloth or other needs. What he could not understand was where it came from originally—the bank, of course, but how did it get there. Even native cashiers have been known to think that the bank just makes it, as much as it wants, and when there's a demand.

When the method of paying the government tax by money rather than by goods came in, the puzzle was greater than ever. Obviously the collector D.C. put it in his own pocket, why then with all that money didn't he buy a new hat or have a better house? Of course the Bwana D.C. tells us that nearly half of it (40 per cent) will be given back to us, but if so, why take it at all? Truly the ways of the white man are hard to understand.

Yet in some respects the African can be very shrewd in his

direct way as is shown by a story concerning *Nkufwi* ticks. These are a special kind of tick usually to be found in old native huts, which transmit a very unpleasant disease, a fever followed by partial paralysis. One day this D.C., then at Kasungu, stopped to chat to five men coming down from the north to work at Lilongwe and he saw that each had a short length of bamboo plugged at the end. He found that these contained a few of their own northern *Nkufwi* ticks which they would place in their huts at their new location. They were, in fact, transplanting the ticks to which they were by then immune, on the principle of 'Better the *Nkufwi* you know than the one you don't know.' The D.C. felt he must warn the medical people of this spreading of ticks, and they in turn found out that it was quite a regular practice and very difficult to combat. This D.C. had a very special interest in the ticks since, years before, he had picked up the fever from his own tent which had been left in an old hut for some days by his carriers. The nature of the fever was not diagnosed in time and it was only when the after effects of paralysis came on that he received the proper treatment, almost too late.

The worst of the effects passed off after a year in England for this treatment, when he promptly returned to his duties, but there are still signs even after twenty years of the bad time he had. He may not like me for adding here that his popularity with both white and black in Nyasaland is such that his friends feel almost an affection for the slight tic in his facial muscles when he speaks and the slight drag of one leg. They are visual reminders of the courage he showed in carrying on in spite of these disabilities.

He told me of one way of combating the tick nuisance, possible in places like court-houses. The ticks like to sleep off the effects of their blood sucking meal in a crack or fold of material, as in the folded tent. One can provide such a fold by tacking overlapping pieces of tin low down all round the wall of the building. Once a week or so a boy goes round this tick refuge with a blow lamp, roasting them to death, a more certain method than using insecticides.

It is natural enough that D.Cs. of this calibre should gather to themselves personal boys who are devoted to them, who look after their things while they are away on leave, and move from station to station with them as a matter of course. With them their Bwana comes first and all the time, long before the Bwana Governor and equally in front of the Dona D.C.

The curious thing about such associations is that the boy (who of course may be quite old) often acquires characteristics such as bravery when with his Bwana which he does not normally possess. There are plenty of instances of Africans coming to the rescue of their masters in big game hunting when they have risked, and sometimes met, instant death.

I met one such in the person of Saleh, a tiny wizened old man of sixty who has been with his Bwana D.C. for 25 years. He lost sight of him for a year or two while he was with the Army in East Africa, but when the fighting there was over this D.C. was made a political officer on the always troublous borders of Abyssinia. He therefore got Saleh up from Nyasaland to look after him. As political officer he did not carry arms but one morning after camping in the bush he was sitting down at his camp table in the open air for his breakfast. Saleh had just put a plate of eggs and bacon in front of him when they heard that characteristic 'Ping-phut! Ping-phut!' of bullets whistling past their heads. They looked round but could see no one, when the noise was repeated and they realized they were being attacked by a wandering '*Shifta*' or band of guerillas. Saleh grabbed the eggs and bacon and put them under the table and then stood up looking in the direction of the attack, shouting, '*Chipongwe! Chipongwe!* The cheek of it! The cheek of it! How dare you shoot at my Bwana when he is having his breakfast.'

As they were unarmed there was nothing for it but to leave their camp gear and go off in their jeep, Saleh shouting to the last that the villains had no manners, to interrupt his Bwana and make him forgo his eggs and bacon.

All D.Cs. have to be magistrates of greater or lesser degree according to their experience and their legal qualifications, and it is in this capacity that they are seen most closely by their people, especially where there is no court house and everyone can study the course of justice, even as with cases tried by the chief.

In fact, it is regarded as essential by both winner and loser of a civil case that there shall be full publicity, as though the loser wished to show how hard he had tried to rebut the accusation.

Even when the D.C. is completely fluent in the language he usually prefers to have an interpreter in these cases. For one thing it gives him time to sort out the evidence in his own mind before he has to put the next question. One would think that the outward majesty of the law, so impressive in an English court, must be absent when the magistrate is in shirt and shorts and there is a crowd of spectators sitting round haphazardly with totos running about in the background. Far from it, there is a great solemnity even in frivolous cases, and the uniform of the D.C.'s messengers with bright buttons and red fez caps more than makes up for the D.C.'s careless garb.

A great deal of the litigation concerns wives, wives scorned, run-away wives, bride price unpaid and so on, and in these the D.C. often needs the wisdom of Solomon. But even if he has not that at his command the whole court and all the bystanders know that he is trying to get at the truth, and is completely unbiased one way or the other, which in the native courts is obviously not always the case. In fact his people do their best to make things easy for him and soon learn the white man's idea of justice, even if it seems to take forms which to them are queer. They are quick to understand his jokes, and a D.C. who is a tease is much liked; it oils the proceedings to have a wisecrack or two from the magistrate.

The African is usually a great orator and likes to hear himself speak, so cases can be long drawn out and wearisome to the D.C. who must never show impatience.

The judgment and sentence are received with just the same awe as those of a High Court judge, but no one thinks very much the worse of the delinquent in minor cases when he is given a month in gaol, least of all the man himself.

There are many jokes about the gaolbirds or convicts, how they live at Government expense, how they are more terrified at being locked out at night than locked in, and the ripe old story that the sentences are heavier in the dry season when the Dona D.C. wants more water carried for her garden by the convicts. They are not now allowed to do any personal service of that kind, not that they would mind much if they were.

I was once allotted a team of convicts to do some hand drilling for me for water at a station. They included two murderers, but all were intensely interested at the queer job I gave them of twisting a pipe down into the ground and were as excited as I was when the material brought up became more and more moist. I used to go with the six-year-old daughter of the D.C. to watch the operation and hear her prattle to them and occasionally have their remarks interpreted to me. It was quite a party we had with the criminals, the only bored person being the policeman with his burdensome rifle.

To be a competent D.C. takes time, of course, and in his earlier years he is constantly having to do things he had never dreamed were going to be expected of him. For instance, I arrived to visit one who had been a former student of mine and was instantly impressed by him on to two jobs which were quite strange to him. He had had an order to build police lines, that is, brick huts for his police, but he had not the shadowiest idea of how bricks were made. He showed me his convicts making bricks to his formula, his first mixing producing blocks of clay which were so cracked as to crumble away, and the second being melancholy pats which had slumped into mounds. The remedy was simple in that case, but the next was just as much outside my experience as his, a very sick cow in the 'Boma herd' which he was supposed to look after without advice except for a visit once a quarter from a very busy Agricultural Officer.

Perhaps we have spent long enough on this description of the men who are the backbone of the administration in Nyasaland, the men who are in direct contact with the people. We can only add that the people themselves appreciate them as their guides and their friends, to whom they can go with complaints or questions. That having been their practice with all the new regulations that have come to the villagers from headquarters in the past one can imagine what they thought when in the matter of this federation idea the D.Cs. flatly refused to advise. If the Bwana D.C. himself would not tell them what best to do about it obviously it must be something rather shady or dangerous, something to be avoided at all costs.

To the true villager at all events the very best way to put him against a proposal is to tell him that he must not ask his D.C. about it. To the town African it is rather different; he has other ways of finding out; he can even see English newspapers occasionally. He often feels that he has grown beyond need of a D.C. to consult, he is ready to think for himself in an egotistic way. In such a situation he sees his chance for advancement, perhaps even leadership and suitable rewards. Moreover, he can say whatever he likes, publicly, within reason, for this is a free country, the police won't touch him for talking politics.

The D.Cs. hated this order for silence just as much as the people, for whether they thought well or ill of the federation scheme, they were letting their people down by not answering questions.

Lest it should be thought that D.Cs. become too earnest in their lonely stations here are two stories to show that even in their magisterial capacity they find room for humour.

One of them was reported to the police by the Medical Officer for allowing an open vessel of water in his compound which would breed mosquitoes. The police were scandalized at having to put in a charge against their D.C., but they managed to find some exposed water in the M.O.'s compound. The D.C. thereupon fined himself and the M.O. the same amount, five shillings, for their offences. In due course, word came back from Zomba that a magistrate could not fine himself so he won that round with the doctor.

On another station, which had pretensions to being a township, the D.C. fined his A.D.C. for riding a bicycle without a light when neither of them had lights. The next court was taken by the A.D.C. and he fined the D.C. double the amount for the same offence, because, as he carefully wrote in the court proceedings, 'he felt he must be severe so as to check a habit which was becoming chronic'.

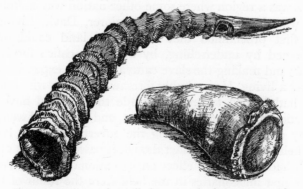

Horn trumpet and small drum made from a gourd
of the size to fit into a man's hand

9. THE MISSIONARIES

IN the era when Napoleon said that we were a nation of shopkeepers we had few footholds in Africa. When the Industrial Revolution had got into its stride Dr. Livingstone was beginning his journeys.

At some time then or perhaps later the slogan arose, 'Trade follows the flag'. It was usually a wishful utterance because the flag, under the direction of successive home governments, refused to go first.

In Nyasaland it was very much the reverse of that slogan and the sequence was rather that the missionaries led the way; they enlisted the association of trade to help in undermining slavery and the flag only followed when it was shamed into doing so.

One might, of course, say that it was precisely because we were a nation of shopkeepers that we refused to let the flag lead the way; we declined to take on new commitments over and over again in Africa for fear it would lead to expense, or else because it might offend some other nation. If ever a nation acquired an empire with reluctance, it was ours in the latter half of the nineteenth century. One might almost say that the most unpopular man in Westminster was the British explorer or missionary or administrator who turned up saying that here was a good country, where there was slavery to be combated or this was a region where some other nation was encroaching.

It was the missionary-turned-explorer, David Livingstone, who first proclaimed that slavery on land could only be challenged by underselling, by bartering calico for ivory or copper and making the slave caravan a more expensive way of getting a living. He probably foresaw that even when missionaries had helped to organize trade there would have to be protection by the home government, and he himself went as far as any one dared in warning the government that Portugal was sheltering slavery in fact though it passed all sorts of edicts which had little or no effect on its nationals in East Africa.

The first missionaries in the field were the result of Livingstone's appeal in a speech at Cambridge in 1857. This led to a party from the Universities of Oxford and Cambridge under Bishop Mackenzie who went out while Livingstone was still on the Zambezi.

They had hardly arrived at Magomero on the Shire Highlands when they were faced with the problem that beset all the later missionaries in Nyasaland, namely, how far they were to interfere with the slave trade going on all round them, or in plainer words, were they justified in fighting for the enslaved?

Bishop Mackenzie answered this question in the affirmative and reluctantly took part in repelling the attacks of some slaving parties trying to recover some slaves he had released.

This, in the view of the raiders, amounted to a declaration of war, with the missionaries always on the side of the weaker party. Nevertheless, it was not his action in this matter that caused the retirement of the Universities Mission from Nyasaland, but deaths from fever and the difficulty in getting supplies through from the coast.

It was not until ten years later, in 1874, that a second attempt was made, this time a more or less dual effort by the Free Church of Scotland and the Established Church of Scotland.

The statement is made in that form because it reveals one of the great hindrances to missionary effort all over the world, the fact that it has been and still is, actively and sometimes violently sectarian, and constantly competitive.

It seems to have been inevitable since in the homeland the differences between sects have been so fierce. Perhaps the least harm done was that resources were divided and the worst was that it published to the pagan world not only that Christianity was far from being one and indivisible but that one's soul's safety lay in choosing the right brand of Christianity.

It would be amusing if it were not so tragic reading the letters of such great men as Dr. Robert Laws; in which they often deplore this state of affairs and in the next sentence urge that their own Church should get in ahead of a rival church in a given area.

Dr. Laws himself belonged to the United Presbyterian Church and the fact that he worked all his life with the Free Church shows how little fundamental difference there was between them. Yet there was a tremendous pother to let him go and he would not have had permission unless someone had suggested he might be 'lent' by the U.P.s to the Free Church for two years. He himself had a broader view and asked only that he be 'sent, not to the Free Church or the Reformed Presbyterian Church, but to the work itself'.

Missionaries often complain that they are unduly criticized, but in incidents such as the above they certainly have invited it freely. In actual fact the two missions, Free Church at Livingstonia and the Church of Scotland at Blantyre, succeeded in working together very well on the whole and they certainly gave each other mutual help in the mundane field of sharing stores and even teachers. It would have been interesting to hear from the elders of the Church at home how much more hope of salvation a pagan convert had under the banner he was offered by their particular branch of Christianity. It was no wonder that occasionally a pagan chief, scenting this disunity in the missionary world, uttered his own equivalent of, 'A plague o' both your houses.'

The ethics of missionary practice in the field must be extraordinarily difficult to agree upon, or even if agreed upon by the Committee of reverends at home, remain difficult when faced with the questions of the heathen themselves as to what they are about to receive. There are so many obvious pitfalls in the technique of proselytism.

It is a melancholy fact that the majority of the benefits of Christianity as announced by the missionary must appear, to the heathen, as a form of bribery. If he does certain things, even utters certain words, he will be saved, which to him merely means that he will be ahead of his companions in some way.

It was perfectly natural for the wild Angoni, when shown the Sacred Book by Dr. Laws, to plot his assassination to get this Book by which apparently the white man could become successful in battle.

Moreover, it was so easy to become, in the eyes of the native, a competitor with his own medicine men. For those who firmly believed in the efficacy of prayer the problem was worse still for, putting it bluntly, if he prayed for rain and it came he could hardly help profiting by it, if it did not come he had to invent reasons for the failure.

In the eyes of the African until he had learned the real inner meaning of Christianity, the missionary was a very superior kind of medicine man.

Again, it was, and still is, very difficult for a missionary to dissociate the material benefits of his civilization from the spiritual blessings of the religion he was proffering.

In the larger field of what was really diplomacy Dr. Laws found himself cornered in this way by shrewd chiefs like Mombera, the paramount of the Angoni. To the chief's question of, 'How shall we get calico, how shall we learn to do things like the white man?' it was so easy to say, 'Let us bring the Book and start schools and you shall have them.' What to Dr. Laws was a grain of hope for saving their souls was to Mombera nothing but a bargain.

In the smaller field of mission education the same thing is true. The boy sees that if he attends the mission school he will acquire merit, position, even wealth above that of his play-fellows in the village. Many will look upon it merely as a good bargain for him, the only price he has to pay being to learn what to him are phrases, shibboleths, and catchwords which he can discard when he has acquired his black coat and white collar.

That is why the settlers tend to cry down what are known as 'mission-boys'. Their reputation is far lower than it should be and many will say that they are sly, arrogant and dishonest compared with the boy who has stayed in his village and learned by the discipline of his seniors that being proud or smart or false gets quick punishment. Unfortunately, what would not be tolerated in a personal boy by a settler can be suffered in a junior civil servant, who, provided he does his six or seven hours a day with dispatch and discretion, can go away and be all kinds of a villain in his own time.

We need not blame mission schools more than government schools in this matter, it is rather the system of education, which has emphasized learning rather than formation of character, which is responsible.

Nevertheless, as one missionary remarked to me, 'It is difficult to turn a boy away from a chance of education, even when you are not sure of his character.' Moreover, what is a peccadillo for a village boy is magnified by Europeans into a sin if it is committed by a mission boy, so their reputation is so much the more vulnerable.

133

Some would say that the real value of missionary work in a completely raw environment is the character of the missionaries themselves, the example they set in all the ordinary decencies of behaviour. When it comes to ethics in the proper sense they are not so well placed because what is good in our eyes is apt to be taken for weakness or cowardice in the eyes of men who despise the peaceful, who revolt at the idea of turning the other cheek and to whom gratitude in our sense of the word is almost unknown.

The great men amongst the missionaries of the past in Nyasaland, and there are many of them, most certainly swayed their native people by their deeds, usually more than by their words, which were only partially understood. If one may particularize amongst many fine qualities, then those of sheer courage and honesty of purpose must rank uppermost. It is possible to name a dozen men in the first ten years of missionary work there who faced appalling risks, constantly visiting hostile headmen and chiefs unarmed and practically alone.

They must have won through many times just because such courage could not be understood and was taken to be backed by some occult or magic power. It has been said that the puniest of men if faced by a lion may get away with it if he will walk slowly towards the lion with complete assurance, and certainly Laws, Hetherwick, Johnson, Elmslie and many others were constantly doing just that.

So whatever opinion we may hold with regard to the value of missionary effort or the methods employed, we must give the highest praise to most missionaries as men of great courage both physical and moral, and that is probably true today though the risks have decreased.

The body which selected the first mission party from Scotland had learned several things from the failure of the English party of ten years earlier; it must also be admitted that it gave the planning much more thought. Consequently we find that there was only one full missionary in the party, Dr. Robert Laws, and he was accompanied by men who were the crew of their mission vessel, the *Ilala*, with a carpenter and an agriculturalist. Another full missionary, Mr. Henderson of the Church of Scotland, was attached to his party for a while almost as a member of it. It was realized that the establishment of a station and providing the barest amenities for the party was the prior duty.

There can be little doubt that it was very wise to choose the lake shore for the first station and that the possession of a steam-vessel raised their status tremendously in the eyes of the lake-dwellers in a way that nothing else could have done. Possibly it was the *Ilala* herself which gave the slaving chiefs pause when they might have descended on the party and destroyed them, even though she was only 48 feet long.

At all events, for at least a year the situation of the infant settlement at Cape Maclear at the south end of the lake was precarious beyond belief. Even more so was the establishment of the Church of Scotland mission at the present Blantyre. Mr. Henderson, after a few months with Dr. Laws, disappeared into the wilderness of the Shire Highlands with his baggage and one interpreter and for months nothing was heard of him.

The early history of almost every one of the mission stations is similar in some degree to these two early ones and excites the amazement of anyone who reads it, for the dangers faced, the problems met and the constant threat of illness and death by fever as well as the risks of land and lake travel.

Dr. Laws soon had to grapple with two major problems and he did so firmly. One was that already mentioned, the action if any to be taken towards the slave trade. It was not the question of fighting it, that could not be done in any case, but of receiving runaway slaves. He wisely decided that he must not do so and he kept to that decision despite immense temptation. A parallel problem was whether the mission should take sides in disputes, either inter-village or inter-tribal. Again he had to steel himself to complete neutrality even to the extent of seeing the Angoni raid villages close to the mission and murder the people whom he was trying to teach. The most he could do was to advise the victims of these raids, the Atonga, to unite and resist, but he also made a perilous journey, several times performed, to the chief Mombera to ask him to stop his men raiding. One gathers from reading the accounts of these parleys that it was not the reasons that Dr. Laws gave for his pleas that weighed with the chief, but the fact that he had an admiration for the missionary, who was so weak in material things but so fearless in asking the wellnigh impossible. There was at least one occasion when the missionaries at Bandawe, half-way up the western shore of the lake, had to pack up all the goods they could carry, ready to go aboard the *Ilala*, and fly from utter destruction.

Another problem was whether the missionaries could or should exercise powers of justice and punish men who had committed crimes in the precincts of the mission. Dr. Laws, whenever possible, sent the criminal to be judged by his own chief, but there were cases when this could not be done. There were complications too from the fact that the Established Church allowed far more judicial powers to its missionaries at Blantyre than the Free Church did for the Livingstonia party.

This latitude given to the Blantyre Mission was to be very nearly its undoing, when some of the junior members of its staff

'Goree' or slave stick in use

abused the measure of civil jurisdiction implicitly allowed them and sentenced men to floggings which ultimately got into the newspapers in England. A mission had to be sent out from the Church of Scotland Assembly to inquire into the allegations of cruelty, which were, in the main, upheld, and nothing but a drastic dismissal of the Europeans responsible saved the Mission from closing down.

In a letter from Dr. Laws at this time there is a very wise statement on this matter of civil jurisdiction: 'Personally my opinion is that the less a missionary has to do with the government of the country as an active agent himself in its administration, the closer he will get to the hearts of the people and the greater influence he will have on their lives', a dictum which has its application even today.

He expresses himself plainly on these matters and shows his eminent broad-mindedness in referring to 'the sickening sectarian differences in Scotland' and fears that they may turn up in Nyasaland too, which they certainly did.

At the end of five years the Free Church mission was moved from Cape Maclear to Bandawe, where it was much more immediately in touch with the inter-tribal wars and in no more healthy a place than before. Unkind critics referred to the balance sheet of the Cape Maclear residence of five years as 'Five missionaries dead of fever for one convert', a grossly unfair way of putting it, but not disturbing to the spirit of Dr. Laws whose plans were already made for very different balance sheets in the years to come.

In fact the most notable characteristic of that great man appears to have been his capacity for long-term planning, to which must be added the faith to carry it through.

From the very beginning he was looking for a healthy and therefore a high-level station, though he took sixteen years to find it. In some of his early letters too he made it clear that ultimately Christianity must be taught to the people by their own kith and kin; the white missionaries and the native deacons from South Africa were to him only the first phase of a truly African and Nyasaland Church.

Therefore he built his famous Livingstonia as a Training Centre, not a mission in the ordinary sense.

Finally, one can detect in his writings (which were few, he being so busy with his plans) that he put handiness next to godliness, so he taught trades alongside The Word at his Centre. He poured out builders, masons, carpenters, and they were dispersed all over the country: Livingstonia became a password for good workmanship, and its effect in establishing the reputation of Nyasa boys has been tremendous.

The settlement above the Lake at Livingstonia became a model technical college as well as a school for native clergy and in Dr. Laws' day it was the pattern of efficiency and even of architectural merit. Placed on a comparatively level spur jutting out from the east of the great Nyika plateau it was difficult of access and short of water. These were small matters to a planner of his calibre; he constructed the famous road with its hairpin bends; he led water in large pipes from higher up to give power and light; he opened up a quarry, built terraces for agricultural produce, started orchards and, in fact, made the Centre self-supporting in food.

It was a wonderful concept and as wonderfully carried out but one can imagine that his principles did not all appeal to his committees in Scotland. Nor did his application for a very large grant of land meet with approval from the Administration of a later date and he had to content himself with many score less square miles of territory than he had envisaged.

Thanks to his energy and vision there was created an institution quite unique in its day and, as we have said, of tremendous influence over the young Protectorate.

Perhaps it was inevitable that when he retired its character should alter somewhat and its light be somewhat dimmed. At all events its reputation for hospitality, tidiness and close union with the African no longer shines so brightly. One gathers that the mantle of one great man has now been divided to rest upon many committees and possibly that is why the name Livingstonia no longer stands high above all others in the Nyasaland picture. In particular, it has transgressed Dr. Laws' own dictum that missionaries should not take sides in politics and in so doing it has lost some of the respect it used to command.

Turning back to the very first missionary venture, that of Bishop Mackenzie's party with Livingstone in 1861, it will be remembered that it gradually withdrew from Nyasaland and renewed its energies at Zanzibar. From there, however, under the guidance of Bishop Steere it approached Nyasaland once more, and from a very different direction. In the late seventies the Bishop and others toiled up the Rovuma river, along the route that Livingstone followed on his last journey in 1866.

Now known as the Universities Mission to Central Africa (U.M.C.A.) it essayed this much more difficult gateway to the lake, through tribes far more hostile than those on the Shire and without being able to carry with it steamers and quantities of trade goods with which to impress the people.

It showed, if possible, even more determination and disregard of danger than its Scottish allies on the lake and finally established itself on its eastern shore and on the island of

Likoma close to it. Later it opened a branch mission at Kota Kota where its buildings surround a quadrangle in the midst of which still grows the 'magnificent wild fig-tree with leaves ten inches long' under which Dr. Livingstone received the Jumbe or chief in September 1863.

I suppose missionaries get rather tired of civilians coming to ask questions about their work; at all events I rarely had the welcome from them that I had from the administrative officers. I called on the head of the U.M.C.A. mission at Kota Kota, very full of its history, eager to hear more about Bishop Chauncy Maples and Archdeacon Johnson, two of their great men, and if possible to learn about the success of the mission. Perhaps I came at the wrong time or did not announce my purpose with due tact but at all events the wind was definitely in the east that day and I had to be content with being told which was the Livingstone tree and was then bowed out.

That was a pity, but it did not alter my opinion of the great work of the U.M.C.A. people on the lake, working as they were on the most forbidding and dangerous side of it. Their early vessels, as did the *Ilala*, came into the history of the early wars and their hospital at Likoma was second only to that of Dr. Laws for saving the lives of black and white alike.

The U.M.C.A. tended to send out bachelors as missionaries and even to discourage marriage amongst them later. It was not a very wise policy and one result which may possibly be ascribed to it was the high rate of deaths and the degree of comparative discomfort they put up with at their stations.

Even the upholder of the system, Chauncy Maples, writes movingly of the difference in comfort and appearance of their dwellings on Likoma Island when at last two lady missionaries came out to join them. He was one of the real martyrs of his mission as he was lost by drowning when he was returning from England as newly consecrated Bishop. This too makes one feel that practical common-sense was not so highly developed in the English missionaries as it was in the Scottish ones.

The good bishop was so determined to get quickly back to Likoma that he set sail in bad weather from Fort Johnston in a rather unhandy boat with one white man and some Africans. He declined to take shelter at Monkey Bay when his crew strongly advised it, and worse still he declined to sail up the eastern side of the lake where the seas would not be so high, but steered straight for Kota Kota and went on late into the night. Some fault in the steering or perhaps an extra big sea caused the boat to broach to and all fell into the water some two or three miles from land. The bishop was a good swimmer but he declined the offer of the native crew to help him off with his hampering cassock, and told them to go on and save themselves. It was all very heroic and unfortunate but it should not have happened.

The mission of the Established Church of Scotland at Blantyre is best known of the three oldest missions because it is so central. It is a little outside the business centre of the town and is a little colony in itself with its beautiful and famous gardens, up-to-date schoolrooms, pleasant quarters for the missionaries, hospital accommodation and so on.

Its church would be notable anywhere but it is easily the most beautiful and remarkable building in the territory.

It would redound to the credit of any of the great architects yet, in fact, it was designed and carried out by a man who had never had a single lesson even in bricklaying, much less in architecture.

It is constructed entirely of brick, all made locally and laid by African labour. The church is of cathedral proportions, as our photograph shows, and manages to achieve in brick many of the features which one would imagine could only be done in stone.

The most amazing thing about this building is that it was completed in 1895, that is to say, while wars were still going on not many miles away, when the total whites in the country were under 200, before there were railways, and within a few years of there being not a single wheeled cart in the country.

Apart from the genius of the designer, Mr. Scott, it is a standing reminder of the natural gift the Manganja tribe has for handicraft. The mission at Blantyre, in its gardens, in its printing press and in its buildings, showed that works could come before faith, or at least with it, and both become alive.

This church must be a modern parallel to, say, the cathedral at Ely, which arose in its majesty amongst the peasants' huts and low stone quarters of the monks to the greater glory of God and the wonder of the fisher folk of that island in the fens. There cannot have been more than a half-dozen two-storied buildings in all Nyasaland when these towers and turrets and rounded domes arose to the wonder of the Africans.

It will have been noted that in both of the Scottish missions there was a recognition that the education of the African must be both on the practical and the spiritual side. The accusation often heard that the missionary schools always prefer to train children for clerical posts is not sustained, though it is true that the emphasis varies from one mission to another. The African has already developed a certain degree of snobbery and tries to get into the white-collared fraternity rather than that of the artisan; the demand for clerical training comes largely from him.

There are signs, too, that the Africans do not particularly like having their education tied up with proselytism and there is a general move towards having purely secular schools, either from Government entirely or assisted by their own voluntary subscriptions. The enthusiasm over the new school at Kota Kota, described in Chapter 6, is an instance.

There is yet another example of a mission which views its obligations to the people in the broadest way. The Dutch Reformed Church, based on South Africa, was early in the field and at Mkhoma, between Lilongwe and Dedza, it has recently been focusing its activities along somewhat original lines.

Under the direction of Mr. Lou Pretorius it has taken on the function of fostering community development, which in a sense may be called encouragement of self-help and mutual co-operation, a more difficult task than merely teaching individuals to enter careers. The scheme at present comprises a group of 22 villages on rather poor land and involves persuading them or their representatives to get together in a number of developments. They have already done so to the extent of running communal brick and tile works, communal carpentry workshops, pottery, basket-making, etc. These were perhaps the easier forms of activity but the mission is going much further in guiding such less popular forms as the bunding of gardens, the planting of trees, improvement of home life, sanitation and even training in local self-government. The villages subscribe to and put voluntary labour into a flourishing primary school.

I was shown over these various activities and told that very little money had been asked for from the government—only for the teacher's salary in fact. Further developments will come mainly from the income derived from the village industries, each of which will in time be independent of white supervision, and be subject to the direction of local committees of Africans.

The success of such a scheme depends very much on the personality of the director, of course, and in this case there is no doubt on that point, as Mr. Pretorius seems to be cast in the mould of Dr. Robert Laws.

The Roman Catholic missions are in no sense behind those of the other denominations. Their more ceremonial forms of service seem to have a strong appeal to the emotional temperament of the African whom it is strange to hear chanting in Latin.

The missions run by the organization known as the White Fathers, with its headquarters in North Africa, are of particular interest. In spite of using French as their main language, and in spite of their somewhat ascetic mode of life, they give a warm welcome to the passer-by, of whatever religion. I had the impression that their approach to education for the African is more rational than that of most other missions, since they place more emphasis on handicrafts. Their discipline, too, seems to be firmer. The White Fathers, in fact, are a very potent influence and no one can fail to be impressed with their results in the advancement of the African.

We cannot end this chapter without saying something about the reaction of administrators and settlers to the missionaries.

There was a time, when the administration was just getting under way in the early nineties, when there was a wide gulf between it and the mission. The latter had been in Blantyre already for ten or a dozen years and had been forced to take on powers which had to be handed over to the civil service in due course. This it was loth to do and Consul Johnston met great opposition, and unkind tactics too, in trying to adjust the situation. He was not noted for his tact, it is true, but he says that the opposition he met made 'his life and the lives of his subordinates unbearable.'

So it is all the more interesting to read his account of missionaries written in 1896 and to note his admission that 'they have done more good than armies, navies, conferences and treaties.' While thus pronouncing a verdict almost entirely in favour of the value of missionary work he notes the prejudice and dislike of missionaries shared by other white men.

He ascribes these feelings to two things, the cant which, as he said, 'seems to be inseparable from missionary work', and secondly, an arrogant demeanour often assumed by missionaries towards their colleagues in the protectorate. He then very handsomely proceeds to explain or modify these accusations so that one ends the chapter feeling that these faults were small matters compared with the outstanding services rendered to the community.

Perhaps these and other strictures on the missionaries owe their origin to the behaviour of the lesser brethren and have acquired undue prominence, but there is still an echo of Sir Harry Johnston's assertions. Those whom we regard as the great men of the brotherhood, like Dr. Laws, certainly did little to offend in these ways. He never stooped to counting souls saved and contriving a balance sheet of converts at so much cost per head. He would point, with proper pride, to the numbers of useful citizens and workmen his mission sent out, but in his rare summings-up of the situation in regard to true Christianity he would shake his head in comparative disappointment. He would probably have agreed with Sir Harry Johnston that 'it takes at least three clear generations before any full appreciation of the principles of morality, truth, gratitude and honour can penetrate the intellect and curb the instincts of the negro.'

It is perhaps natural for the missionary who labours so hard to inculcate these virtues in a single generation to persuade himself that he has done so, and there may well be instances where he has succeeded. He is so eager to succeed that he is apt to think wishfully and even more apt to pat his initiates on the back too early. Even the wisest of the missionaries appear to have this fault.

The broad-minded settler, of whom there are many, seems inclined to hold much the same opinions now as Johnston did 60 years ago, which might be expressed in a somewhat different way: that missionaries as a whole were doing a good job but were apt to overrate themselves and to consider that no one else could attain to an equal enlightenment about the African or what was best for him.

Certainly many of their ardent supporters are occasionally dismayed when the missions project themselves into the political field as they unfortunately do, especially when they counter or even contradict the administrative officers, who have no axe to grind and must be permitted to have the welfare of the people equally at their heart. A visitor to the country must, as we have already pointed out, give his true impressions. I confess that going there charged with the history of the missions by my reading and a readiness to believe that there were still Hetherwicks and Chauncy Maples and Laws at work in Nyasaland, I came away slightly disappointed in the missions of today.

Two Sansas (or Sansis). They have wooden sounding-boards and keys of welded iron, and are played by the thumbs pressing down and releasing the ends of the keys, the fingers holding the sounding-board. Usually there are 7 keys, sometimes 5 or 9

10. THE PEOPLE

THE word *Bantu* means people, men, folk, in the major language of Southern Africa, and it is a convenient alternative to that very hard worked name 'African'. Fashion in group naming is a little fickle, and it is said to be distasteful to the Africans to call them 'natives'. On the other hand, the most intelligent chief I met in Nyasaland told me that he did not consider it in the least derogatory and would rather be called a native, which meant that he belonged to the country he lived in, than an African, which labelled him as coming from somewhere in a vast continent of many types of people.

The singular is *Muntu*, which in Southern Africa has been shortened down to 'Munt' and is sometimes used in much the same way as we use the word 'Yank' for a single American. The Bantu of Nyasaland number a little under two-and-a-half million and that works out at a population density of nearly 60 to the square mile, which is very high for Southern Africa. We may compare it with the following:

Tanganyika	about	30	to the square mile	
Portuguese East Africa	,,	20	,,	,,	,,
Southern Rhodesia	,,	10	,,	,,	,,
Northern Rhodesia	,,	5	,,	,,	,,
Union of South Africa	,,	12	,,	,,	,,

Another way of putting it is that in the new Federation, Nyasaland covers only one-thirteenth of the total area but has one-third of the total population. When we add that Nyasaland follows an almost entirely agricultural economy, with no industries of any consequence yet, it becomes striking enough to require some explanation

Part of the reason for this density lies in the climate, that is to say, chiefly the rainfall. There are no large areas which are frequently subject to drought.

In the two Rhodesias there are large tracts of plateau country with a comparatively low rainfall coupled with a scarcity of perennial streams. The only parts of Nyasaland in that category are the areas near the boundary with Northern

Rhodesia. Further, with its high mountains and abrupt slopes Nyasaland has more chance of getting some rain in the dry season, particularly near vast high masses like Mlanje, the Vipya and the Nyika. Even if rain does not actually fall on the lower country it keeps the streams perennial. The lake itself and the Shire River provide perennial water for a long 'shore line' suitable for habitation. The soils of Nyasaland are consequently slightly more fertile than those of the other two territories.

This by itself is hardly reason enough for the great difference in density. We have seen already that there has been tremendous immigration into Nyasaland from neighbouring territories, and that is a highly significant factor, which is based mainly on the security promised by the white settlers and their administration, and which springs from the fact that Nyasaland got an early start with a settled government and a demand for labour, and more particularly with education by the missionaries.

The result was that the Nyasa peoples were a little more intelligent, a little more pressed for room and therefore a little more industrious than their fellows in the two Rhodesias. Just as the proverbial industry of the Indian and the Chinese is largely due to the struggle for existence so in a very minor way the large numbers in Nyasaland had a consciousness that they must work a little harder than people who were not so closely packed and it has become somewhat of a tradition. This may surprise some of the employers of labour in Nyasaland, but if they were to go into the thousands of remote villages in Northern Rhodesia they couldn't fail to see that the people there do very much less hard work than is done in Nyasaland.

The people living in Nyasaland today present such a complex and baffling mixture of tribes and sub-tribes, indigenous and foreign, raiders and raided, that we cannot hope to give a picture of them to satisfy an anthropologist or ethnographer.

We can simplify the subject by naming the lake itself as the centre of a vortex of movements by these peoples for the last two centuries at least.

The Bantu, the chief inhabitants of East and Central Africa, have always been migratory, not always willingly perhaps, and they have also been fairly ready to absorb or be absorbed by newcomers. Consequently it is very difficult to decide when a group or tribe is really a tribe and not a mixture of elements.

What we can do is to give a name to the chief disturbers of the peace, the most warlike tribes who set the vortex in motion, and either walked through the more peaceful tribes or pushed them into corners or round the ends of the lake. In doing so, however, they tended to lose their character either by attrition, since they did not always have it their own way, or else by dilution, that is to say, by intermarriage with the conquered.

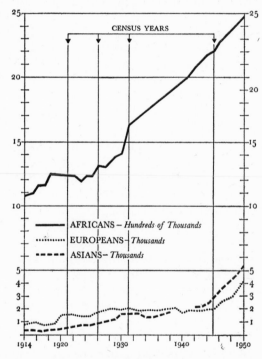

Graph showing how Nyasaland's population has grown
(*Note the difference in scale*)

The Angoni, or Ngoni, were originally a people living in Natal who rebelled against the Zulu tyrant, Chaka, and migrated slowly northward to the Zambezi, raiding as they went. We can fix the date of their crossing of the Zambezi as 1835, since it took place during an eclipse of the sun and obviously at a time of year when the river was low.

At this stage they were probably not formidable in numbers, but they had brought with them the military discipline and

147

tactics of the Zulus, the crescent form of attack with encircling wings and hand-to-hand combat with the stabbing assegai.

They had to increase their numbers by recruiting young men from the conquered and they took care to train them in their own method of warfare.

In a few years, therefore, we find them marching north and dispersing in branches, some even as far as the southern shores of Lake Victoria, and some turning back and raiding on both sides of Lake Nyasa.

The number of people put down in the Nyasaland census now as Angoni is about 200,000, so it is obvious that the dilution of the original few thousand warriors who crossed the Zambezi is so overwhelming that the use of the name is hardly more than a token. They have all but lost their language, so characteristic with its Zulu clicks, and now each section of the Angoni use the local dialect. This loss was almost automatic, as the warriors' wives brought up their children to speak their own local language. In some respects the invasion of the Angoni can be likened to that of the Normans into Saxon England; the conquest was nearly complete but the invaders were swamped and absorbed by the indigenous people.

When I was able to interview two of the major chiefs, Mbelwa in the Mzimba district and Gomani in that of Ncheu, I tried to find out how many of the truly Zulu customs still obtained. Mbelwa himself, being in more direct line of descent from the original leader, looks the Zulu all over, but Gomani did not. Both, however, were anxious to persuade me that Zulu customs were still practised, though they had to rack their brains to think of any. When, for instance, I asked whether any of them wore the Zulu ring of matted hair and gum, betokening prowess in war and command Gomani admitted there were none but that when he was young he saw several men wearing it. On the other hand, both were anxious to demonstrate that their dances incorporated the use of the assegai. In fact the son of Mbelwa, dressed in a zoot suit with a very flamboyant American tie, threw off his coat, grabbed a spear from a bystander and worked himself up into a perfect frenzy in front of me, repeating the motions of stabbing me to the heart over and over again. It must be admitted, on the other hand, that some of the Zulu psychology has been faithfully transmitted to their very mixed

descendants, including their arrogant assumption that they are
superior to all other tribes. This is to be seen in the Shire
Highlands, where Angoni labour has long been used and where
the Nguru and Manganja labourers give a wide berth to their
Angoni colleagues, who are apt to take offence and seek a fight
with true Zulu zest.

This love of fighting and tendency to lord it over all other
tribes have been used with effect by the Administration by
picking Angoni for the troops and for the police. It may have
been Dr. Laws who introduced that way of making the best of
them. Sir Harry Johnston wanted to invade and conquer the
Angoni to put an end to their persecution of the lakeside
people, but Dr. Laws said, 'Don't conquer them, enlist them,'
and later on that simple method prevented a lot of bloodshed.

Anthropologists seem to disagree concerning the Zulu-like
qualities of the Angoni and some say that it was their organization and weapons rather than their aptitude for war which
made them conquerors

Without being very intelligent the Angoni seem to have had a
sense of military tactics which was quite foreign to all the other
tribes except possibly the Yao, and they were constantly winning battles against superior numbers, which in itself was partly
responsible for their haughty manner.

This commonsense in war comes out especially in the story
of the massacre of Mount Hora, and though it was told to me by
a venerable old grey-haired Angoni parson there was an
occasional flash of martial pride in his tribe as he told it. He
was telling it to me in front of some hundreds of his tribe and
though he began in good English I asked him to continue it in
Chi-Nyanja so that his comrades could hear it. This was guile
on my part for I could not only get it more slowly through the
interpreter but I could see the effect on the ranks of Angoni
sitting on the ground all round us. It was about 1880 when the
Angoni had cowed the Tumbuka tribe into a form of servitude
and my orator began by saying it was all the fault of Baza, the
Tumbuka chief, who cheated Mombera, the Angoni chief, by
sending him a small tusk of ivory as tribute instead of a large
one. War was declared and Baza thought of a way of keeping
the Angoni assegais at a distance and spoiling their usual shock
tactics. He led a thousand or two of his tribe up the rocky slopes

of Mount Hora and they armed themselves with rocks to throw down on the warriors trying to come to close quarters. But the Angoni were far too wise to attempt to storm the position and they merely encircled the hill and waited for starvation and thirst to conquer for them. They dispatched the parties that came down for water as they arrived and lost hardly a single man of their own. Only two of the beleagured Tumbuka lived to tell the tale and they were the chief Baza and one other, who climbed down one night at a place which seemed impossible and sought refuge with Mwase, the chief of the Chewa tribe. The grunts of approval from his hearers as they heard the details of the oft-told tale were in fact a parallel to the cheers of any English audience in Stuart times when some old salt told them how the Spanish Armada was defeated.

It was chiefly due to the personality of Dr. Laws that we never had to go to war with the northern section of the tribe under Mombera, which would have been a big undertaking for an army which consisted then of only a hundred Sikhs. A still greater triumph claimed for that eminent peacemaker was that when he came to build the final Livingstonia it was Angoni men who acted as his carriers up the terrific slopes while the Atonga idly watched their aforetime lords doing all the hard work.

At that time the Angoni had only been in the country for some 40 years and their Zulu manners were still very much to the fore. It may therefore be of interest to compare the reception of Mr. Elmslie, Dr. Laws' understudy, by the great Mombera in 1880 with my own reception by Chief Mbelwa in 1952.

Mr. Elmslie writes in his very notable book, *Among the Wild Ngoni*—'When we had been invited to enter the hut we did so by going down on our knees and crawling through the doorway which was only a couple of feet high. As each entered the royal salute had to be given by raising the voice, and saying *Bayete*. Mombera sat on a reed mat, beside which was a huge pot of beer. A smaller pot, made of grass deftly woven so as to be quite water-tight, was held by Mombera, who took frequent draughts and sometimes handed it round to the people in his presence. If he did so, or rose from his mat, all shouted *Bayete*. If any one rose to go to another part of the hut, or to leave the royal presence, he shouted *Bayete*.'

Of his dress we note that 'the chief part was the numerous

beautiful ivory rings . . . and his clothing was completed by a few yards of coloured calico, carelessly thrown over him.'

Mombera was a short, corpulent man, with a shrewd look in his one eye and the old Zulu ring on his head.

'It was a trying ordeal to be stared at by Mombera's one eye over the beer pot and to know that his remarks about one's appearance were causing amusement to all in the hut, for until one has been greeted by the chief he must be silent. It was the custom of the chief to refrain from the greeting for some fifteen minutes after the visitor had come into the presence.'

'The Ngoni salutation is, "We see you," and when Mombera had greeted us thus, all were free to do so and tongues were loosened.'

Angoni head-rest or wooden pillow

'The present we had brought for Mombera consisted of some coloured calico, brass wire, beads and some trinkets. He looked at it and demanded a kind of bead of which we had none. With the most barefaced impertinence and incivility he said he would not like to insult the new white man by refusing what he had brought but as there was nothing to be seen he would ask me to bring something with me another day.'

And now let us see what the passage of 70 years has done for the mode of reception by an Angoni chief.

We had arrived at the village early in the day, always a wise procedure with chiefs, so as to catch them before beer drinking has gone very far, and were very impressed with the buildings of brick, the chief's house painted white, several favourite wives' houses, a dormitory for the royal children and so on. We were told to wait as the chief was robing and the D.C. who was with me but was new to the Angoni said that there were all the signs of a big show being laid on. After a while a number of elders went off to the chief's house together with warriors garbed in old style and there a procession was formed which came towards us with shouts from the men and shrill lu-lu-luing from the women.

I turned to the D.C. to ask what we were supposed to do but he grinned and said he 'hadn't the faintest', it was up to me to decide.

There was at least no doubt who was the chief, a burly figure in the Zulu style with many ivory rings on his arms and a cloth thrown over with 'The British Lion' on it, exactly as in our photograph.

I still do not know what I was supposed to do, but I advanced slowly towards the procession, past the warriors stabbing at the air and the procession had to halt while I addressed the chief, 'I am pleased to meet you, Inkosi Mbelwa.' I had at least remembered the Zulu 'Inkosi' and he shook me warmly by the hand. Then I introduced my wife who tried, 'How do you do?' to which came the gracious reply in perfect English, 'Very well, thank you, Madam.'

Then I fell in alongside the chief and the procession continued with songs and war cries and dancing till we came to a table and four chairs set in the midst of about 600 of his people, who all stood up and at some invisible signal, roared out the famous *Bayete*.

Then I was motioned by the chief to the armchair while he sat on a rickety one alongside me and the proceedings began.

No waiting till he 'saw me' you'll notice, perhaps because I saw him first and spoke out of my turn, no remarks about my appearance, as far as I could tell, and certainly no beer. Nor indeed had I any presents to be criticized.

My impressions of the vivid two hours that followed were that Mbelwa was a pleasant jovial country gentleman, ready to leave

'Angoni warrior.' The artist was 'that most versatile of Governors, Sir Harry Johnston'.

(*Above*) A progressive Nyasalander with his family on the verandah of their home. (*Below*) Township types listening to a speech. The white cap is favoured headwear for houseboys. These are mainly Yaos.

(*Above*) 'Mganda' dance performed by the Chewa for pleasure and on ceremonial occasions. (*Below*) Blantyre Market is an organized affair, a place of gay colour.

Mount Mlanje from the top of Mount Zomba. Part of Zom

d, Mount Chiradzulu in the middle distance to the right.

H.E. the Governor greets the late Chief Gomani, head of the southern group of Angoni

Typical barge labourers on the Lower Shire at Port Herald.

Chief Msusa of
Kota Kota.

Mbelwa, Paramount Chief
of the Northern Angoni.

Mwase, Chief of the
Chewa at Kasungu.

ewinner and mother
at a baby show.

The woman's task:
pounding the grain.

Women have learnt
the value of spinning.

(*Above*) A classroom in the Livingstonia Free Church Mission founded by Dr Laws. (*Below*) The Church of Scotland Church at Blantyre, designed by Mr. Scott, an amateur, and built in brick in 1895 by African labour.

most of his politics to his sub-chiefs and councillors, well able to grace a formal gathering with a royal presence, but on the whole preferring his beer and wives to taking a leading part in a conference.

He is not happy at English though he could understand simple sentences. He visited England with other Nyasaland chiefs a few months later and was seen on platforms. He also spoke in his own language on these platforms and as reported his sentiments were so much the opposite of what he had said to me, that I inquired later of a D.C. who was at the meetings. I was very pleased to find that what his interpreter, with an axe of his own to grind, told the meeting Mbelwa had said was very different indeed from his actual words. One of the listeners at an Edinburgh meeting told me how surprised he was when after a long sentence or two given with a winning smile from Mbelwa they were told by the interpreter that he had just said that federation could come only over his dead body and that of every man, woman and child. What would have happened to that interpreter in the good old days of Mombera, if his very free translation had been detected, would have been something very short and sharp.

Mbelwa's Angoni are about 50,000 in number and being in the partially-developed North are less sophisticated than the 30,000 under the chieftainship of Gomani round Ncheu, who are so 'diluted' that they do not fully deserve to be called Angoni.

My visit to Gomani at his village three miles from Ncheu was therefore much more civilized. He and his elders received me in his offices, they having suspended a session of his court to do so, and all the people in the room were in European clothes.

Gomani was not very old, but he had some form of Parkinson's disease which shook all his limbs, and talking to him was difficult when his arms and head were twisting from side to side.

The proceedings began by his son Willard, a former Boma clerk, handing me an address of welcome, for which I thanked the chief after I had read it, but I had spoken too soon as I had to hand it back to Willard for it to be read out to the assembled company. It included the somewhat ambiguous sentence—'Sir, I trust we will be patients to listen to your problems and hope will be more interested.'

Our conversation was mainly about the history of the tribe, the shortage of land, stories of man-eaters and so on, and I carefully avoided the subject of federation.

At one stage when they had admitted a little sadly that there were very few of them who were of original Angoni stock they were visibly cheered by my saying that the English nation was a mixed one just like theirs with a mixed language and customs.

Before we adjourned to the court the chief made me a present of a vast bowl of eggs and as he handed it to me all the people shouted *Bayete*, and Gomani nearly embraced me when I made a remark that 'that was more like the true Zulu spirit.'

Again my impression was wildly different from what may have been underlying at the time to lead to the civil disobedience of a few months later. All the people who spoke, except Willard, who was a little inclined to *chipongwe*, seemed contented with everything except that they were being crowded for land by having people from over the border wished on to them by the Portuguese. When someone asked me about the Queen and Buckingham Palace they listened eagerly to my description and I should have said with the deepest feelings of loyalty. They clearly appreciated their D.C.

Afterwards I sat through a long court case, to which I was invited by Gomani, and had bits of it explained by the D.C.

These two are not the only sections of the Angoni in Nyasaland but I had only casual contact with those near Fort Jameson under Mpeseni and others near the lake under Chiwere.

We must now turn to a tribe which may be described perhaps as the second most warlike and virile, the Yao people.

These originally came from the direction of the Rovuma river, which is the border between Tanganyika and Mozambique. So for some centuries they had occasional contact with the coast Arabs. It is not surprising, therefore, that most of the Yaos are Mahomedan in religion and were quick to learn the art of slave raiding. Like the Angoni they are late-comers to Nyasaland and the greater number are still in Portuguese East Africa, but they did not invade the region in a body or indeed in any organized way. Their coming was more in the nature of an infiltration and they were just establishing themselves as overlords of the more peaceful Manganja when Dr. Livingstone first met them and called them the Ajawa. It is possible that

they were set on the move by the Angoni who came round the
north end of the lake, but they were quick to learn also that
raiding other tribes for slaves was preferable to being raided
themselves by coast Arabs. They now are the predominant
tribe in the Southern Province and have even spread up towards the south-west of the lake, rather exceeding the Nguru
except on the Shire Highlands.

They are agriculturalists rather than cattle people, possibly
because most of their territory in Portuguese East Africa is

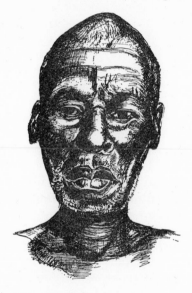

Head of a Manganja man, drawn from a photograph
taken at Zomba in 1912 by Dr. H. S. Stanus

ridden with the tsetse-fly. They are great wanderers so they
furnish a good proportion of the emigrant labour from Nyasaland to the Rhodesias and South Africa. A majority of the houseboys in Nyasaland are Yaos and with them it is not so necessary
to lock up the drinks, though their Mahomedanism is not always
capable of resisting the temptation.

The people they first enslaved and later settled amongst were
the Manganja, more peaceable than the Yaos and far better
artisans. Their language, Chi-Nyanja, has been made the
official one for most of Nyasaland, largely because they were

155

the indigenous people where the Administration grew up on the Shire Highlands.

After 60 years of peace the various tribes have inter-mixed a good deal and their differences of custom and even of character have become somewhat blurred.

It is therefore of little purpose to describe the tribes in great detail, but we must refer to one or two which are remarkable either for numbers or for character.

Easily the largest group of people in Nyasaland are the Chewa, over half a million in number, and they occupy most of the Central Province, enclosing the separate Angoni groups. It was natural therefore that they clashed with those warriors and suffered from them. However, partly by indulging in the slave trade themselves and procuring guns with which they were nearly a match for the Angoni and partly by making treaties with them and paying tribute, they suffered less severely at their hands than did the smaller and perhaps more stubborn tribes, the Tumbuka and the Atonga.

Their chief's name is Mwase and the present centre of such power as he wields is Kasungu.

The Tonga tribe may have been an offshoot of the Tumbuka but they have evolved more recently into a unit of their own and a very interesting one. In common with the other tribes on either side of the Vipya plateau they were conquered and enslaved by the Angoni under Mombera in the middle of last century. But after a while they took heart, retreated down to the lakeshore and actually repulsed the Angoni army that came after them. It is true that they expected reprisals and had to fortify every village with stockades, but a little later Dr. Laws established his second station amongst them at Bandawe. The missionaries resolutely declined to take sides in a tribal war but there is no doubt that it was very embarrassing to Mombera to have his friend Laws living in the midst of the people he wished to annihilate. It is almost certain that they would have been dispersed if not exterminated but for the presence of the missionaries, and in fact it was due to them that a formal treaty of peace was made between the Angoni and the Atonga in 1887. The tribe was naturally taken under the wing of the mission for education and the people, being very intelligent, took full advantage of it, especially in the trades they were taught. They soon acquired a reputation for their skill and were able to earn high wages in South Africa. This was likely to prove the undoing of the tribe and at one time the proportion of able-bodied males absent as migrant labour was 60 per cent. On the other hand, most of them returned to their tribe after their contracts were up and were not added to the number of the 'lost ones', the name they give to migrant labour which fails to return. The district has the highest emigrant figure of all but it has a low percentage of lost ones.

In the plain behind Karonga at the extreme north of the

Wankonde hut, with a man playing a 'Zeze'

territory which has been called the northern funnel of the Rift Valley there survives the tribe of the Wankonde which is rather distinct, culturally at all events, from those we have mentioned. There are only about 60,000 of them, which is roughly the same as the Atonga.

They had a rather complicated system of hereditary chiefs who took the name Chungu, who seemed to have powers much nearer the feudal type than most African tribes, with something approaching the nobles or barons of our own medieval times. The simile can be carried still further in that the barons were frequently at war with each other.

The Chungu has great prestige, much of it of a religious

character, and he is usually very wealthy as he profits by the system of free labour from his subjects for a set term of days.

They had the usual trouble with the Angoni but they came to terms with them in similar fashion to the Chewa, by paying tribute and at the same time repelling the occasional small raid. They fared far worse at the hands of the Arab slave traders who challenged the British attempts to stop their trade. The Arab parties with their guns were able to decimate the Wankonde, and when Sir Harry Johnston finally defeated and hanged the Arab leader, Mlozi, the tribe was down to a few thousand only in number. They are cattle people but are also skilled iron-workers and more recently have produced a useful surplus of rice. The villages are quite different from those of the southern tribes in plan; they are tidier and the huts of a special pattern. As mentioned before the D.Cs. who have ruled them from the rather remote and unhealthy Boma at Karonga tend to prefer the Wankonde to all other peoples they have governed.

It will be seen therefore that in Nyasaland there are various types of Bantu, warlike tribes and peace-loving tribes, cattle people and agricultural people, father-right and mother-right patterns of society.

All appear to have had beliefs or religions based on spirit-worship and ancestor-worship, and in connection with these there were severe disciplines and sanctions when the cult of the tribe had been violated.

We need not pretend that it was an orderly form of society but it did have a pattern, and it was far from a primitive one. Its material culture was not advanced but there were workers in iron and in weaving cloth. There was, in fact, some knowledge of the lever but none of the wheel.

Into this grouping of societies there first broke the coastal Arab culture, bringing war and slavery, both of which they could understand and a smattering of Mahomedanism which could be roughly fitted to their own beliefs. The muskets and cloths they bought were worth the shocks their pattern suffered.

Hard upon their heels came the whites, adding the shock of colour-difference, still better guns and better cloths, magic wheels and steamers on the lake, and a strange philosophy.

It was no wonder that the Bantu thought that the white man came out of the sea, that they believed there was magic or great medicine in the Book that these men looked at and spoke from. The doctrine of Love which these men taught was too new to be assimilated at all quickly but in the meantime there were plenty of other benefits to come from making friends with them.

That is probably too simple an account of how the white man came to fit into the Bantu society but broadly speaking it is correct, mainly because the missionaries made first contact.

Then followed fresh shocks but nearly always delivered gently or gradually. The white man was not going to 'eat them up' nor was he going to take their land, but he insisted on peace and he could quickly punish offenders. Also he had a great sense of justice and fairness and would always listen to both sides in an argument. He would confer benefits like making roads and buildings, but they had to be paid for by a tax. That too was fair enough though sometimes it was excessive and the young men had to go away and work for the tax amongst the white men.

By and large, therefore, the arrangements made by the white men were a tremendous advantage, and so different from the old days that it was a new world for the people. And it all came to pass within the lifetime of those who were boys when first the missionaries came. What seems remarkable to us must appear to be incredible to them.

As Chief Gomani said to me, 'Things are very well with us, we can go anywhere we like in the country, we are free to work for anyone we choose, there is only this matter of the Portuguese pushing our people back across the border.' He did not say, what he might have felt, that federation would be a bad thing because the fashions of South Africa might be introduced.

I must repeat that, to a visitor spending four months in the country in 1946, Nyasaland was the most contented territory in all East and Central Africa.

Not that we should pat ourselves on the back too much; we have made blunders in plenty and will continue to do so, but we have the grace to admit them and to permit criticism.

There is a series of excellent studies of the situation some years ago written by Mr. Frank Melland and Mr. T. Cullen Young. These men speak from long experience, one in the administrative and one in the missionary field, and what they say merits attention.

Put very briefly I think their message is that we have paid insufficient attention to the merits of the Bantu culture and organization, we have in fact been too paternal. That may be true, perhaps we have foisted too quickly upon them our experiments with Direct or Indirect Rule, perhaps we have too readily cast aside their old religious background as utterly pagan and worthless. Only fellow experts can debate these assertions with them.

What we can claim, however, is that we have done these things with the best of motives and there is nothing dishonourable in our treatment of the Bantu.

We must also be careful that the pendulum does not swing too far in the other direction. If these two very wise critics are right in saying we have rated the Bantu culture and wisdom too low, others, mainly in England, have rated it too high.

If we admit that the undoubted contentment of the Nyasa peoples of a few years ago was the result of our system and not mere chance, we ought to inquire into the principle of that system, which I would call Partnership, a word which is full of meaning in spite of the hard words now showered upon it.

The Zeze is a one-stringed instrument, introduced from Madagascar by the old Arab caravans trading from the coast. When played it is held with the gourd resonator upwards, the string being plucked by the fingers as shown in the drawing on page 157

11. THE WAYS OF THE PEOPLE

THE last chapter can have done little more than introduce the reader to the main sections or tribes of Nyasaland, and he cannot from that have much idea about the life of the people or their general character. We have seen that tribal differences are gradually disappearing, that there are signs of a new difference appearing, the town folk as opposed to the village folk. With federation a new outlook on the Africans and from the Africans must come.

What we need, of course, is a fuller understanding of them, their attitude to life, their aspirations, their needs, and perhaps most important of all, their capacities, their potential for advancement from backwardness to a status of partnership in which they must take on more and more responsibility.

We need a real understanding of the African, if we are not to make mistakes, and yet it is extraordinarily difficult for any European to have anything like intimate knowledge of them.

Perhaps the missionary comes nearest to understanding the ways of his flock, but he has his own inhibitions and degrees of bias. The administrator observes a good deal but not on such an intimate scale, and he too must have his prejudices, usually in the direction of ordering his Africans to do certain things rather than persuading them. The settler or manager who employs them has a point of view also, perhaps less trustworthy than either missionary or ruler, but his must be taken into consideration because it is as employees that many of the Africans must live in the final resort.

We have seen from the last chapter that Nyasaland as we now know it was somewhat of a melting pot even when Livingstone got there, Angoni from the south conquering, Arab influence from the east infiltrating with slave-raiding and Islam. The earlier inhabitants fitted in as best they could between the jaws of the pincer movement, with the very different Wankonde at the north-west perhaps the most promising tribe of all.

With British protection the melting pot has not boiled over so violently but diffusion of the different elements has been going on steadily. Even so we cannot talk of a typical Nyasa African and for the sake of brevity we must confine ourselves mainly to the Central and Southern Provinces.

That means leaving out about one-tenth of the total population, which would not matter so much were it not that that tenth includes the people who came under the influence of Dr. Laws and his Livingstonia, a factor of importance out of all proportion to the numbers included. We must, therefore, keep the intelligent Atonga and the northern section of the Angoni in our minds even if we do not include them in the few statistics we may use.

At this stage we should take note of two well defined splits in the country, one being in religion and one a fundamental difference of attitude in their social life.

The split in religion is between Islam and Christianity, the Yaos being mainly Mahommedan and the remainder part pagan part Christian. As far as the national character is concerned, using a rather vague and unsatisfactory term, this split is not of great consequence.

The other cleavage is that the Angoni follow the patrilineal pattern in their social structure whereas the rest have the matrilineal, which can be understood better if we use the words 'father-right' and 'mother-right'. The difference is a major one but for our purpose we may simplify it by saying that the Angoni give priority in descent to the father and son whereas the Chewa and related tribes give it to the mother and sister. Thus it would be normal for the son of an Angoni chief to succeed him whereas in the Chewa tribe it would be the brother or other male relative of the mother, or the son of a sister. Another consequence is that on marriage the Angoni wife would go to her husband's village and be absorbed there, whereas in the 'mother-right' system the husband may transfer himself to the village of the wife.

This is a radical difference in what we might call 'loyalties' perhaps but I doubt whether it has any overwhelming influence on this average character of the people we are trying to assess.

It does mean that with the Chewa the influence of the women is possibly greater than with the Angoni, and that should, and perhaps does, lead to a more settled disposition, less warlike, less wandering than would be natural to the father-right people. Perhaps we should describe it as a greater conservatism, more suspicion of change in the mother-right section. There seems to be historic evidence for that in the way in which under Dr. Laws the Angoni made what is little less than a *volte-face*, a complete reversal of policy, in abandoning raids and accepting a form of Christianity when the Atonga were still stubborn in their traditional ways.

Perhaps we need not emphasize these two forms of cleavage any more since the fundamental characteristics we are seeking do not seem to be greatly affected by them.

Of these characteristics we might begin with what the European is apt to call laziness if he be anti-African and love-of-leisure if he be pro-African. If we are thinking in terms of the Asiatic peoples with their habits of industry we tend to regard this attribute as a racial one, but I believe that is too simple a solution, and I would rather call it a historic or traditional one.

Africa has been a relatively empty continent; there has been little competition for land and hardly any pressure of population. Broadly speaking, when the African felt himself crowded he went elsewhere to live a life with the leisure he preferred. There was, in fact, plenty of competition in the arts of war but little or none in the arts of peace, if one may include ease of subsistence as one of those arts.

By itself that cannot account for the backwardness of Africa; racial differences obviously come into the argument. One has but to think of the Chinese civilization leading the world a thousand years ago or the number of deeply philosophical religions in Asia to realize what worlds apart are the Asian and African capacities. But for the question of industry alone the lack of competitive effort may be a prime cause of the easy-going Africans we meet in the southern half of that continent.

There is a calm logic about their love of leisure which we must admit even though it confounds our plans to get Africans on the path of what we call progress and development. The case of refusal to pick more cotton than was sufficient for buying their requirements for the next season is an example of this logic. Or the case of the boy who works on a tea plantation until he has earned the price of a bicycle and then stops. There is no answer to his plea that he has got what he was after so why work for more than he needs? If we tell him that he had better

163

go on working and be able to buy two bicycles he will reply that he can't use two at once, and in so doing he would merely be working for someone else's benefit.

We cannot say that such a point of view is new and strange to us, for it is what we are up against in our boasted welfare state. We too, whether we are miners or electricians or doctors, are liable to seek that equilibrium between our work and our leisure whereby we ease off as soon as we have earned enough for our needs, saying that if we earn more most of it will go to the state in the form of P.A.Y.E. or Income Tax. Moreover, any stump orator can get up and say to a certain trade or community that the more they produce the more the state will ask of them, and down goes the rate of production at once.

What else is it but a welfare-state version of the belief in the Lower Shire cotton-growing district that if they picked more the Government would expect more in the future. A perverted form, if you like, of the Law of Diminishing Returns, that the harder you work the less of the proceeds will be yours.

There is, too, a very real brake on individual profits which comes into the picture in that village life is communal to a large degree. If one man has more food in his garden than the others he is expected to share it out. If he does not do so, if he sells it and spends it on himself and his family he is liable to ostracism or worse.

This, too, we recognize as one of our own practices, only we have gone further and laid it down in black and white regulations, in some circles, that no one shall work harder than the average and that anyone who does not cease work within a minute of the allotted day shall be fined.

The sharing of profits or food amongst relations is so much a tradition in the African mind that it has the force of a sanction which can rarely be avoided. It is even claimed by those in a position to know that many of the 'lost ones', those who go away to earn money outside the territory and stay away, do so because if they come back they will have to divide their earnings amongst their kith and kin. There is a rather successful Nyasalander in England who is a shining example on a high scale. He ran away from Nyasaland when a boy and by dint of energy and intelligence became a doctor and has never returned to his homeland. He was asked why he did not do so and his reply was that he would be a poor man if he did, as he would have to support anyone who claimed to be a relation in his tribe.

Here then are reasons other than racial ones for the love of leisure in the African.

If we consider too the aforetime natural division of labour as between man and woman we find another good reason why we must not expect a quick and radical change to European ideas of men being the breadwinners.

Sixty years ago, only two generations, that is to say, the respective duties were very clearly defined and for ample reasons. The woman was the breadwinner, the slave of the hoe and the cooking pot while the man was the bread protector, to defend with spear, to build stockades and food stores with axe and to provide luxury relishes like meat and fish when there was opportunity. As their own stories show the man had just as much right to demand to be fed by the woman as she had to run to him for defence, and in those days the men were often as fully occupied as the women.

Along came the white man with his Bible, his ordered trade and, later, with his soldiers and police, all of them suggesting, in Milton's words, that the men should now seek 'meek eyed Peace' and that 'the idle spear and shield should be up hung'. The general effect was to give the men more time for leisure while keeping the women as fully occupied as ever. Shrewd administrators like Sir Harry Johnston and Sir Alfred Sharpe then devised the hut tax, for which the men were liable, so achieving the double purpose of paying for benefits conferred and of keeping the men occupied.

Even so the men could not easily invade the woman's sphere of growing food and they usually hired themselves out as labour elsewhere for part of the year.

You may meet, in a journey through Nyasaland, nearly all the phases of this change-over. In the busy and populated Southern Province you come upon very few spears and in a village you see groups of men sitting talking under the trees while the women are pounding maize or going for water. At certain times of the year there will be no men at ease under the tree, for they are away working for the white man; but when they come back they have little to do. As you go north to what we may still call the wilder parts you see more spears, not for war any longer but for protection against animals or for hunting; always the man's job; and there are fewer men at ease beneath the tree in the day-time.

Tradition dies hard; it wears a snowy beard, but it does die in the end, and we can see signs now of a change in the respective functions assigned to men and women in the social organization. Two factors are prominent in this change; one is the absence of so many of the men as migrant labour and the other is the increasing number of girls sent to school. This latter, as we have seen, is in itself a break with tradition, and the crack is widening steadily.

It is well known that the conservative element in the population is the women and it is also understood by us now, but tardily, that they are not the down-trodden slaves and chattels of the men that we took them to be at our first glance; they have well-defined rights and privileges and they exert a great influence on certain aspects of native life. A wife is in some measure a form of property but she is aware of her value and within limits can use that value, even if it is only by becoming a nuisance. We have long since abandoned our first ideas about the system of *lobola* or bride price as being quite unwarranted. Africans do not buy their wives as we used to think, rather they worked out a curious form of insurance, mutual insurance of the behaviour of each partner in marriage. A very rough parallel would be an arrangement between buyer and seller of say, a horse, that the money should be returned if either the horse misbehaved or the new owner ill-treated it. We may in our arrogance consider that *lobola* is a crude and clumsy system, appearing to be, like the British Constitution, quite loose and unworkable on paper but we must continue the simile and admit that it somehow works in practice.

So much then in explanation or extenuation of the alleged idleness of the African. We have had a choice of reasons for it and it's quite certain that we shall do more harm than good if we try to hustle him out of it. The Administration must go on inventing incentives, such as putting gaudy scarves under the noses of the women, because that is one way of raising the African to our level of self-respect and of inducing him to take a proper place in the world's economy. It will no doubt go on making blunders occasionally but no one can say that it is trying to exploit the people, still less that it is dispossessing them of land.

For his part, no doubt the Nyasaland African will go on inventing grievances, often with his tongue in his cheek, and dodging responsibilities which he is not yet ready to assume, yet in his heart of hearts realizing more and more that his future there is tied up with the white man, who is giving him a fair deal and enabling him to reach a standard of living which he could never have attained by himself. There has been a partnership of a kind over sixty years, and with certain provisos there is no reason why that partnership should not bud and blossom into something very new in the world's history of racial relations.

One of those provisos is that both sides, if we may call them sides, shall go slowly, and another is that they shall not have interference from outside, however well intentioned. That is tantamount to saying that we in England must trust the man on the spot, a cry that has gone up for centuries from far-flung dominions and colonies and has often been disregarded.

Well, the new Federation is a move in the direction of putting more trust in the man on the spot and that is a real gain, however much the extremist press may proclaim it as a loss, and suggest that it is all a Machiavellian plan of getting more work out of the native people. More work must be asked of the leisure-loving African, it is true, but it can be for his own good, and what is more, for his own safety. How long, we may ask, would the industrious Chinese and Indian peasant slaving ten hours a day be content at seeing the African working only four hours a day in a world whose population is chronically on the verge of starvation.

Readers may consider this treatment of the leisure question as rather couth and cursive yet it is all we have room for here, especially as it is not a question for Nyasaland alone.

We will pass, therefore, to another problem which has also been bedevilled by using a question-begging phrase, the 'colour-bar'.

We must say at once that in Nyasaland there is no colour-bar but there is a culture-bar, precisely as there is in England. This will be denied, of course, for someone is sure to say that no African there may go into a hotel or store and buy a whisky and soda. That is as true as it is wise.

Again, no African is, normally, allowed to be a patient in a European hospital, but, conversely, no European may be a patient in a native hospital. There are many sensible reasons for this separation of colour, one of which was brought home rather rudely to a certain lady who was visiting Nyasaland. She was, so the story runs, accusing the Matron of a white hospital of the grossest colour prejudice in saying that African women could not come to the white women's hospital, and would not even wish to come to it. The visitor insisted that she herself would not in the least mind sharing a ward with an African woman. The Matron tried her best to remain polite by merely repeating that the African woman wouldn't like to share a ward with the great lady until at last the latter cornered her by asking, 'Why not?'. The answer to that was, 'Because she would hate your smell, Madam,' and is said to have ended that particular conversation very abruptly.

There are, of course, plenty of instances of white men, particularly those of the skilled artisan class, adopting an attitude of the worst colour-bar kind, just as there were cases in the past of chiefs treating whites as almost beneath contempt.

In general, however, the whites insist only on a culture-bar which has but an accidental connection with colour-bar, and that too meets the desires of the black man as well as the white. It would, in fact, be an act of gross unkindness to ask a man to dine with you when he had never used a knife and fork and plate in his life; it might even rank as an insult to him.

The proportion of senior Nyasaland Africans who now feel at ease with our table manners and culture is rapidly increasing. There are certain places in Africa where you may meet colour-bar in reverse, where you will be edged off the pavement because you are only a white, but that is not to be found in Nyasaland.

And that topic leads us naturally to a very real bar to what we may call culture equality between black and white, something so fundamental that we almost despair of changing it, namely, a belief in witchcraft.

And yet we ought to be able to understand it better than we do since we have only recently emerged from a stage of culture wherein witches and their crafts were not only recognized but legislated against. In the days of Cromwell, for instance, it is computed that between three and four thousand people suffered death for witchcraft in England. Many of these, no doubt, were the victims of a famous witch-finder, who hanged sixty of them in one year in Essex alone. The biter in that case was finally bitten as he was tested by his own rule and thrown into a river to sink or swim. He did not sink so he was executed as a wizard.

In other countries of Europe there are yet more recent examples of a firm belief in witches, and do we not still in England plant the Rowan tree (or Witchen) in our front garden in a vague hope that it will ward off witches if indeed there be such things?

We nevertheless find it baffling to explain the workings of this belief in witchcraft, because it comes out in the most unexpected ways and in people whom we had thought to be educated beyond what we now call such a primitive stage.

For instance, there was a skilful and well-educated mechanic who was a driver of an ambulance at the copper mines of Northern Rhodesia. He was called to drive to an accident but after inspecting his ambulance he came back and refused to go because he had found that his steering wheel had been bewitched by some enemy. In fact he lost his job because he was determined not to handle a bewitched wheel.

We must be careful to distinguish between witch doctors and witchcraft, a distinction which is commonly omitted in the earlier books concerning Africa. The duty of the witch doctor or medicine man is primarily to exorcise or even explain instances of witchcraft. He does, in fact, make use of his powers with a fine disregard of morality, so he can be accused of practising witchcraft as well as dispelling it.

Nevertheless, he is a professional man and must be so regarded by us if we are to understand the attitude of his clientele. To put him in prison because he is occasionally an impostor does not in the least affect his prestige with his people; it merely convinces them that we are not likely to be helpful in their difficulties with magic and evil spirits. Nor does it help in the least to tell them that there is no such thing as sorcery or evil eye; it only makes them less likely to quote examples of it from which we might come to understand better their behaviour.

We tend to suspect and even proscribe the witch doctors, who are usually the most intelligent men in the community, when really we should be trying to co-operate with them.

There are those, such as Mr. Frank Melland, who hold that an open scoffing at witchcraft, and our legal clumsiness with regard to the native methods of dealing with it by spells, ordeals and so on, form the greatest barrier to co-operation between white and black. When we punish a witch doctor for finding a witch we run entirely counter to their way of looking at the matter; we have punished the wrong man, and their sense of justice is deeply injured. For an analogy we might quote the case of cattle disease coming to a district. We set our veterinary officer trying to find the man who brought the diseased cow into the area and commend him highly when he has located and fined the careless fellow. We should be very indignant if the African came along and said that cattle disease was not contagious, and that we really ought to fine the veterinary officer for believing such nonsense.

Our attitude towards their belief in witchcraft has driven it underground, as we say, and caused a gulf to form between us which will not easily be bridged.

We are now tackling this gulf in a more sympathetic way: our anthropologists are trying to explain their beliefs and our education is very slowly raising them beyond the reach of the more absurd forms of it. Dr. Mitchell, the Director of the Rhodes-Livingstone Research Institute, has tackled it in Nyasaland, and he suggests that the native believes in sorcery because he must have an explanation for every happening; he is not content with saying, as we do, that it was just bad luck that the branch of the tree broke and the man was killed, or that it was pure chance that one man got tick disease and the man next to him did not.

Where we might say that some quite inexplicable misfortune was the 'Will of God', they say, 'Some evil person has wished this thing upon us'. They would even claim that ours is a doctrine of despair, to fold our hands meekly and say it was bad luck or the will of God, that they are being far more practical in finding out who was responsible and punishing him.

Dr. Mitchell considers that 'the belief in sorcery is not only a causative principle', illustrating their passion for finding a cause for every effect, but that 'it also interlocks with their moral code and social structure'. For that reason he fears that the formal education we are giving them will not of itself undermine that belief in witchcraft which seems to be so universal.

We cannot follow the experts further into a problem that is so baffling, but we must record that it is a very real one and has a great influence on the race-relations of the future.

To those of us who believe that education will be at least a factor in reducing this bondage to evil spirits, if only by degrees, progress in educational facilities must be of great interest, and it is indeed a matter for congratulation to the Administration.

It was estimated in 1951 that over half of the children in the Protectorate attended school for short periods between the ages of five and eighteen. It is true that very few pass beyond the lowest classes, and only 339 of whom 17 were girls passed the standard VI examination. But it is estimated that in 1955 the total of boys and girls passing their primary course will be over 1000.

If we take another yardstick, the standard of literacy, we find that for the whole country there are in every thousand people, of all ages, 65 who can read and write.

The number of literates per thousand goes up to 72 if we confine ourselves to those between five and eighteen years of age, and curiously enough the proportion is nearly 140 per thousand in the Northern Province. That is probably a reflection of the influence of Dr. Robert Laws plus the unusual intelligence to be met with in the Atonga tribe.

The mere counting of literate heads like this does not tell us much, however, and it may convey more to the reader when we say that the yearly expenditure on education is roughly the same as on the Medical Services and on Agriculture. As the mission stations are still responsible for a good part of the teaching this hardly represents the total effort on the part of the whites to educate the blacks.

Almost everywhere in the whole continent the attitude of the African towards education is nothing less than an intense hunger, and it is the subject on which community effort is more easily roused than any other. This is unquestionably a very healthy sign for the future of the African, but as we have pointed out elsewhere, it can be interpreted by him in terms which are not quite so healthy, as a means of getting an office job rather than sharing in the duller production jobs.

There has crept in a sort of snobbery over careers which has to be watched very carefully by the Education authorities. From this rapid growth of education there has arisen the awkward situation that the teen-age boy is often smarter, though no wiser, perhaps, than his father and his uncles, and, more to the point still, that a clerk in the post office may understand the directions of the Government far better than his chief or Native Authority.

The Jeanes Training Centre near Zomba, now known as the Government Teacher Training Centre, attempted to counter this tendency by having classes for chiefs and senior men, and their wives, but this could only be a palliative.

The moral seems to be that it is possible to progress too fast with education unless you can somehow manage to educate the seniors as well as the juniors. Certainly the impact of schools has done something to upset the discipline of the tribes and the family and to place some degree of authority on shoulders which are often too young to use it with wisdom and tolerance.

It has often been remarked that the greatest enemy of the African is the African: it was so in the days of slavery and is still so now that authority of another kind is given to those who have acquired education. Formerly it was the possession of guns which placed one section in a position to bully another, now it is the possession of certificates in education. We must not overrate this academic arrogance; it is not universal by any means, but to anyone who watches a native post office clerk dealing with requests over the counter from his less tutored brethren it will be clear that there is a very distinct social step between them which can easily be turned into a form of great rudeness if not actual persecution.

The plain fact of the matter is that Education with a capital E has failed in Africa to teach nobility of character, and is not even very good at teaching the ability to command.

It would be wrong to leave it at that, because a very little thought shows that there should be considerable sympathy for the educated African who is, at present, an odd-man-out.

It was the wife of a settler who asked me to put the case, in this book, for the African intelligentsia, that small but growing class which has out-distanced the others. It is a group which has acquired that little learning which is liable to be a danger to those who possess it, since it is not enough to put them on a level with the white man, yet has raised them far above the standards, and earning capacity, of the bulk of the people.

As yet there are very few who have attained the standard of the West Africans in educational accomplishment, but there is no reason for thinking that they will not reach it in the long run. Chief Mwase seemed to me to have almost done so already, but that is the special case of a clever man who is also a chief. It is rather of the village boys who have profited enough by education to become junior civil servants that we are speaking now, a group which finds itself placed midway between two strata of society, too well-educated to mix contentedly with the one below and not enough to take its place alongside the one above.

There are people, mostly well-meaning but sometimes mischievous, who will point to this isolation of a class as a deliberate instance of race-prejudice and colour-bar. I would say that it was the working of a perfectly natural culture-bar and no more malign than the fact that sixth-form boys will not associate with those from the third form, while they, in turn, have the greatest scorn for the 'kids' at the preparatory school. It will tend to be remedied in much the same way, but at a much slower rate, in that a proportion of the prep. school boys do ultimately achieve the status and responsibility of the sixth form. It would be an odd schoolmaster who ventured to suggest to the third form that, by rights, they should have the privileges of the sixth form.

The issue of the so-called colour-bar problem is so often confused by that kind of suggestion that perhaps an instance of this should be quoted. It was in a recent annual report of a famous Missionary Society that it was pointed out, regretfully, that one could see proof of discrimination on grounds of colour in Nyasaland if one 'compared the airy houses of the average European with the small, often single-roomed, shack in which his "boy" lives.' One can hardly blame mission boys, reading such statements from their august teachers, if they acquire a false and unhappy perspective of their lot and feel that sufficiently shrill cries of 'Colour-bar' may get them the airy houses which the European needs if he is to endure the climate at all.

Nevertheless, as the settler's wife assured me, we do not do very much to make the African intelligentsia contented with their lot and perhaps we have concentrated too much on the welfare of the lower strata of African society and neglected that of the African civil service. It is not an easy thing to do, to find activities and interests for a class which is a little apt to resent advice, and suspect advances, from the European. Nor can one ignore one of the motives behind some of their study to reach the grade in which they are. In a report on students in Nigeria who were specially selected for a course of training for responsibility and leadership the Principal gave several instances of the disappointments he had had, and we may quote from his speech.

'It puzzled me at first that so many of the students, when we discussed the work they might do when they went home, chose literacy, leprosy or latrines. Later I discovered the reason: these were the lightest labours. Literacy classes were sit-down work; leprosy they understood as meaning that they should simply tell lepers to get treatment; and latrines because every one knew that sanitation is dear to the heart of all colonial officials.'

I am glad to say that I could offset that story with many instances of energy, devotion to their work and a sense of responsibility in educated or semi-educated Africans such as Boma messengers, head *capitaos* or foremen, agricultural demonstrators and even senior personal boys. I would call attention, Pharisee-like, to a common denominator in that list, namely that they are jobs in which the African is in constant close contact with his European senior. They are also jobs which have a constructive end in view, a purpose which can be shared fully by the junior assistant. I have a suspicion, which may be ill-founded, that discontent and envy are more likely to grow amongst those whose jobs, while requiring considerable intelligence, are of routine character, like some post-office and accountancy work, in which they feel they are only part of some unintelligible machine.

If it is a rule that the African is apt to be uninterested in the job itself then I can assure the reader that there are plenty of brilliant exceptions to it, and there will be more still when the intelligentsia grow in number and have more attention paid to their off-duty occupations and relaxations.

Now that we have called attention to some of the short-comings of the Nyasaland peoples we may conclude by making some comparisons with other Africans and these are undoubtedly to the advantage of the territory. The Nyasa boys have a high reputation beyond their own country, for loyalty, for intelligence and for industry. They do not always get on well with their cousins in the Union and Southern Rhodesia, who are apt to call them arrogant and quarrelsome, but they are so often put in command as foremen or *capitaos* that such a verdict is perhaps a natural one from those who are commanded.

The number of Nyasalanders who migrate is rather staggering, the official number estimated in 1953 being 159,000, of whom two-thirds went to Southern Rhodesia and one-third to the Union of South Africa. Some tribes, notably the Atonga in the Northern Province, are thus deprived of a serious proportion of their able-bodied males, and a whole series of social and economic difficulties arises from it. Originally this migration was largely due to the difficulty men had in earning their hut tax within the protectorate but now other factors enter into the matter, particularly the high rate of wages in Southern Rhodesia. The migration is now under more control than it was but it remains a serious problem for the Administration, and will continue to do so even under federation. The Nyasa boys think little of walking nearly a thousand miles to the Transvaal mines and back again, but so valuable is their labour that now they are usually taken by train or plane. They are in a sense well aware of their value and it is quite false to think that they are under any duress at the scenes of their labour.

I was once coming by car from Southern Rhodesia to Nyasaland, and was passing a European farm. I had just passed a group of Nyasa boys walking along the road when I stopped to ask a white man if I could be of any assistance to him as he was standing by his car looking furious. His tale of woe was that he had just stopped that party of boys to engage three of them to work on his farm as he had done in previous years. The bargain was nearly completed when the leader of the party pulled out a piece of paper and asked the farmer for his name. When he gave it the leader said he was sorry but that name appeared on his black list, so none of the party would work for him.

In that and other ways the sins of the employer at last recoil on their own heads, so the Nyasa boys are under full protection both from the Government and by being able to pick and choose their employers.

One may meet them very far afield in Africa and the 'lost ones' are not lost in the real sense, they have married elsewhere and settled down, if any Nyasa man can be said to settle, when they are such inveterate wanderers.

You find him almost always in a senior position, most often as a well paid house boy or cook and that is partly because he is innately polite, he is less afraid of work than local boys, and usually has a contented disposition.

We have seen that the Africans of Nyasaland are apt to be superstitious, and we know that they are readily roused to a state of emotion or fervour, whether by inflammatory speeches or by dancing and drumming.

Drums, carved from single pieces of wood, over 4 feet high

To a European their dances seem to be monotonous and repetitive, in spite of their amazing variations in rhythm. Yet it is in that repeating of stampings and shufflings and tattooing on the drums that the emotional effect of the dances lies. It is significant that not only the performers share in the dances; the spectators down to the tiny totos are all being moved by the rhythm and join in it as far as they are able. The small children on the outskirts of the circle trying to keep time are under the spell of the dance just as much as the principal performers. The dances are, of course, very varied; some are merely to entertain, some are to arouse stronger emotions, but all are intended to sway the people in some direction or another, and to satisfy some urge of their being.

The studies of Mr. Hugh Tracey and others are showing how very informative their music is, how much a part it may be of their inner mental life. Music and rhythm, of their own kind, come naturally to them and are clearly an outlet to their thoughts and feelings.

The drum is, of course, the chief instrument, but they have others, like the *marimba*, which is a sort of xylophone, the *sansa*, illustrated on p. 144, and a form of flute and Pipes of Pan, as well as a single-stringed type of fiddle. Our guitar and banjo have appealed to them and moderate performers on them can be met in most of the larger villages. These are for the most part used in the sort of recitative or in solo songs, whereas the drum is the obvious accompaniment to the dance.

The proper setting for the dancing is a moonlight night, with the drums thudding, but one or two of the ceremonial dances require more light and are to be seen in the daytime. Such a one is the *mganda* we have pictured, in which a team of flautists marches up and down, keeping step to its music, without any drums.

Their decorative arts seem to be at a more primitive stage than their music, the ornamentation put on their pottery consisting mainly of criss-crossed lines done without much care, though in a great variety of patterns. This is curious because their iron-work shows great manual dexterity and the symmetry of their spear heads and hoes is nearly perfect, and all done by eye. No doubt this symmetry is functional, the spears and hoes must be carefully balanced if they are to be useful, whereas the decorations on walls or cooking pots are merely to catch the eye.

Their carving of wood and ivory, on the other hand, can be

very good indeed, though never so elaborate as the work of the West African tribes. Like the blacksmithing this carving seems to be hereditary and localized, with Kota Kota as its centre. Livingstone remarked on the standard of carving there in 1861 and there is still a family of an old man with two sons turning out excellent work. Sets of chessmen made by him in ivory and rhinoceros horn are valued highly and show originality, but the sons' work is mainly repetitive and clumsy. The old man showed me his lathe, a European one, of course, but most of the carving is done with a knife. He seemed far more anxious to show me his many grandchildren than samples of his work.

Probably their most skilful work is in plaiting. Their mats made from split reeds and various kinds of grasses are beautifully done and their patterns with interwoven dyed grasses are

Basket-making

far more symmetrical and original than those found on their pottery. The settlers use these mats for carpets, and the coarser ones as curtains or even ceilings. They make baskets of every size and closeness of weave, and the Atonga and Wankonde still make flasks of fine grass which will hold beer or water. The usual receptacles for water are gourds and for cooking they have clay pots. These are nearly always made by the women, baked in a rough kiln and finished off with graphite or some other sealing substance which will stand heat.

178

It is in the field of dramatic art that Nyasalanders show at their best. They are accomplished orators at any time and they are fond of stories, which are acted very naturally. Now that they have had a little coaching from Europeans and have been given the idea of a stage and a plot they have achieved a high standard. A brief description of a play by a native dramatic society in Lilongwe will show that they will go far in due course.

This society has been organized by one or two Europeans, but the acting is all done by Africans, and the play was given in a small cinema-hall on a tobacco estate, the proceeds going to Red Cross funds.

The manager of the estate was afraid that the native audience would be small as they are given the weekly film-show free of charge, whereas they had to pay 3d. a seat for the play. Nevertheless, the house was packed and they took £4 from the native audience and £4 from the dozen or so Europeans.

There is no script in the play, the actors know what is the subject of each scene and they talk impromptu and spontaneously, with never a silent or a dull moment. The play was given in Chi-Nyanja, except for a few remarks made by European characters, played with much verve by Africans.

A man and his wife (who carries her tiny baby on her back throughout the play) have grown their crop of tobacco and are seen with it at the tobacco market. The grader throws out bad leaves and this arouses ire on the part of the man and his wife, torrents of language about it from all three, ended by the grader shouting out, 'Shut up, bloody nonsense talk,' a remark which brought the house down.

They get £40 for their crop and take it home where the agricultural supervisor (really a European) advises them to put the money in the Post Office Savings Bank, but a seedy friend persuades them otherwise and then steals it.

There is a terrific scene when they discover their loss, the wife bobbing round, looking everywhere, the baby being shaken violently at every movement but never waking up. The wife was, in fact, the star performer and her 'business' of trying to keep her clothes from falling off her shoulder was in itself a cause for almost continuous laughter from the audience.

They go to the chief to complain, a scene full of 'take-off' and the stage crammed with people. The chief comes on singing

'Poor old Joe', with his attendants harmonizing the chorus. The complaint is sustained and the prisoner is brought before the chief's court, marched in by a policeman. This scene is a violent one, everyone on the stage doing 'business' of his own as side play. The audience howled with merriment at the by-play between policeman and prisoner, knocking each other's hats off, a real slap-stick comedy, which somehow did not interrupt the trial.

The next scene is where the case is tried at the D.C.'s court, complete with interpreter, the D.C. writing down the evidence in a book and so on, while the prisoner is as violent as ever. The wife as witness is nervous and trembles from top to toe, the baby's head vibrating vigorously but without waking, while the mother continually re-wraps the clothes round it, without pausing in her torrent of words. Everyone on the stage is doing some sort of by-play but the talking is not interrupted except by the shouts from the audience, especially when the prisoner says, 'Good morning, Bwana D.C.,' exhibiting *chipongwe* (cheek) to a degree which staggers the whole court. The money is restored, there is a very rowdy beer-drinking scene, they lose their money again and there is another realistic arrest. The final moral is plain, that the best way to avoid losing it is to put it in the bank.

There was never a dull or halting moment throughout, and most of the actors had not been able to attend rehearsals, though they had given one performance a week earlier, to the Governor. I was told that on that occasion the words and the by-play were quite different though the plot was identical. The whole play, in fact, was a brilliant improvisation, the speeches extemporized, the action fast and yet rarely out of hand, and the characters never at a loss for a moment. Perhaps the most impressive aspect of the performance was that although it was screamingly funny the actors themselves never smiled or lost control in any way.

The evening ended with a memorable song, given in Chi-Nyanja by all the characters assembled on the stage and conducted by a tall Post Office clerk, accompanied by two guitars. The harmony and modulation of this song were wellnigh perfect.

After seeing such a performance one came away feeling that for this form of art the African has a natural gift and one which is worthy of encouragement. The play had a moral which was driven home very skilfully and one wonders whether the native stage is not a very good medium for propaganda in a wider field, on bigger issues than how to keep money from being stolen.

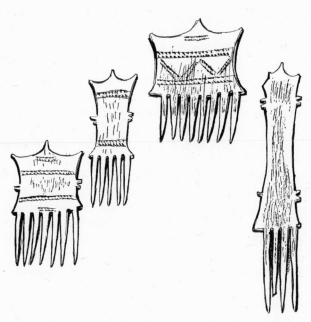

Ivory combs from the H. H. Johnston collection

12. THE MAN-EATERS OF KASUNGU

PERHAPS I had better begin a chapter with such a grisly title by stating that I have never yet seen a lion in daylight in Nyasaland though I have spent some six months there, mostly travelling about.

Nevertheless even now there is an annual death rate amongst Africans of up to a dozen due to lions and twenty years ago it was over a score. These contrasted statements are to be explained by the fact that while there are plenty of lions in Nyasaland, they mostly hunt by night, and that the African has very little defence against a real man-eater, whereas the white man has, for he carries a rifle in suspect country and he sleeps in a house with stout walls instead of a comparatively flimsy hut, with perhaps only a loose wicker door to it.

We have already heard that lions are no respecters of European towns and often pass through exalted places like Zomba at night. They do, however, have a distrust of the houses themselves and particularly of the wide verandahs the white man puts round his dwellings. They also are nearly as fond of dogs for food as are leopards. These two characteristics were both shown in an incident in the middle of Fort Johnston which can only be given at second hand as it occurred twenty-four hours before I went to stay with the white man concerned. Late that night he had gone out in to the street outside his house for a stroll in the cool night air when he heard a rushing sound coming towards him and wisely stood quite still beside the signpost which is in the centre of the crossroads. Just visible in somewhat poor moonlight he saw a large dog tearing past him followed by a lion. The dog dashed on to the verandah of the house but the lion swerved sharply away, not daring to follow and made off. This must not be taken as an invariable rule, however: lions do learn to disregard verandahs as sanctuaries, as I learned next day.

My host slept outside on his verandah at a corner surrounded by somewhat fragile wire netting, but he wouldn't hear of my sleeping on another part of the verandah where there was no netting. You can, in Central Africa, buy a stout wire called lion-wire because it is specially meant for keeping lions off verandahs.

This only goes to show the truth of a remark made to me, in 1913, by Mr. F. C. Selous, 'There are no rules for lions, they are all individualists, and you never can tell what the next one will do.'

Another thing to remember about lions is that whatever they decide to do they will do with lightning rapidity, a characteristic of the feline race which we know well enough from seeing our domestic cat lying lazily on the hearthrug yet shooting out a paw in a flash to catch the ball we dangle over it. Whether the lion is a coward at heart or not is perhaps one of the rules which has many exceptions but it is quite certain that if you stand still and face a lion you have got some chance; if you turn and run you have none whatever. There are many cases in which that has been proved, especially when the lion is not actually hunting but comes upon a human by accident. You can then outstare him and he may lose interest and go his way.

Lastly we may add, since we have embarked on how to treat the lion, that he will not climb a tree after you; there is safety there, for the simple reason that he knows his body is far too heavy to be held up by his claws and he will not risk injuring them by trying to imitate leopards and lesser cats.

Experts differ in their opinions about the character and ways of lions in general and the man-eating lion in particular. Many hunters will tell you he is a cowardly and even a lazy beast far removed from the noble creature we depict on our flags and heraldic emblems. Others will have a better word for him, and say that normally he's rather a nice old thing, rarely out to make trouble.

It is fairly generally agreed that a lion does not take to human victims unless for reasons of age or other disability he is unable to capture the bucks that are his normal source of food. This does seem to be the rule but like all rules has some striking exceptions. The fact is that once a lion finds that humans are vulnerable, and, no doubt, tasty, he may, however strong and healthy, take the easier way and prefer humans to animals. If, for instance, a lioness for any reason has to become a man-eater, then the nearly full-grown cubs who stay with her for a couple of years after birth may acquire the habit and so the abnormality, for such it is, may spread. This, at all events, is one of the reasons given for the undoubted fact that one area may acquire a bad reputation for man-eaters whereas another with just as many lions does not.

One of these areas in Nyasaland is that of Kasungu, which has long been known for its wild animals. It is a centre rather than a town, some 80 miles north of Lilongwe and 100 miles south of Mzimba. It is not far from the watershed leading down to the rift valley of the Luangwa river in Northern Rhodesia where there are few villages and the game of all kinds is numerous. As we shall see it is not only lions that can be a menace in the Kasungu district.

A few miles from the Boma, under the high kopje after which the district is named, there is the village of the chief of these parts, Mwase, whom we met in Chapter 10.

In my first call on him and his elders, in November 1952, I was anxious to establish friendly relations, which could not have been done if I had mentioned the federation proposals. So I hit upon the idea of asking the half-dozen seniors gathered round me for their experiences of man-eaters. With the pleasant D.C. of Kasungu beside me to interpret I got far more than I could assimilate and in nearly every anecdote the narrator was the principal of the story, able, and anxious, to show the marks of the encounter.

One and all told me that leopards were really far worse than lions, and I understood them to say that with luck you could frighten a lion but whatever you did to a leopard it only angered him more, or in other words, that a leopard would fight to its very last breath while a lion might give in or try to escape.

Only four years earlier a leopard had been killed which had got 37 people and was so renowned for its fury and cunning that Mwase's people would not let him join in the final hunt.

When I asked whether anyone present had had to face a leopard unarmed the others called on Kamiza, who showed me his chest and arms and went on to relate how he had tried to drag away a man held down by a leopard, which would not let go of his first victim so could only make vicious passes at Kamiza with a spare paw. Even so, it was only driven off by men rushing up with burning brands to thrust at it.

This hanging on to its capture by the leopard led to a very interesting tale which shows that it is not nonsense to say that the best way to deal unarmed with a lion is to pull its tail.

The incident had occurred only a year before in the village of the councillor who told the story. A lion had got into a hut in which a boy was sleeping, probably by falling through the thatched roof and could not find its way out again. The yells of the boy brought father and mother from the next hut and when they had pushed down the doorway they saw the lion with its forepaws on the boy and its stern towards them. The man caught hold of its tail to pull it off his son but the lion dug its claws into the ground and the boy and held on. The man then bit the lion's tail but that too had no effect so he got his head farther into the hut and bit the lion's rump, still pulling the tail. Then the woman crawled into the hut to try and pull the boy out, but with a lightning sweep of one paw the lion felled her and held her down and he did the same thing with a man who also attempted a rescue. The father had to keep up the pull on the tail or all would have been killed, but finally a lamp and an axe were brought. There were then others to help in the tail-pulling and the father reached under the lion and cut the foot that was holding down his wife. Finally he reached over the back of the lion and killed him by hitting him on the head. All the wounded recovered and are alive today and who can say, in the light of that story, that the African is not brave and resourceful?—the resource in this case being to keep up the pull on the lion's tail so that its feet were occupied in keeping itself in position over its captives.

Though the confirmed man-eater usually attacks unaccompanied women or men, its spoor and characteristics soon become known to the villagers and it is then that the call goes out to the nearest D.C. or other white man to come and shoot it. I stayed for some time with the Provincial Commissioner of the Central Province who had spent most of his time at Kasungu and so had been in the thick of the man-eating hunts.

I managed with difficulty to get the story of some of his hunts out of him, and the very natural lead-up was the skin of a lion in his office at our feet. For months this lion had outwitted him in his efforts to kill it, till finally its greed (or hunger) was responsible for its end. It had taken a woman from a village in the early morning and my friend got early news of it and made good time on his bicycle to the scene. In wiser or less hungry mood the lion would have left the woman's body and escaped, but on this occasion it kept on dragging the body from thicket to thicket followed by the D.C. This went on for half the morning over several miles till it paused by an anthill and a steady hand put a bullet through its mouth to end its career of crime.

These stories all show that the typical man-eater becomes very cunning and wary, rarely returning to its kill, and moving about the country so that it cannot easily be located.

One such was hunted by the same D.C. for a long time and always eluded him till its end came from a lapse in its cunning, or from excessive hunger, after it had taken at least 60 Africans and was known far and wide. One of the difficulties in getting word of the man-eaters is the conviction held by many Africans that a man-eater is a reincarnation of a former chief. Not only does that superstition increase the terror of the villager when he meets the lion but it seems to have some effect on his reporting its depredations. After all, it would be a little unfair to one's great-grandfather to go and tell the police that he was responsible for the last murder down the road.

To his great regret the D.C. arrived half an hour too late to be of active help in ending this particular lion, but he knew all the details of the story.

The headman of the village and his son had gone to wash at the local stream and the lion killed the man but the boy escaped to arouse the village. Some went to summon the D.C. but the insolence of the lion taking the headman himself seems to have spurred the villagers to attempt some action on their own account. Accompanied by an ex-askari (soldier) armed with a spear and an axe the villagers approached the lion, which was busily eating their headman. He left the body and took a few steps towards the rabble, whereupon all except the stout-hearted askari, Chiteka, fled. Emboldened perhaps by this flight the lion continued to walk slowly towards Chiteka, who himself confessed that he knew then that it was a case of a fight to the death. There was apparently a certain amount of dodging round a large tree as a preliminary, but when the lion finally sprang at him he managed to check it with the spear in its chest and in the next round crash down the axe on its head to finish it off, the courageous askari being absolutely untouched.

There was an interesting sequel to this story, for the D.C. noticed that the lion's jaw had peculiar features, so he preserved the skull and took it home with him on his next leave, and presented it to the British Museum without telling its history. A little later he saw the lion's skull expert there who told him that the skull was particularly interesting as the jaw was malformed in such a way that it could not have dealt with normal prey, that in fact it ought to have been a man-eater. It must have been very satisfying to both men when the full story of the lion was told.

Perhaps the most horrifying story I had from my friends in Mwase's office was one of a man-killing elephant and that too was only a year or so before, and witnessed in fact by the chief himself from that very office. The elephant when killed proved to have a festering sore on its rump from an old bullet wound, which explains its behaviour. On its way up from the Lake back to its usual territory in the Luangwa valley it had killed two separate men, the evidence later showing that it had hunted the men and had not just stumbled across them.

When it neared Kasungu it came upon a woman gathering firewood, carrying her baby on her back as usual, and accompanied by a small boy. The elephant first disposed of the boy with one sweep of its trunk and then attacked the woman by bashing her and her baby with the bundle of firewood she had put together, opening up her abdomen. The woman pushed back the intestines and somehow managed to get back to the village but both mother and child died. The elephant walked on past the chief's office and found at a waterhole a woman whom it killed. By this time men with rifles had been summoned and the elephant was shot.

It must be owned that retaliation by animals for being shot at can hardly be censured and in that category comes the action of a hippo in the same district. In a bad drought this hippo had adopted the last waterhole for its abode, so a man shot three slugs into it to make it go elsewhere, whereupon the hippo left the water, caught the man running away, and literally bit him to pieces.

It is common knowledge that the African exhibits a sort of fatalism with regard to risks from wild animals, and especially towards that most insidious of foes, the crocodile. The heaviest mortality is amongst the women whose duty it is to fetch the domestic water from the lake or river. Yet there are innumerable instances of utter carelessness by women even after their friends have been taken only a day or two earlier. It is perhaps

Elephant about to charge

a parallel to the pleasant fiction of British soldiers that if the shell is marked with your name it is no good trying to dodge it, and it is certainly linked with the African theory of causality, which always refers sickness to ill-wishing on the part of someone and may lay the blame less on the crocodile than on the catty neighbour who willed the crocodile to seize the victim.

This does not prevent attempt at rescue, however, and there are tales of the utmost heroism in saving people whose limbs a crocodile has seized.

The encounters with wild beasts are all duly recorded in their memories and become oft-told tales, and in almost any gathering you will find someone who has had a narrow shave.

At the meeting with Mbelwa's Angoni I asked if there were any present who had killed a lion single-handed. There were eight who stood up and the Chief selected one of them to come forward and tell his story. As he warmed to the subject he became more and more excited and so did all the listeners. When he had given the *coup-de-grâce* he startled us by roaring like a lion and all those round took up the lion song, the warriors jumping up and stabbing the air with their spears and the women shuffling round outside them with vigorous lu-luing. He must have been a celebrated hunter as well as a popular entertainer because when I asked for someone who had killed a leopard the chief called the same man forward. He had killed no less than three and told us all three stories, the last one being graphic beyond all belief. In that case he had only wounded the beast and had lost his spear, so the contest resolved itself into strangling by the man versus scratching to pieces by the leopard, all mixed on the ground as they rolled over and over. For this contest he had many scars to show, on his thighs and arms but still more noticeably one on his forehead where the leopard had got in a vicious bite.

There was then another paean of triumph in song and dance which I unfortunately spoiled by offering him a cigarette, which he accepted and subsided into silence.

Moreover, the true man-eater becomes very cunning and will not seek trouble. My friend the P.C. of Lilongwe had pitted his own cunning against one such at Kasungu for weeks on end but could never persuade him to come to a kill specially arranged for him. His closest shave possibly was from this beast which did come to the kill but from the wrong direction.

Half a zebra had been laid out with every precaution in making it appear natural and unhandled by man, and a shallow pit was dug and covered with thorns in which my friend sat up for many weary hours, peering out towards the kill. When the moon went down the chance of a useful shot rather diminished and it occurred to him, for no particular reason apparently, to look out of the peep-hole left at the other end of the pit. He was idly looking at the stars from that viewpoint when suddenly and without a sound they all disappeared in total eclipse. For a moment this puzzled him as a very mysterious thing, when it suddenly occurred to him that it might be the lion's head just in front of the peep-hole that had got in the way. He couldn't see any outline to go by but, on the other hand, his bush covering was very slight so he guessed where the central part of the shadow might be and fired. He guessed correctly. It was the man-eater and he was only a foot or so from the muzzle of the rifle, preparing to spring.

Both lions and leopards have the ability to approach absolutely in silence, in fact one should welcome roars and grunts from them as a sign that they do not, for the moment, mean business. There was a very famous man-eater in a nearby district, which had some dreadful total of victims to its credit, and was, I believe, known as 'Monty'. Three white men had prepared a bait for it and were going to sit up in a tree platform to shoot it. They were yarning at the bottom of the tree until it was rather dark when one of them failed to answer a question. The next moment a rifle was fired by their askari who had met the lion dragging the missing man by the shoulder so quietly that no one had heard it. The lion was frightened off and the man still lives.

It may seem curious that the best defence against lions is a comparatively thin fence of thorn bush, of which there is no lack in Africa, provided it is broad enough or high enough to prevent the lion jumping over it. It is in fact the standard fence all over Africa in protecting the cattle kraal at night. The reason is that the most vulnerable part of the lion is its pads, and it knows well enough that if it gets a thorn well embedded in a paw it can be disabled for a long time, hence no doubt the story of Androcles and the lion. In a district of Northern Rhodesia there is a minor weed with a seed which has four sharp little corners to it, like miniature caltrops. There are no lions to be found in that district when, in the dry season, these caltrops litter the ground.

From what has been said it must be clear that a still better defence is plenty of the natural prey for lions, but we cannot turn the clock back in that way. The antelope tribe is slowly but surely disappearing from Nyasaland as the population spreads and the lions will follow suit. In the meantime it is even more difficult to teach lions the difference between domestic cattle and wild game than it was to convey the same thing to the little Bushmen of Cape Colony a century ago. It was noteworthy that lion trouble became much more common when the rinderpest plague of the nineties of last century suddenly swept away a great deal of their prey. Possibly it is from that date that the man-eaters of Kasungu began their bad habits.

Six-stringed instrument with gourd resonator

13. SOIL AND WATER

IN the centre of Zomba, half a mile below the key building, which is the Secretariat, there is a low spreading edifice which might be regarded as the spare key, since it is the Department of Agriculture.

Nyasaland, as we have seen, has little to sell except what it grows, so the Director of Agriculture is a kind of king-pin, on whom the wealth of the country depends.

You can tell that at once if you meet him. He changes every few years, of course, but the three whom I have met have all been big men in every sense of the word. To be head-farmer of two million people on twenty million acres is no small job. Like every farmer he has got to be many other things besides a grower of food. On this scale he has got to be a scientist, an engineer, a business man, a politician with a seat in the Legislative Council, and a diplomat, because he has to handle all kinds of men, both senior and junior to him. There are a few other lines on which he must be competent too as the following circumstances will show.

On the Lower Shire flood plain there is a promising cotton-growing industry. It is entirely a native industry; all the cotton is grown by the villagers and it has had its ups and downs. It has had to accommodate itself to the vagaries of the river which, as we have seen, is dependent on the variable level of the lake. So for a period of years there is plenty of cotton land available and that is followed by a period when much of it is flooded out. To control the river and the lake is the engineers' job but the Director must be aware of their plannings and surveys. Then there are seasons when there is rain at the right time and others when it is at the wrong time or comes not at all.

To control the rainfall is beyond human power but there is irrigation which can only pay when a series of 'ifs' can be answered. If the water can be got on the land cheaply, if the peasant cultivator can learn how to work his water furrows, if it doesn't encourage malarial mosquitoes and so on.

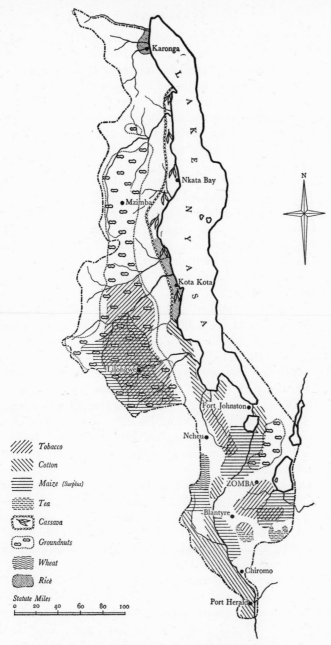

Tobacco
Cotton
Maize (Surplus)
Tea
Cassava
Groundnuts
Wheat
Rice

Statute Miles
0 20 40 60 80 100

Distribution of crops, based on information received
from the Director of Agriculture in 1952

The most ominous of the threats to the cotton growing industry is that of pests, the pink boll-worm and various other little terrors with long scientific names and complicated life histories. Even when, with the help of research by the scientists of the Empire Cotton-Growing Corporation, you have found how to attack these pests you are little better off, as the cotton is grown in native gardens, mixed up with other plants and cultivated by people who could not or would not use sprays and chemical poisons.

However, a way of circumventing the pests was devised, which, put simply, amounted to sowing the cotton earlier than the pests had bargained for so that the boll or seed case full of the fibres could keep a lap ahead of the insects. That was fine and promising but, of course, the growers had first to be persuaded to this change in their routine and that was a major operation in itself, and took two years of persuasion with a modicum of coercion.

Still, it was accomplished and, in the year I am speaking of, the yield of cotton in the fields was nearly three times as much as before, to the astonishment of the growers and the delight of the planners of this scheme.

With ordinary growers that would have been a complete answer but not with those of the lower Shire, to whom bounty on that scale was too much of a good thing and, of course, meant more work in picking the cotton. So they proceeded to pick a little more than half of their crop and leave the rest in the fields; in fact they picked just as much as they could spend in buying goods and no more.

The Director of Agriculture and his associates had to save some of that good cotton somehow and they were driven to a curious expedient. They hurriedly collected any traders they could find, got licences for them and sent them up the river in canoes and boats with trade goods to tempt the growers to pick more cotton with which to buy more goods.

That is a very much simplified form of this true story; for instance, the agricultural officers wanting to get their peasantry to buy more luxury goods hoped that the traders would sell more coloured and patterned cloth for the women. They found that even in Nyasaland fashion was fickle and even obstinate, and most of the women stood by their tradition of wearing the drab indigo-dyed cheap cloth and waved away the coloured prints as garish and gaudy and, we presume, unladylike.

It seems then that there will have to be yet another expert in the office of the Director of Agriculture, a man who can persuade the native women to appreciate colour and design in their wrappings and encourage them to turn out like their sisters in Uganda, with shirt-waists and coloured sashes, the glass of fashion and the mould of form in that very advanced community.

In parenthesis one may say that some such innovation in the dress of Nyasaland women is long overdue and is not by any means just an underhand trick of traders to make more money. The women there are not downtrodden by any means but they certainly are the hardest workers and, except in the towns, they have not yet found time or inclination to increase their attractions by the clothing they wear. It may be that they hold the view that silks and satins put out the fire in the chimney, or perhaps their husbands do.

It will be seen then that running the farm that is Nyasaland requires something more than ability to farm. Possibly it requires most of all the good humour with which the then Director told me that story; truly the white man needs an angelic temper and a sense of fun if he is to teach the black man to better himself. We have saddled the Director himself with this Pooh-Bah range of accomplishments but, of course, all his juniors in the Department have to undertake a like diversity of jobs. The most baffling end of their duties seems to be that concerned with the marketing of the villagers' produce. It requires not only technical skill and judgment but also a great knowledge of human nature to get across to the African the most simple of farming axioms such as that it is more profitable to produce a little cotton or tobacco of good quality than a lot of inferior standard.

I was able to see these qualities being used to the full by a young A.O. (Agricultural Officer) at a tobacco market in the Central Province. The sellers in this case were all women and they were putting before him their small parcels of leaf for comment and grading. His manner with the different women was worth watching and though I could not understand what he said to them the gist of it was plain enough. A good honest round-about of a woman with babe on back would push her basket in front of him—he would rummage in it and find good average quality and pass her on with a pat on the shoulder. Next would come a sly one who had put all her best leaf on top—hers was emptied out and she was treated to heavy-handed chaff which she would take a little time to live down. To some he would explain what they ought to have done, while a sloven presenting really dirty tobacco was shouted at and turned back. She, not a whit abashed, formed at the end of the queue again, having shaken off some of the dust and dirt from her bundle,

Cotton harvest

and came up again brazen to the last. She got through at her third attempt but only under threat from the A.O. of decapitation at the least if she didn't do better next year.

From these two stories one might say that the heading given to this chapter is the last one should choose for a chapter on agricultural officers, who have so little time left for the study of soil and water.

Yet those are the two all important elements in the economy of the country and they have to be under review all the time. The African knows as well as anyone what is good soil and long ago he occupied it where circumstances of water supply, security from war and other hazards permitted. In that hilly country, however, there is not a great deal of perennially fertile land which can be cropped continuously or with only the occasional fallow. He learned long before the white man came that burning the trees over his garden gave him up to four years of reasonable yield, after which he moved on, the famous system of shifting cultivation found all over the tropical world. If he could wait about twenty years before having to re-occupy his first plot the land recovered sufficient fertility for his needs, but as soon as population increased enough to bring the period of fallow down to eight or twelve years his returns fell and he found himself entering a vicious circle of more and more land producing less and less food. He had avoided sloping ground in the beginning but now he had to use some and that started soil-erosion, and a quicker descent than ever to unprofitable farming. It was worse than that, of course, because soil lost in one area meant ruining areas lower down either because of the increased flooding or because the waste soil and rubbish swamped existing good land.

For the last dozen years or so therefore soil-erosion has been the chief headache for the agricultural officers, especially in the most crowded province, the Southern, where the Nguru from the Portuguese territories were coming in in thousands. It was not a simple problem of technique either, for every one, including the African now, knows just how to combat soil-erosion, and terracing or 'bunding' on slopes has now become almost a standard practice, provided the A.O. can get round his area often enough to see that it is carried out. It was much more than that, for to make full use of the land, now too scarce for shifting cultivation, it was necessary to have good farming and industrious farmers, or in other words, common sense and hard work.

We have said already that the African woman is a hard worker and it is she who hoes the ground for the food for the family. For cash crops, whether of food or fibre, the man is more or less responsible and that is where his confirmed love of leisure comes into the picture. Africa on the whole is a 'take-it-easy' continent though Nyasaland by the general standard is perhaps less take-it-easy than the rest. Yet by comparison with China or India or Burma or Java, any one of the teeming lands of Asia it is a downright lazy territory. There is plenty of land even on the populous Shire Highlands if it is farmed with energy but the habits of centuries do not vanish in a generation.

It is a slow process teaching the African that his former technique no longer will work in the new and more crowded conditions, but the day is not far off when he will farm on a more intensive scale, with attention to manure and the use of the plough. Not that the African has not got something to teach the European in turn about some of the crops; for instance, we began by denouncing the habit of sowing crops mixed together as untidy and thriftless and we tried to alter his pattern into neat rows in the European style. The plants then did not do so well and we discovered that there were very good reasons for the practice, the shade of one plant being useful to another, the surface rooting of one class helping to check the water for those with roots at a lower level and so on. Their intercropping in fact was a sound practice and we have had to retract some of our denunciations.

Even when the A.O. is undoubtedly right in laying down a technique or a method of growing a crop, he cannot order that it should be done, unless of course it is something essential to saving land, such as terracing the ground on a slope. Nor can the Director of Agriculture order what cash crops should be grown, though he can do a good deal of gentle persuasion.

The growers of cash crops, chiefly cotton and tobacco, are very sensitive to the prices they get and, of course, are usually rather ignorant of the external factors which affect the price, like the incidence of deficits or surpluses in other parts of the world. Consequently, in the earlier years, a low price for cotton one year would mean that the villagers would swing over solidly to some other crop the next year and possibly regret it when prices again rose.

The Government has put some of that right by organizing markets and stabilizing funds to tide over lean years, and there is no doubt that the growers are coming to see that there is method in the madness of the white man. Perhaps that is not the best way of putting it, for it might be more accurate to say that the grower does not understand why there are Cotton Associations and Tobacco Marketing Boards but he does know that the A.O. is always doing his best for him, always backed by the D.C., and that when sixpences are deducted here and there for some incomprehensible scheme the money is certainly not going into the pockets of these officers, to whom the scheme only gives more work than ever.

Moreover, the general rise in the standard of literacy has meant that councils and committees have come into the agricultural field as well as into the social field.

Agriculture, however well organized, is always at the mercy of the weather, and the ups and downs in the curves or graphs of crop production are mainly due to good and bad seasons. I believe that if you could get an Agricultural Director quite privately in a corner he might admit that an occasional bad season is not half a bad thing; it enables him to drive home lessons which would never be learned otherwise.

That appears to the outsider to have been the case with the crop failure of 1949 which, but for prompt action by the Governor and his Directors, would have become a serious and crippling famine.

Feeding camps had to be established, grain had to be imported, volunteers had to be got from the European community and there were all the paraphernalia of the big famine reliefs in India of which Kipling wrote so graphically at the end of last century. The relief measures cost about a quarter of a million sterling, which is about ten per cent of a normal year's revenue, so it was a heavy charge on the country.

It gave a great fright to the Administration and, what was more important, it scared the villagers into action.

I happened to be travelling up from Beira just before the rains in that famine period and the scene from the train on the Lower Shire was a great contrast to what I had seen four years earlier. In 1945 there were occasional native gardens alongside the railway from Port Herald to Chiromo with a few women at work in them, but very little of the soil was ridged ready for seed in November. In the same month in 1949 there were almost continuous gardens along the same stretch with both women and men at work on them and all the land was ridged. Much of it was box-ridged, that is to say one set of ridges was crossed by another so that the general effect was that of a huge waffle-iron, each little 'box' ready to hold the rain when it fell and to keep it from running along eroding the parallel trenches.

It is true that the piccaninnies helping in the fields were, one and all, without that distended tummy so characteristic of that age and their little ribs were clearly outlined. Already the shortage of food was thus evident and the onset of what the official reports liked to call 'acute malnutrition', but what we should call 'near-starvation', had begun.

An unhappy feature about this famine was that so many of the sufferers were left unsuccoured by their fellow-villagers, particularly the dependants of men who were away working in Rhodesia or the Union. As the Report put it, 'The tradition of charity among African villagers, so much a characteristic in the past, seems to have died.'

It may not have been so much the death of the tradition as its suspension when the villagers saw the Europeans, both official and private, buckling down to coping with the famine. In almost any activity in Africa in which the Government takes a leading part there is an obvious drawing back on the part of the Africans, and even a demand for payment for things that in the old days they would have done gratis and automatically. It is as if the people were saying, 'Let the Government be paternal, it's now their affair.'

Whether it was the result of the firm measures of the Government or the fright given to the villagers by the famine, there was a bumper harvest the following year. Possibly the moral is that however tactfully the agricultural officers encourage foresight and correct methods in native agriculture nothing much happens until some external pressure is exerted such as a serious fall in price for poor products or the onset of a pest or disease or an actual famine.

The African has a naturally happy-go-lucky attitude to such things as purity of drinking water, risk from crocodiles, the danger from bush fires, and he carries that attitude into his garden economy. In justice to him we should add that until this century he was quite right to adopt a fatalistic approach to life, a feeling that he was at the mercy of influences over which he had very little control.

'What use,' he would say, 'to grow extra food when we can't store it, when it attracts the robber or the idler, when a raiding party may sweep it all away in a night's dastardly attack?' Security of a kind has come to him but he has not yet grown to a full appreciation of it.

(*Above*) Mowing hay on a mixed farm estate with Zomba Mountain in the background.   (*Below*) Tractor-ploughing at Zomba.

(*Above*) A farmer and his wife pluck cotton on their own farm, cleared from the bush. (*Below*) Girls grading according to length in the Tobacco Board sheds.

(*Above*) The irrigation of farm lands envisaged in the Shire Valley Project would make large rice fields such as this a common sight.
(*Below*) Tung trees in flower. The nuts are crushed to yield a quick-drying oil.

Serried orderly rows of vivid green tea bushes at the base of Mlanje Mountain.

(*Above*) Mudi Dam, Blantyre—Limbe Water Supply Scheme, showing shaping and planting of grass on downstream slope of earth embankment.
(*Below*) A communal effort at Domasi. Filling in one of the larger eroded gullies.

(*Above,* *left*) A class of Agricultural Assistants at Makawapala Agricultural Training School. (*Right*) An Agricultural Demonstrator.
(*Below*) An African blood-donor group at Zomba African Hospital.

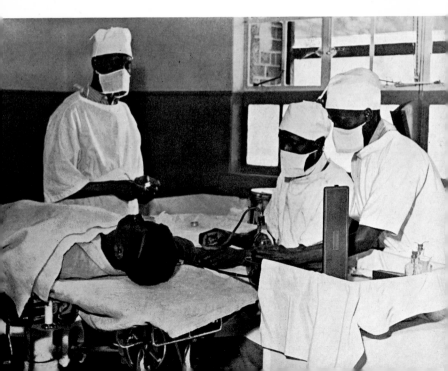

(*Above*) His Excellency the Governor (Sir Geoffrey Colby) and Lady Colby greeted by the Mayor of Blantyre on the Diamond Jubilee of Nyasaland, 1951. (*Below*) Lord Llewellin arrives at Blantyre on his first official visit as Governor-General of the Federation, January 1954.

When Livingstone was making his last voyage up the Shire in his four-oared gig the slave raids by the Yaos were in full swing and there was misery and starvation all along the river. What impressed him most was the apathy of the survivors; 'They could not be aroused from their lethargy. Famine benumbs all the faculties. We tried to induce some to exert themselves to procure food—but failed. They had lost all their former spirit, and with lack-lustre eyes, scarcely meeting ours, and in whining tones, replied to every proposition for their benefit—"No, no!"'

In view of this readiness to accept whatever comes with resignation it is clear that one of the major duties of the Department of Agriculture is the putting across of propaganda and that, of course, has to be done by the junior A.Os. who alone are in close contact with the growers. Several such have told me, ruefully enough, that all their intensive training at their university and at institutes for tropical agriculture was often enough quite subordinate to their ability to persuade their villagers to do something which was not agriculture at all but sheer common-sense. The most disheartening aspect of this propaganda push on their part is that a single agitator, usually a literate from a nearby town, can wreck any progress they may have made simply by telling the villagers that the white man wants them to grow more so as to give them a lower price for it, or that if they grow more and show the white man it is good land it will be taken away from them.

Propaganda can be thus easily undermined by a word or two to sow suspicion in the minds of the people so unused to anything like philanthropy or good will on the part of a ruling class.

One of the deterrents to this undoubted brake on progress is the encouragement of co-operative societies of one kind or another and this falls on the shoulders of the D.Cs. and the A.Os. It is curious that these have succeeded far better in the Northern Province than in the more populated Central and Southern ones. It is stated that the people there are less conservative and have a better business sense. It is also possible that the early influence of the Livingstonia Mission under Dr. Laws made them more community-conscious. There are also, be it noted, no large townships there.

With all these responsibilities towards the African growers it will be realized that the Director of Agriculture has not much time to give to the European farmers. The settlers are liable to complain on this score. Perhaps it is the essence of the partnership basis of the white man in Africa that the greatest assistance must be given to those who most need it—the weaker partners.

Now that we understand some of the difficulties that face the Administrative and Technical Services over agriculture we should attempt to present a long-term view of the situation.

Any country that depends for its prosperity upon agriculture is really putting its trust in the two natural resources of Soil and Water, for it is these, combined with suitable temperature, that grow its products.

Of these water is actually more important than soil, and there are cases, such as Denmark for instance, where poor soil with ample water can become fertile if used with industry and intelligence.

The soils of Nyasaland, of all Central Africa in fact, are not very good, except where there has been deposition in valleys and estuaries. Elsewhere the rain and tropical temperatures have leached out much of the best constituents for plant growth and have left a deep layer of decomposed rock, high in iron but deficient in phosphorus and potash. This deep soil has little or no humus and the result is the rather poor savannah forest, that is to say, trees rather far apart with coarse thatch-grasses growing between.

Even this land will produce reasonable crops for a few years if, as we have seen, the trees are burnt on it in the fashion of the shifting cultivation with a 16 or 20 year rotation. If stock can be kept on the land the rotation could be much reduced, say to four years.

To a certain extent then one can quote the old saying about the Romney Marsh in Kent, that it keeps ten sheep to the acre because ten sheep to the acre have been put on it. In Africa that saying would have to run, 'if you keep one beast to four acres with good management the soil will keep its balance,' that is to say it won't run down in fertility. But this can only be done if there is water, and that is the difficulty in Nyasaland, where there is a dry season of six to eight months every year, and a variable rainfall.

So water comes even before soil.

Yet it is possible to make the same kind of remark about water as about sheep to the acre, that is to say the more water you conserve the more you spread it out over the dry season, to which there is a corollary, that the higher up you conserve it the more valuable it will be.

There is no mystery about such a remark if you remember that those deep lateritic soils will hold a great deal of water and give it back slowly farther down a slope, and that the best place to store water in the tropics is underground.

It would be idle to quote maxims and formulæ of this kind if there were no examples of their validity to be quoted also, but there are such examples, many in other parts of the tropics and even one or two in Nyasaland itself.

There are, in the Shire Highlands, two or three farms, perhaps more, where the soil and the water supply have been so improved that the capacity of the land has steadily gone up and is approaching that of good farms in England where the aim is to leave the land as good as, if not better than, you found it.

The secret in these few Shire Highland farms can be put in a few words: continuity of ownership, good management and ploughing back of profits. These are not new maxims, they are but the wise saws of olden times complete with modern instances. Nor is it sensible to wave them aside as so far beyond the capacity of Africans as to be useless. In fact the African is a good imitator when he sees advantage in the imitation; what he lacks is energy and incentive.

The story of the cotton on the Lower Shire which was not picked may be likened to the parable in St Matthew's Gospel of the talents entrusted to the servants, provided we tone down the harsh words of the owner of the land. The non-pickers were slothful but they were not so much wicked as suspicious, foolishly so, since the Director of Agriculture does not own or want the land and therefore does not reap where he has not sown. These 'unprofitable servants' need not be cast into outer darkness therefore, but equally they cannot be made rulers over many things until they learn that talents must not be buried in the ground.

The suspicion that comes into the cotton story is curious and is found in other activities as well, so it needs some explanation.

The wife of a D.C. gave me a good instance of it. She had started a knitting class for the women in her neighbouring village and used for it odd balls of wool that were in her house or coaxed out of European friends. The women could not believe that they would not have to pay for this wool though assured that it was gratis from the beginning. Even a year later there was a strong rumour that sooner or later the Dona D.C. was going to charge them 10/- each for the instruction she had given them.

I would venture the suggestion that this suspicious nature is due mainly to the fact that the idea of true gifts, sheer generosity, does not come into the African's code, he cannot understand it, it's too good to be true. The idea of barter, a quid for every quo, is so innate in his mind that he cannot realize that the white man, whether administrator, missionary or settler, sometimes feels that it is more blessed to give than to receive. The teacher of knitting went further than that and was of the opinion that there was a distinct absence of sympathy in the African mind; she gave as an instance of it that they would not bring their sick people to the hospital until they were at the point of death. But of course there may be other reasons for this than lack of fellow feeling.

One soon falls into this habit of giving after taking, for at every camping place the local headman will give a 'present' for which you give a return 'present' which must be at least of equal value.

I once thought I had found an instance to the contrary. It was in Northern Rhodesia in a large swamp. When I arrived at an island and had set up camp, there was the usual visit of the chief, a venerable old man I had met before. He made me a present of a white fowl and, following precedent, I had, after consultation with my cook-interpreter, given him about twice its value in money, but strictly as a present and nothing to do with such a sordid thing as payment for the fowl. In the ensuing chat I showed him his own picture in a book I had written about my former visit. Soon after he had returned to his own little island there came a procession of women carrying baskets of cassava and pots of native beer for me and my party.

I was much alarmed and called up Sandy my cook to tell him I couldn't afford to pay for all this largess and he must tell the women to take it all back again. Sandy replied, 'No, Bwana, there is no money to pay, this is a gift, not a present.' At last, then, I had found a chief who was not commercially minded, who perhaps liked my face or thought me worthy of a gift as well as a present for some other unknown reason. Later I questioned Sandy further and he told me the truth, 'The chief is pleased with you, Bwana; you put his picture in a white man's book.'

If these suggestions are correct perhaps we should not use the word suspicion over the cotton-picking incident or that of the gratis wool, but explain it rather as a reluctance to take something for which they could not pay. I think that would be putting too good an interpretation on some of these incidents because there is ample evidence that a few insidious words from an African who is anti-white will persuade the people that the whites have the worst motives behind all their actions.

The fundamental importance of water has perhaps not been recognized in Nyasaland as quickly as it might have been, possibly because there is such a large quantity in its vast lake, where, as we have seen, most of it is useless.

Individual D.Cs. and A.Os. have recognized it, and so have Directors of Agriculture but the Higher Command has been apt to say that priority shall be on other counts. There is no doubt that water conservation is an expensive business, especially on the grand scale advised by some visiting engineers, but it pays dividends fairly quickly and there is no reason why the scale should not be a small one in the beginning. I am reminded of a small scheme, involving only a hundred acres or so which I was shown by its supervisor and planner, an A.O. in the Central Province, in 1945.

There was a tiny spring at the head of a small valley which gave enough water to maintain a rill down the valley for most of the year. A neighbouring village had spoiled this spring by cutting down the trees near it for firewood and clearing the channel occasionally so as to make the streamlet flow faster. Originally it had formed what in Nyasaland they call a *dimba*, that is to say a boggy patch extending along the bottom of the shallow valley.

The A.O. had somehow, by means unknown to me, persuaded the villagers to do several simple things. First to put a veto on cutting trees and grass near the head of the valley, and that increased the yield of the spring. Next to divert the rill just below the spring into two runnels, one on each side of the valley, flowing so slowly that their water seeped down gradually into the peaty soil of the *dimba*, which itself had tiny little drainage canals leading in a herring-bone pattern to the original stream-bed. That made it possible to grow all manner of things in the *dimba* which was no longer sour from stagnant water. They were so excited at being able to grow food on formerly useless *dimba* and on the stream becoming perennial that they were about to go further still, and were digging a large pond or lagoon below their cultivation to be used as a fish pond, and on the soil thrown up on the lower side there was already a strong growth of what they call *bango* reeds. This they use for their fences and a myriad other things and the belt of reeds was acting as a sponge below the pond, letting the water seep down the valley slowly and making the stream perennial where before it had always run dry for part of the year. Better still, they had increased the number of their cattle because there was more grass in the valley and were at least within measurable distance of using the manure from the kraal or night enclosure for their gardens instead of letting it dry and be blown away or washed away in the rains.

That is an example of a small scheme and it required nothing more than a persuasive A.O. and a trusting village. There are now training centres for African agricultural officers and demonstration plots to be shown to those who are willing to profit by example. If the population can only increase naturally and not by occasional mass invasions from Africans flocking in from outside there seems to be no reason why agriculture should not provide food for all and something over for export. The native cash crops, cotton, tobacco and perhaps coffee in the future must increase also if luxuries like A.Os. are to be paid for, and the cash sense of the growers should in time triumph over whatever it was that caused the non-picking of cotton we have used as our awful example.

We have made no mention of tea, which next to tobacco is the most valuable crop grown, and which in fact provides most revenue in taxes, because that is a plantation crop and is not, and cannot be, a native peasant crop. Its acreage continues to expand and though it requires rather special rainfall there are still areas in the territory into which it can expand.

Being entirely a European industry it has been left to its own resources. It can indeed provide all its technique and management itself without help from the Government which, as we have seen, has its hands full with native agriculture. The tea people are liable to complain that it is taxed to the limit and is carrying the country, and it is not for a visitor to say how far that may be true. It is an industry which must always be very sensitive to labour supply and that is its Achilles' heel.

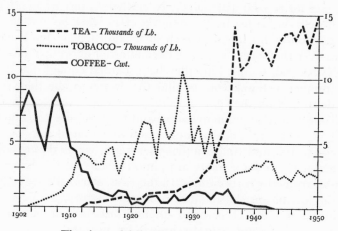

TEA – *Thousands of Lb.*
TOBACCO – *Thousands of Lb.*
COFFEE – *Cwt.*

The rise and fall of European-grown crops

Apart from the more obvious factors affecting labour supply, such as its migration to Rhodesia and the Union, and the need for large numbers to pluck tea for a short period of the year, there is the fact that the African is not really or fully dependent on earning wages.

As one report puts it, 'he places a high value on leisure and is inclined to work sporadically when it suits him and for a limited purpose of his own.'

Practically all the casual workers on tea estates have homes with an acre or two of garden round them and subsistence is easy enough for any energetic worker. Moreover, he may desert his work to go and dig his own garden just when the tea flushes most demand his labour. Almost every year there is a good deal of tea left unpicked because of this shortage. The net result of these factors is that the African is in a very strong position and the tea industry in a weak one, even a precarious one at times.

We might ask those good people in England who say that whites are robbing Africans in Nyasaland to think for a moment of the feelings of a manager of a tea estate in the Mlanje district. He has been obliged by the Government to provide increased incentives to his labour in some form or another. It may be better housing, recreational facilities, some free meals or bonuses for regular attendance. Nevertheless, just when a flush of growth on his tea bushes requires extra work he may find a proportion of his labour, much of it Nguru, who have come from over the border but have been allowed to occupy gardens in Nyasaland, telling him they have earned enough for their requirements, thank you, or that they want to hoe their own gardens, and off they go.

European production of cotton and tobacco, the two annual cash crops, is negligible in comparison with that of the African growers. Tea and tung, on the other hand, which do not come to maturity for some years are almost wholly in the hands of white farmers or corporations. In the case of tea, the treatment of the leaf means skilled work in a large factory.

Coffee, on the other hand, though originally a plantation crop in Nyasaland, can be grown by peasant growers and harvested by unskilled hands. This has been shown very clearly in Uganda, and also on the slopes of Kilimanjaro. In fact, the *Robusta* type of coffee plant was indigenous to Equatorial Africa, though the more valuable *Arabica* has been introduced.

Coffee-growing is coming back again though it is now in native hands and mainly in the Northern Province.

Rice has been grown for a very long time, having been brought into the country in the slaving days. It is grown on the lower Shire, but its chief centres are on the lake shore, at Karonga in the north and Kota Kota half way up the lake on the west side, where there is also a mill for milling the rice.

The story of the Rice Co-operative Society at Kota Kota is such a good example of partnership that it deserves telling in some detail.

Rice, as introduced by Arabs before the white man came, was grown sporadically on the low wet lands near the lake shore, and the product was a low-grade sample.

The first thing to do, therefore, was to introduce a better strain and see that it alone was sown. This had to be done by the then D.C. by original methods, since the growers took no

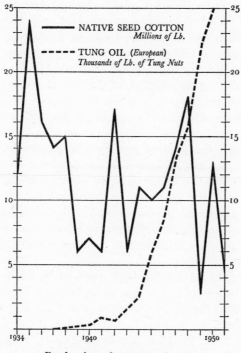

Production of cotton and tung

account of such things, and it cost the D.C. a great deal of effort and not a little expense.

By 1938 the administration was able to form a loose type of co-operative society entirely of Africans and obtain some Government help for purchasing machinery for the mill. With the rise in price consequent upon the war shortages the white advisers, chiefly the particular P.C. who comes frequently into these pages, were able to induce the African committee to embark on a programme of expansion. A very active and able man,

209

who hailed from Central Europe, came as manager and its present flourishing state is largely due to him. The plans for the new mill were drawn up by an expert, who had never been to Africa and had assumed the existence of things like steel and cement which the builders could not get.

The D.C. and the manager were not to be put off by little difficulties of that sort and they made the foundation of very large stones cemented with mud, which in fact has stood the vibration of the heavy machinery perfectly well. They met their Waterloo, however, when the foreman bricklayer refused to build the walls as laid down by the designer, because he said the walls would fall outwards and he would be blamed. So they had to disobey the instructions of the expert overseas and trust to Saidi, their bricklayer. It was a tremendous struggle to surmount all these obstacles in 1942, but it has been a triumphant success. The Society now mills over 2000 tons of rice a year; it has increased the area of rice-growing enormously, is financially sound and has African directors.

In its essentials this seems to be the ideal form of co-operative effort for Africa, the spur coming from the local administrator, the money advanced by Government, the management by a skilled European and the organization more and more in the hands of Africans, while the raw product is entirely grown by Africans.

Reviewing the agricultural prospects of Nyasaland we must remember the great change that took place when the white man came and asked the African to grow more food than he needed: food for reserve stocks, food for labour which was not growing its own and later, food for occasional export. Food tended to become cash crops as well as subsistence crops, yet with the exception of sugar these were not profitable enough to rank as plantation crops.

The new system put a strain on the energies of the villagers, who, although they were able to endure it were not organized for it. A man and his wife could easily grow enough food for the family. If he went away as migrant labour the family could still be kept going in normal seasons, but when there were dry seasons and urgings to grow more than enough for subsistence the real limitation appeared, the capacity of the hoe.

Both men and women are artists in the use of this their sole tool for all cultivations, but they cannot cover more than a restricted area with it and the digging is rather shallow. A spade would dig deeper but cover even less ground, and could not touch the harder soils. Also the hoe is a magnificent tool for cutting out weeds.

Introduction of the plough and animal traction is so obvious that one wonders it hasn't made much headway, until one talks to A.Os. who are trying their hardest to introduce it.

Quite apart from the initial capital cost the use of oxen with a plough by villagers demands rather radical changes in native methods of cultivation, such as mixed cropping, small scattered patches in amongst tree stumps and apportionment of the work between men and women. So the plough is coming in very slowly and mainly because Nyasa boys have learned its scope from working in Southern Rhodesia. The A.Os. are anxious to see it become the regular thing because it works in very well with the contour terracing they have been at such pains to inculcate, because it makes it much easier to measure up the area under crop, which is one of their duties, and because the deeper cultivation is beneficial to soil and crops. It is, in fact, the thin end of the wedge for mixed farming and the use of manure from stock. It will come because the African does understand that it will increase his production and therefore his cash, but that, as we have already seen, is not so pressing an incentive as it would be with Europeans or Asians.

Nevertheless, there is no doubt the ox and the plough will gradually extend over the country and the people will gradually become peasant farmers rather than gardeners.

Meanwhile, the administrators with the help of social anthropologists are wrestling with the complicated systems of land tenure that have ruled in the past and are endeavouring to bring them into line with a new agricultural economy.

To those who will take the trouble to read the yearly reports from the Department of Agriculture it will be clear that the story of progress in production is one of a working partnership between white and black.

It has been a very one-sided partnership so far because the white partner as represented by the Government has had to furnish most of the capital and all the management and research. The dividends have so far failed to reimburse the

Government, but they have advanced the black partners beyond belief.

The last word to fit this kind of partnership is exploitation,
yet it is still used by stump orators on African problems and
accepted by a proportion of their audiences.

An example of contemporary woodcarving

14. PROFIT AND LOSS ACCOUNT

THERE is a school of thought today which seems to hold that wherever Britain has assumed protection in Africa it has been for the purpose of exploiting the African. It is one of the penalties we pay for free speech that all sorts of people can get up and impute such motives, and if they do it skilfully enough they will persuade some people that their perversions of the truth are battle-cries for freedom. Nyasaland must have been a great disappointment to these people since it is very difficult to prove that Britain has benefited in the least from that Protectorate.

The premise to their argument is that if, as Cecil Rhodes used to say, 'philanthropy must have its five per cent,' then it is the work of the Devil. A false premise, of course, for Philanthropy must die if it cannot expand or find new fields with its five per cent. In fact, the Protectorate cost the British taxpayer a goodly sum, and in the beginning it was the pennies and sixpences of Scottish Sunday Schools which launched the Nyasaland we now know.

It was shrewd Scotsmen like Dr. Livingstone, Dr. Laws and The Rev. A. Hetherwick who saw that philanthropy must pay its way or cease; and it was their creation, later called the African Lakes Corporation, which had to take the job of finding a five per cent to permit expansion. It took them ten years to produce even two-and-a-half per cent, but long before that there were people who murmured against a corporation which endeavoured to make some money, in an open market, for missionary work.

The story of the A.L.C. is a fascinating one, too long to tell here, but if we are compiling a list of people without whom there would be no Nyasaland today, we must add to it the names of John and Frederick Moir, the first managers of the Corporation. Both of them proved that it is possible to be devout Christians and hard-headed business men at the same time. Both were wounded in battles against the Arab slavers at Karonga and both had to provide that measure of common sense and business ability, the lack of which has often been the cause of failure in missionary endeavour. The A.L.C. has altered its character somewhat now but it is still more commonly known as 'Mandala'. This word is the native name for reflection of light from a surface, and arose because John Moir wore spectacles. The provider of cloth and beads in exchange for grain and ivory was therefore Mandala and that word is over the doors of all the A.L.C. stores throughout Nyasaland and Northern Rhodesia.

But of course Mandala was just as much at the mercy of the hard facts of geography as any other trading concern: it could not pay its way without getting its goods to market at a profit.

At that time, in the early eighties, there was only one commodity which could stand the cost of transport to the coast and that was ivory. Moreover, the Moirs were in competition with equally hard-headed and far more hard-hearted people in the persons of the coast Arabs, who had solved the problem of transport in a far simpler way, for they captured or purchased slaves to carry the ivory and sold both at the coast.

To undercut the Arabs was part of the purpose, as suggested originally by Livingstone, but it meant making roads, putting steamers on the lake and on the rivers, concluding agreements with the unco-operative Portuguese who could block the way, and a host of other things which never worried the Arabs.

But ivory was a diminishing asset and the Moirs had to look round for something else which would bear the cost of transit. Coffee came to the rescue for a few years, introduced by the missionaries, and later, tea, tobacco and cotton.

That is the end of the list, for practical purposes, except that in recent years tung oil has been added, though still a minor item.

From the very first, therefore, Nyasaland was in the position of a very remote farm, say in the Hebrides, which could sell nothing except what it could grow and had to compete with the luckier farms which were closer to the market. This could not be done without help or without enduring hardship. Both were forthcoming, the funds partly from the sixpences of the missionary committees but mainly from the British Government. Hardship and self-denial came from the missionaries and the settlers, and, in some degree, from the administrators.

It was a losing battle in the early days, and every year there were deficits which had to be faced, promising schemes which had to be postponed, appeals of one kind or another to someone or other to keep the Protectorate going.

There were, of course, shrewd people, at the Foreign Office at first, and later at the Colonial Office, who had to look at the matter from the purely business point of view and it did not need much shrewdness to say that Nyasaland was a liability, and was likely to remain one. Here in fact was philanthropy steadily losing five per cent and that would ultimately be the end of philanthropy.

Here was a protectorate which was a drain on the resources of the Home Government. What could be done about it?

From the purely business aspect the only thing was to rid ourselves of the encumbrance or the responsibility, but it was far from being a matter of plain business.

The Protectorate really was established in order to give protection, and was recognized by Lord Salisbury even then as a liability from the very beginning; in fact he almost said he would do the protecting on condition that it didn't involve any expense. The protection was a dual one by that time, firstly for the native Africans from the slave-trade, an object we had aimed at for some 30 years or so and, as a corollary, protection for the missionaries who were the main if not the only agents on land with that humane purpose in mind. It was also, in a very short time, protection from the Portuguese, who, in fact though not in name, were still fostering the slave-trade and had no real hold on the country. It is amusing to recall that in 1883 that hold was so precarious that it was maintained only by the assistance of the non-Portuguese. Mr. Frederick Moir was returning on leave to England and had reached Quilimane where he found that all but one of the hinterland Portuguese stations had been taken by rebel natives and preparations were being made to evacuate Quilimane itself.

Moir was elected leader of a polyglot band of 17 non-Portuguese to go up the Zambezi again and save the last of the Portuguese stations, an opium-company's establishment about 60 miles from the threatened or at least timorous capital. Here one Scottish engineer of the company and a few Portuguese were hard-pressed. The rebels had got into the compound and had piled wood against the last building in possession of the

Europeans, when a bold advance of the 17 members of the relief party forced a way into the station. They were still hopelessly outnumbered and there occurred one of those accidental successes which so often turned the scale in that kind of warfare. The rebels were assembled for a council of war about 1200 yards from the building, so Moir gathered the best shots he commanded and they opened fire with their long-range rifles. In Moir's modest account of the action he says, 'We must have done important damage, for the natives, probably considering the rain of bullets from an incredible distance to be some new form of white man's magic, scattered and gradually disappeared. Next morning we found they were in full retreat.'

That victory saved the Zambezi for the Portuguese but there still remained the Shire for the British. This unconquerable leader therefore landed his non-British Europeans and went on in the little *Lady Nyasa* with three other white men and 20 natives to force a passage up that river. British prestige was high and he managed to come to an agreement without any further fighting, the essential bargain being that the British might pass, but no others. Moir concludes with the delightful sentence: 'Peace having been re-established I was able to resume my interrupted journey home.' It was by that narrow margin and by that foreign assistance that Portugal continued to hold the Zambezi.

By the nineties the 'protection', still only in the hands of consuls and not proclaimed, was also against the German claims for territory in East Africa.

Even then, the British Government was not prepared to find money for administering these missionary districts round Lake Nyasa and it was Cecil Rhodes who saved the infant Protectorate by promising £10,000 a year for the time being to finance development and administration in those districts.

The praise for establishing Nyasaland rests therefore on the shoulders of a handful of missionaries and their associates of Mandala, and on those of Cecil Rhodes. It is curious to reflect that had the Government decided to evacuate the area at that time the kind of people who now cry 'hands off Africa' would have been the first to cry shame and say we had broken faith with the African. To keep faith is still our duty today and we can only do that by continuing the partnership which has raised the Nyasaland peoples in half a century from misrule and savagery. In doing so we must now also keep faith with the settlers who in actual fact have carried out many of the functions of the partnership.

For all those years we as the Protecting Power have been trying to make Nyasaland pay for its keep and we are now within measurable distance of doing so. How that has come about is the real subject of this chapter.

The story of coffee in Nyasaland is a brief but romantic one. When that far-seeing gardener, Mr. John Buchanan, arrived at the Blantyre Mission in 1876, he wrote home for various tropical seeds and plants to be sent out. Amongst these were three small coffee plants of the *Arabica* variety which had clung to life in the Edinburgh glasshouses. The move was too much for two of them but the third survived and after two years it produced a crop of 1000 beans and these again produced 400 plants which became the parent stock of all Nyasaland coffee for many years to come. Tea came along just in time to save the situation when coffee began to fail, and has never looked back. Cotton and tobacco of better varieties were introduced by the white man and have now become the standard cash crops of the native gardens. The last importation of note is the tung-oil tree and that has established itself, though its future is somewhat at the mercy of price fluctuations.

So Nyasaland gradually established itself as a producing country, but that is not the same thing as a solvent country. In the fifty years of this half century there have only been ten when the Revenue and Expenditure accounts have shown a surplus. We have already noted many factors—lack of communications, distance from markets and so on—which have been a drag on prosperity, but in recent years one has been added, lack of labour, which now claims our attention.

The problem of migrant labour is a very pressing one for the Administration and it is greatly complicated by the fact that Rhodesia and the Union are very anxious for more and more Nyasalanders, both as skilled and unskilled labour. They are able to offer better pay than the territory itself and to some extent the migrant is free from the family and social commitments he would be liable for if he stayed at home. Moreover, the Nyasalander is a great wanderer; he will face long journeys in order to see other lands, especially as he now knows that he can find work easily.

He may go out under contract with one of the two associations which have permission to recruit labour in the country. These are given a quota for each year and they are not only under control by the Nyasaland Government but they are very well run and the migrant is well treated, being given transport to his work and back again. There is nothing harsh about this recruiting and there are careful arrangements in the contract for sending remittances of pay back to the man's family, for deferring some of his pay so that he shall bring back a reasonable sum when he returns and so on.

Yet the majority of the migrants prefer to go independently and without a contract, especially to Southern Rhodesia, where they can pick and choose their employment within reason, and where they are free from the atmosphere of regulations which surrounds them in the Union.

The migrant has to get an identity certificate before he leaves his country and every effort is made to prevent him getting 'lost'. He is supposed to return home after two years' absence and his employer has to remit some of his pay to his family left behind. He may even take his family with him to Southern Rhodesia or send for them when established in employment.

The missionaries also help by keeping in touch with the family left behind and by endeavouring to trace the 'lost ones'.

It is not generally understood in England that the system of 'passes' issued to Africans in Southern Rhodesia is as much for the benefit of the African, to prevent him becoming lost and destitute, as it is to prevent surges of population going to places where they cannot find housing or employment. There are no passes in Nyasaland; a man is free to go wherever he likes, but the crowding in the few larger townships may become a disadvantage both to black and white and may yet require some sort of control.

The evil of detribalization and of overcrowding in an urban centre as delineated in *Cry, the Beloved Country* is plain enough, and must be prevented when, in course of time, industrialization comes to Nyasaland.

We have seen that the original reason for labour moving about the country was the need to earn sufficient to pay the native poll tax but that is no longer a dominant reason for this mass migration outside the territory.

The poll tax due from all males over 18 is now 17/6 per year, of which the Native Treasuries receive 5/-, which is their chief source of revenue.

The lowest paid grades of unskilled labour receive about 1/- a day for about six hours' work and their *posho* or rations of food, so it does not take long for a man to earn his tax, if he lives in the Central or Southern Provinces. In the Northern Province, where there are very few European estates or industries, work is not so easy to find and the proportion of labour going outside the province is therefore high.

There is a belief outside Africa that labour must be very cheap there, and if it were judged solely by the rates of pay that belief would be justified. When we remember that the cost of *posho* is added to the wage, that the day's work is rarely more than five or six hours and that the rate of work is rarely more than half that of a European labourer we note that it is not so cheap. An important item is the necessity for constant supervision, by foremen or *capitaos*, who do little work themselves, and they in turn need supervision by Europeans. Casual labour is not cheap, but in skilled jobs such as in tea factories or public works departments no doubt the Nyasalander is worthy of his hire.

And now—what of the future?

For sixty years Nyasaland has struggled on as an isolated protectorate, contentedly enough perhaps but always behind-hand in its development for lack of a boost from mineral resources.

Its progress was steady but never spectacular and it rarely came into the headlines for either good- or ill-fortune.

Now it joins a federation of an entirely new kind and its horizon at once broadens, its scope increases and so does its prestige.

It was intensely interesting to be moving round the territory in 1952 when the proposal for federation was being discussed by everyone, whether he was capable of balanced judgment or not. It was a difficult time for everyone but if I were asked to point out who were the main victims of the way in which the matter was handled I would have to say the D.Cs. and the chiefs.

At one stage the administrators were muzzled and they felt

that they were letting their people down, and the chiefs, who are in fact junior administrators under the D.Cs., felt very lonely as a result.

It is difficult to describe how puzzled and confused and unhappy the situation was during all these negotiations but we might attempt a simile of a kind in the following way.

Let us imagine that a County Council decided that an isolated and struggling preparatory school in the country should be

Mothers with their babies and a seller of pots

affiliated to two larger and more prosperous central schools. Normally the Council would confer with the local governors of the school, and the headmaster, and put the affiliation into being.

Let us now suppose that they acted abnormally, and ruled that the children themselves should be consulted, and that the staff of the school were forbidden to advise the children, who had to get the idea mainly through reports. The children would begin by asking what affiliation meant, and most of them would never understand it. Someone might tell them that they would get more jam for tea but that they would have to come under new rules and have more examinations. If the Council allowed complete outsiders to visit the school and tell the children either that it was a very good idea or a very bad idea the confusion would be worse confounded. Some of these busybodies might even get the bright boys of the school together and tell them that the jam they were promised would be sour, that they would be loaded down with intolerable new rules, and that much the best thing to do would be to break away from the County Council altogether, which they could do if they refused to obey any rules at all.

What on earth would be the result of such a procedure? The ruck of the school, disgusted with the staff for not advising them would say, 'Let's stay as we are.' The bright boys would start intimidating the ruck and telling them how they could get more jam than ever.

At that stage the whole County Council changes its personnel and the new lot tells the school that it is going to be affiliated anyhow if one of the other schools says so, and sends still more drafts of the new constitution with complicated things in it called safeguards. The bright boys, further prompted, start disobeying and are astonished to find that their own masters won't allow that and expel them for doing what the outsiders suggested. The school which had been so happy before is now thoroughly confused and discontented yet, since the children are really very little interested in such remote things as governing bodies, they settle down when the affiliation is passed, and slowly realize that the jam is worth the bother of new rules and that the masters are really friendly after all but hindered by that distant County Council.

This pseudo-parallel is not as extravagant as it appears, and in any case is no more ridiculous than were some of the claims put forward in the press on either side.

Our sympathies in such a situation must chiefly be with the Governor and his staff and nothing but wisdom and firm handling averted more serious trouble than did actually occur.

This is no time for recriminations or post-mortems. The change has been made and it is for everyone concerned to join in this novel experiment of a mixed population trying to work out a prosperous future for Central Africa.

The impact of the new Federation status on the future of Nyasaland and its people is a very interesting topic, and one on which a good many people have already expressed themselves a little rashly.

In the economic field there must be general agreement on its advantages, since Nyasaland has had a long struggle to keep its head above water and has had to cut down on many promising developments because of its penury. This scraping and saving had for a long time hindered a full survey of its natural resources though the advances from Colonial Development and Welfare funds have in recent years enabled that survey to be carried on at a greater rate. We have seen already that the most promising lines for careful investigation are those connected with power and communications. Control of lake-level will enable hydro-electric schemes to take shape below the Murchison cataracts and that could be the beginning of an industrial future for the Southern Province. The bauxite deposits on Mount Mlanje, the source of aluminium, would be investigated more fully in consequence and certain secondary industries could start, making some of the consumer goods which at present cost so much to import.

The future of communications is vital to the territory since all its exports have to bear heavy transport costs. If the lake transport can be improved by stabilization of its level, bulk goods will be able to be moved within the territory at much less cost. Better communications by water would also open up an entirely new avenue to the seaboard via Tanganyika, but this could only be made possible if the coal deposits on each side of the northern part of the lake prove suitable for development.

Such an all-British outlet to the sea would be of great interest to Northern Rhodesia and it is certain to receive more attention now that all three territories will have a common aim with regard to oversea trade.

There can be little doubt in anyone's mind that as far as economic development is concerned Nyasaland has everything to gain by its federation with the Rhodesias.

Services like Defence and Education will also be greatly improved, more or less automatically under the new status. In truth it is not until one views the political consequences that one can see any possible disadvantages, and even those seem rather shadowy ones.

It is, I suppose, just possible to imagine that because the white settlers of Nyasaland will have only four representatives in the Federal Parliament they may receive less attention than they feel they deserve, but federations do not usually work that way. Tasmania, in the Australian Commonwealth, is the smallest of the constituent states but one only hears very occasional complaints that its voice is not sufficiently heard at the Federal Capital.

For the black population of the territory we have been treated to a great deal of prophecy in the political field. Most of this has more sound than sense in it and is based on absurd claims for the political maturity of the inhabitants. Fears have unfortunately been planted in the minds of the semi-educated people which will die hard, but the most absurd ones will have a short life, such as that federation means that land will be taken from them, that pass-laws like those in the Union will come into being, and so on.

Until a more responsible and intelligent type of African can be got for their representation we shall continue to hear such demands as universal suffrage, equal partnership in every respect for black and white and several other slogans imported from overseas. Yet there are wiser leaders among the Africans and they will gradually come to the top. It was an African member for Southern Rhodesia who recently spoke as follows, as reported in the Press:

'On the question of equality,' he said, 'there could never be equality between black and white, just as there could not be equality between people in a family. People could not be forced to mix and no African could object to separate hostels in a university, but classes should be multi-racial.'

At the very same debate, however, an African member from Northern Rhodesia said that partnership would only be practical if the children of all communities could learn together, play together and eat together. A Nyasaland representative then went on to say that he would reject anything less than equal partnership for his people.

We must not be too severe on a class which has emerged so recently, a small literate class with oratory at command but no

223

great experience or wisdom; it will take time to produce the same statesmen which we know they can provide, after the pattern of Khama or Tshekedi.

As long as the clever boy gauges his superiority only over his illiterate parents or the duller boys of his village he is bound to get a false sense of his ability and it will not be until he has measured himself in assembly against the white man that he will acquire a proper respect for him or assess his own capacity.

The *nouveau* 'literate', like the *nouveau riche*, takes time to find his true level and it will probably not be very long before his own fellow literates see through any cant or hypocrisy that he puts on to increase his own importance. As we have remarked before, the worst enemy of the African is the African. It was so in the days of slavery and it can still be so when authority without responsibility is given to one set of Africans. Intimidation of one kind or another comes very easily to them, and when, as with the Mau Mau oath, it is clothed with superstitious rites of a loathsome kind it is a very effective weapon of the few to sway the many in a course of action. That is one reason why any talk of universal suffrage in Nyasaland is worse than nonsense; it is an invitation to intimidation.

It is unwise to forecast how the political aspirations of the Congress group in Nyasaland will work out, but I believe that when the economic benefits begin to accrue, the people as a whole will decline to follow those who prophesied disaster and tyranny as a result of federation.

These people have promised so fulsomely and have prophesied so falsely that their reputation is even now in the balance. If only Nyasaland people are left to themselves and not incited from elsewhere there should be contentment under the new régime very soon, a return in fact to the situation a few years ago when there was complete amity as a whole between black and white, and there were all the essentials for a real partnership satisfactory to both colours.

There are many who think that we have striven for political maturity before we have achieved a measure of the economic stability which is a pre-requisite. Let us now look at some of the factors which are essential for a broad-based economy in the territory. Its prosperity is so tied up with its communications that we might begin with the possibilities under that heading.

We have seen already that one of the factors governing the future of transport is the existence of coal at the northern end of the lake. Its occurrence on Mount Waller has been known for sixty years but the reports of its amount, quality and accessibility are still inconclusive. It occurs in a faulted area, as one would expect on the side of a rift valley, and therefore it may not be very extensive. Its quality is described as 'fair'. This is not very encouraging yet it is possible to be too cautious about such a key product as coal. Even if it is but a small field, even if its quality can earn no higher adjective than 'fair', it should suffice for the needs of lake transport for a good long time. Here, one would say, is a project that must not be judged solely on the narrow profit basis that a coal-mining firm is bound to adopt as its attitude. It is more than likely that the coal will not pay for its winning but that is only a part of the accounting that should figure in the balance sheet. If it did no more than provide more transport on the lake it would give a fillip to other projects which are now hampered for lack of it, of which rice-growing can be quoted as one. In a pioneer country in particular one must be ready to assess values on a broader basis than immediate profits in a narrow field. The potential worth of this coalfield is just one of the many possibilities in Nyasaland that has been waiting for a very long time to be examined.

Who can blame her if she sighs at the loss of the money over the Groundnuts affair, one-tenth of which would have settled all her 'ifs' one way or the other. She may even be feeling that the money which was spent on the Nkata Bay Rice Scheme and to no purpose would have been more profitably ventured on proving this coalfield, a far more fundamental need than rice as a cash crop for a small area of the country.

It may well be that the coalfield near Songea in Tanganyika will be more profitable. It is within 80 miles of the lake, but it is still 300 miles from the new port of Mtwara and its development when proved is bound to take a long time.

Now that federation has come the investigation should proceed at a higher tempo since communications in this area become a problem common to both Nyasaland and Northern Rhodesia.

At the other end of the territory there is a more certain promise of power though it will take longer to develop than would a coalfield. The potential water power latent in the Shire River where it drops 1400 feet from the upper to the lower river has long been in the minds of planners. As we have seen, it is dependent on a stabilized lake-level and a comprehensive survey is now in progress. We cannot forecast here what its recommendations will be but previous inquiries on a far smaller scale would suggest that they will include a regulating barrage on the upper river not very far from the lake and a power scheme somewhere along the 35 miles of the Murchison Cataracts. On the same slender evidence one may say that the barrage may cost between £1 and £3 million and the power scheme between £5 and £20 million according to its scale.

These are large sums for a small country whose total annual revenue is less than £5 million.

Yet again we must not judge the scheme merely on the basis of profit and loss on the sale of electricity; its effects will go far beyond that and lead to all sorts of subsidiary benefits which cannot be reckoned in pounds, shillings and pence. Moreover, the Southern Province has the large population necessary for industry, it can grow the required food locally and it is the nearest part of the country to the sea and oversea markets.

In sober fact this hydrological report, soon to be completed, will be vital to the future of the territory, which we believe is now on the threshold of a great advance.

In these last few pages I propose to quote an analogy, to draw a moral and to paint a dream.

The most spectacular and successful development project of the last twenty years is that of the Tennessee Valley Authority in the United States. It began with the prime object of flood control and prevention of soil erosion over an area of about 40,000 square miles and along a river 600 miles long. Its charter was far more comprehensive than that, however, and it went on to develop cheap power, improve navigation, initiate sound agriculture and an immense variety of social services. It was in fact a giant organization carrying out an overall project affecting almost every possible activity of a struggling population in a rather poor valley. Its success has become a classic and its methods have been imitated elsewhere.

It has been aptly described as 'a corporation clothed with the powers of a government but possessed of the flexibility and initiative of a private enterprise'.

As its name implies it was concerned with the whole of a single large valley and it had full authority to plan and carry out schemes for the benefit of the whole area.

The Tennessee River has a greater discharge than the Shire but its effective fall is only about 800 feet, and of course all its reservoirs had to be built, there was no natural one like Lake Nyasa.

The analogy is therefore a reasonable one as far as the size and general physical environment is concerned.

It might be called a long-term business undertaking in that it had to recoup itself in one way or another for the expenditure, and it had to do so by creating the greatest prosperity for the greatest number of the valley inhabitants. It was regional planning on a new and unprecedented scale.

Enormous powers were give to the three directors, of whom one was an elderly president of a technical university who had agricultural experience, one was a hydraulic engineer and the third was a young lawyer, David Lilienthal. It is significant that the two technical directors tended to look upon their sections of the whole project as separate compartments and they were succeeded by the lawyer who had a clearer vision of the ultimate aim and carried it through.

Now Nyasaland is in somewhat the same position as far as powers are concerned, for its Government could promote overall development on the same scale; it rules over a valley of the same size and much the same natural resources, and its aim is certainly very much the same as that of the T.V.A. charter. Where the analogy breaks down is that the T.V.A. was backed by an enormous amount of capital from the Federal Government and it was able to push its schemes through at high speed.

Nevertheless the territory could work in the same direction at a slower rate, and become an S.V.A., a Shire Valley Authority.

So much for the analogy—now for the moral.

The charter for T.V.A. called for an overall plan to provide opportunity, and in particular power, for every kind of economic and social advance. It was not interested in piecemeal development; all the individual schemes were linked to the common end, and any which did not fit the whole plan were either rejected or altered till they did fit.

Its aim was not to suppress private enterprise but rather to provide a sound background for it and regulate it only so far as to bend it to the common good, to fit the regional plan in fact. It was not socialism nor did it aim at a Welfare State in the sense that everyone was to be provided for whether he worked for it or not. It was in fact nearer to that ideal state which we have never yet seen, one ruled by a benevolent dictator.

Finally the machinery of the Authority was simple and flexible, tremendous power being concentrated in the hands of three men who could decide upon and carry through individual projects without referring back to countless committees and subsidiary commissions. Lilienthal used to call it 'hard headed idealism' and that indeed describes it rather well.

These three points to the moral, the overall plan, the aim of helping men to help themselves and the concentration of power in a few men who held office continuously, are the things to be noted in the American instance.

Lastly, the dream.

How can Nyasaland, with its small funds and its few natural resources, emulate a Tennessee Valley? Let us return to that pitying remark, quoted in the first chapter—'Poor little Nyasaland, she has nothing to sell except scenery and labour.'

The speaker had omitted a resource which comes from adding those two together, in this way. Mountain scenery means water-power potential, power needs labour to harness it, so the two together should be an immense asset if it is developed regionally.

The water resources of the territory are indeed the basis of its future prosperity and the general treatment of those resources can be outlined easily enough in a dream, a dream which could assume reality if funds were only available, and powers to use it for the common good concentrated in another Lilienthal.

His first edict would perhaps meet with opposition and even scorn, for he would decree that every little upland stream should have a series of weirs thrown across it, cheap individually but expensive in the aggregate. All possible slopes would be bunded or terraced, even where they were not to be used for crops, and no cutting of trees would be allowed anywhere near the headwaters of any stream.

By these means he would ensure that the seasonal rains were held in part at the higher levels, to sink underground and seep out slowly lower down. One effect would be that many seasonal streams would become perennial and villages could disperse themselves instead of clustering along the lower ones as they do at present in a kind of ribbon development.

Lower down the streams he would create a series of barrages, that is major weirs impounding some of the water and letting flood water pass on. Some of these would be little more than fishponds, others would be large enough to furnish some power, and hardly any of the water would be used for irrigation until the flatter land was reached, land where that intensive form of agriculture could pay big dividends.

Wherever there was a chance of cheap power, such as at falls and rapids on rivers like the Bua and Rukuru he would have a power station—many would have an output of several thousand horse power—and people would be moved to the site to use it for a local industry, the general idea being to prevent a concentration of such industries in a few huge towns, and to produce food for such centres locally. The agricultural development would in fact work hand in hand with the power development and at the larger power stations the production of fertilizers, mainly nitrates, would have a high priority. The fight against tsetse-fly, malaria and bilharzia would have to keep pace with these advances and a certain amount of control of crops would be necessary to ensure that a more balanced diet was available all over the country. The replacement of the hoe by the plough would be a major operation in itself and there would be no mechanization except on the large plantations for special crops. The peasant or smallholder would not be lured into thinking that imported petrol could replace his valuable oxen. Education would be carefully co-ordinated with the main objects of the plan, and since a supply of artisans would be essential for the many works to be executed there would be great emphasis laid on technical education. The very large and very obvious schemes, for power from the Murchison Cataracts for navigation, etc., would be carefully timed so as not to interfere with the less spectacular schemes elsewhere.

The essence of the regional plan would be that it should continue the process of a growing partnership between black and white which has produced the Nyasaland of today, and even more broadly the attainment of Cecil Rhodes' aim of 'equal rights for all civilized men'.

There is nothing new about this dream, for something like it has been in the minds of most senior administrators for years. It is possible that in their ideas there has been less emphasis on the water resources, particularly that unpopular idea of headwater weirs which seem to give no immediate return, but otherwise every item has been thought of long ago, by different heads of departments, and many ideas have been implemented.

The great difference between the S.V.A. we are thinking of and the Nyasaland Government as it stands is that there would need to be greater continuity in office of the principal figures and less interference from still higher authority. Otherwise most of the machinery is already there and under federation it should be able to function with less delay than at present.

The dream in fact could become a reality and though it would be a far slower process than in the U.S.A. the same benefits of an overall plan and careful co-ordination could come in time.

Nyasaland has been called the Cinderella of British African protectorates but we may remember that Cinderella, beautiful but penniless, became a princess in the end.

Nyasaland version of an almost universal African game

BOOKS CONSULTED

THERE is now a considerable bulk of literature concerning Nyasaland, and a reading list follows. But here we wish to note those which were of special value in writing this book.

First and foremost are the writings of the real discoverer and founder of Nyasaland, David Livingstone. His published books were useful, but better still were his original journals of his many journeys up and down and across the country which he was so anxious to see come under British protection. His rugged style and his keen powers of observation, as well as his devotion to the cause of Anti-Slavery, have made his books known all over the world, and have been the basis for many studies of the man and his mission by a large number of authors. One cannot appreciate the amazing progress of this little territory in such a short time unless one has the picture Livingstone gives of it, before any impact at all from the white man.

More scholarly as well as much more recent are the studies by the late Sir Reginald Coupland on the historical background of East and Central Africa. In his *Kirk on the Zambesi* (O.U.P.: 1928) and *Livingstone's Last Journey* (Collins: 1945), he studied the two men who were chiefly responsible for our first knowledge of the Land of the Lake.

Next in value came the writings of the early missionaries who, though they were usually men of action without particular literary turn, faithfully recorded the country and its people as they saw it.

Their interests were naturally rather more limited than those of the early administrators, who had to see the whole wood as well as the trees which formed it. The most useful book on the early days of the Protectorate is undoubtedly Sir Harry Johnston's *British Central Africa* (Methuen: 1897). It is a monumental work, modestly described by the author as 'an attempt to give some account of' the territory over which he ruled for six years. Hardly any branch of science is left out of this account, ending with notes on the Nyasaland languages, a special interest of that versatile Commissioner. The maps and copious illustrations, mostly from his own pencil, combine to make the book a mine of useful information, still useful though it was published sixty years ago. It gives a vivid picture of the country just as it was in process of being changed from the state of anarchy, war and slavery to one of order and contentment. Since the author was himself, with the aid of his junior and successor, Sir Alfred Sharpe, largely responsible for that rapid change, the book is authoritative, and one easily forgives the slight tinge of egotism which occasionally appears.

The lighter side of administration in Nyasaland is supplied a little later by a number of books by less senior officials. Good examples are H. L. Duff's *Nyasaland under the Foreign Office* (Bell: 1903) and R. C. F. Maugham's *Nyasaland in the Nineties* (Lincoln Williams: 1935).

A wealth of information came from the newspapers which began in the nineties, and in fact they give a better idea of the early days than books written at leisure later on by those who saw the stirring events in retrospect.

Finally there are the Official Reports which have appeared in profusion, some on special aspects of the territory, others, like the very valuable Annual Reports, giving résumés of developments soon after they took place. Without these an author would have very great difficulty in attempting to view the country as a whole or to assess its importance in that part of Africa.

FURTHER READING LIST

BELCHER, C. F. *The Birds of Nyasaland*. London, Crosby Lockwood, 1930.

BENSON, C. W. *A Check List of the Birds of Nyasaland*. Blantyre, The Nyasaland Society, 1953.

BERTRAM, C. K. R., BORLEY, H. J. H. and TREWAVAS, E. *Report on the Fish and Fisheries of Lake Nyasa*. London, Crown Agents, 1942.

BOARD OF TRADE. *The African Native Market in the Federation of Rhodesia and Nyasaland*. London, H.M.S.O., 1954.

BUCHANAN, J. *The Shire Highlands as Colony and Mission*. Edinburgh, William Blackwood, 1885.

CHIBAMBO, Y. M. *My Ngoni of Nyasaland*. London, Lutterworth Press, 1942.

COUDENHOVE, H. *My African Neighbours: Man, Bird, and Beast in Nyasaland*. Boston, Little, Brown and Co., 1925.

DEANE, P. *Colonial Social Accounting*. Cambridge, University Press, 1953. Deals with the economics of Nyasaland and Northern Rhodesia.

EVANS, I. L. *The British in Tropical Africa, an Historical Outline*. Cambridge, University Press, 1929.

FRASER, A. R. *Donald Fraser of Livingstonia*. London, Hodder and Stoughton, 1934.

FRASER, D. *The Autobiography of an African*. London, Seeley, Service and Co., 1925.

HAILEY, LORD. *Native Administration in the British African Territories. Part II. Central Africa: Zanzibar, Nyasaland, Northern Rhodesia*. London, H.M.S.O., 1950.

HALCROW, SIR W. AND PARTNERS. *The Shire Valley Project: A Report on the Control and Development of Lake Nyasa and Shire River*. London, 1954. 2 vols.

JOHNSON, W. P. *Nyasa, The Great Water*. Oxford, University Press, 1922.

LAWS, R. *Reminiscences of Livingstonia*. Edinburgh, Oliver and Boyd, 1934.

LIVINGSTONE, D. *Missionary Travels and Researches in South Africa*. London, John Murray, 1857.

LIVINGSTONE, D. AND C. *Narrative of an Expedition to the Zambesi and its Tributaries*. London, John Murray, 1865.

LIVINGSTONE, W. P. *Laws of Livingstonia*. London, Hodder and Stoughton, 1921.

LOVERIDGE, A. *I Drank the Zambesi*. New York, Harper and Brothers, 1953.

LUGARD, LORD. *The Rise of our East African Empire: Early Efforts in Nyasaland and Uganda*. Edinburgh, William Blackwood, 1893. 2 vols.

MACKENZIE, D. R. *The Spirit-ridden Konde*. London, Seeley, Service and Co., 1925.

MAIR, L. P. *Native Administration in Central Nyasaland*. London, H.M.S.O., 1952. (Colonial Research Studies, No. 5.)

MAUGHAM, R. C. F. *Africa as I have known it: Nyasaland—East Africa—Liberia—Senegal*. London, John Murray, 1929.

233

MOIR, F. L. M. *After Livingstone, an African Trade Romance.* London, Hodder and Stoughton, 1923.

MORRIS, M. J. *A Brief History of Nyasaland,* London, Longmans, Green, 1952.

MURRAY, S. S. *A Handbook of Nyasaland.* London, Crown Agents, 1932.

NTARA, S. Y. *Headman's Enterprise: An Unexpected Page in Central African History.* London, Lutterworth Press, 1949.

NTARA, S. Y. *Man of Africa.* London, The Religious Tract Society, 1934.

Nyasaland Calling, 1891–1951; a Visitor's Guide to Nyasaland Protectorate, British Central Africa, Diamond Jubilee, 15th May, 1951. Zomba, Government Printer, 1951.

Nyasaland Journal, Vol. I, No. 1, January 1948—Blantyre, The Nyasaland Society, 1948.

ROYAL COMMISSION ON RHODESIA—NYASALAND. *Report.* London, H.M.S.O., 1939. Cmd. 5949.

STANNUS, H. S. *The Wayao of Nyasaland.* Cambridge, Massachusetts, Harvard University, 1922.

STEWART, J. *The Zambesi Journal of James Stewart, 1862–1863, with a selection from his correspondence, edited by J. P. R. Wallis.* London, Chatto and Windus, 1952. (Oppenheimer Series, No. 6.)

The Story of Nyasaland Told in a Series of Historical Pictures to Commemorate the Diamond Jubilee of Nyasaland, 1891–1951. Salisbury, Central African Archives, 1951.

TAYLOR, Don. *Rainbow on the Zambesi.* London, Museum Press, 1953.

TEW, M. *Peoples of the Lake Nyasa Region.* Oxford, University Press, 1950. (Ethnographic Survey of Africa, East Central Africa, Part I.)

THOMPSON, C. H. and WOODRUFF, H. W. *Economic Development in Rhodesia and Nyasaland.* London, Dennis Dobson, 1955.

TOPHAM, P. *Check List of Nyasaland Forests and Shrubs.* Oxford, Imperial Forestry Institute, 1936.

VAN DER POST, L. *Venture to the Interior.* London, The Hogarth Press, 1952.

WIEHE, P. O. *The Plant Diseases of Nyasaland.* Kew, Commonwealth Mycological Institute, 1953.

WILSON, G. *The Constitution of Ngonde.* Livingstone, The Rhodes-Livingstone Institute, 1939. (Rhodes-Livingstone Papers, No. 3.)

YOUNG, T. C. *Notes on the History of the Tumbuka-Kamanga Peoples in the Northern Province of Nyasaland.* London, The Religious Tract Society, 1932.

YOUNG, T. C. and HASTINGS, B. (*editors*). *Our African Way of Life.* London, Lutterworth Press, 1946.

INDEX

235

Wt.P67515   K20   S.O. Code No. 88-367*

...commenced to give trouble on
...orders by sending out raid...
...arties and declaring himself...
...ile to the English. Every e...
...as been made to keep the pe...
...nt the last unprovoked att...
...n our outposts necessit...
...rompt reprisals. No doubt w...
...he Angoni are brought to t...
...nses, the reason for this u...
...ected hostility will come...
...ght.

Vol. VI., No 27.   BLANTYRE, B. C. A.,   APRIL 4, 1903.   Single Copies 6d.

[No. 86

RISING OF T...
AN...

On Tuesday...
inst, informatio...
in Zomba from M...